VERNON DENT

STOOGE HEAVY

Front cover photo: The Three Stooges (Larry Fine, Curly Howard, and Moe Howard, dressed as Japanese soldiers) infiltrate a spy ring and confront Vernon Dent (as a Nazi spy) in *No Dough Boys* (Columbia Pictures, 1944). Until now, this photo has never been published. *Courtesy of the Margaret Herrick Library.*

Back cover illustration: Moe, Larry, and Shemp run afoul of their perennial adversary Vernon Dent in this remarkable drawing by Drew Friedman. It has been reproduced with Mr. Friedman's kind permission. Please check out his website at *www.friedmanart.com.*

Vernon Dent: Stooge Heavy
© 2010 Bill Cassara. All Rights Reserved.

Foreword © 2010 Edward Watz.

No part of this book may be reproduced in any form or by any means, electronic, mechanical, digital, photocopying or recording, except for the inclusion in a review, without permission in writing from the publisher.

Published in the USA by:
BearManor Media
PO Box 1129
Duncan, Oklahoma 73534-1129
www.bearmanormedia.com

ISBN 978-1-59393-549-8

Printed in the United States of America.
Book design by Brian Pearce | Red Jacket Press.

VERNON DENT

SECOND BANANA TO THE THREE STOOGES AND OTHER FILM COMEDY GREATS

STOOGE HEAVY

BILL CASSARA

TABLE OF CONTENTS

ACKNOWLEDGMENTS 9
FOREWORD 13
PROLOGUE 17

CHAPTER 1
THE DENT FAMILY IN SAN JOSE 21

CHAPTER 2
SHOW BUSINESS DEBUT 31

CHAPTER 3
THE DEATH OF WILLIAM E. DENT 39

CHAPTER 4
MOVE TO OAKLAND 45

CHAPTER 5
COMING OF AGE 51

CHAPTER 6
JEWEL CITY 59

CHAPTER 7
VERNON IN THE MOVIES 65

CHAPTER 8
**TRIUMPHANT RETURN
TO SAN JOSE** 77

CHAPTER 9
MACK SENNETT STUDIOS 89

CHAPTER 10
THE TALKIES 109

CHAPTER 11
IN TRANSITION 121

CHAPTER 12
VERNON DENT, SECOND BANANA 127

CHAPTER 13
THE THREE STOOGES 135

CHAPTER 14
EUNICE 155

CHAPTER 15
DON'T MENTION THE WAR 161

CHAPTER 16
THE FINAL CURTAIN 169

EPILOGUE 175
APPENDICES 177
SOURCES 243
ABOUT THE AUTHOR 249
INDEX 251

This book is dedicated with love to my beautiful wife and muse, Michelle, my children, Diana and Douglas, and my late father, Sam.

ACKNOWLEDGMENTS

I was first intrigued by the history of San Jose from my father and aunt who were born and raised in this city. My grandfather John Cassara emigrated from Sicily in 1899 and married in San Jose in 1914. He owned The Old Chicago Barbershop, which was located in the city's downtown area. When I was born (in 1951), there were only 92,000 people living within the city limits of San Jose. Fruit trees made up more land than developed acreage.

In 1963, I happened upon a book by Ralph Rambo, a local author and cartoonist who grew up on the west side of San Jose, near Cupertino. Rambo was born in 1895, so his homespun stories of familiar geographical locations made this place extra special to me. The book, *Almost Forgotten*, was comprised of handwritten graphics, along with his unique illustrations. I always wished I could thank him.

While on summer break from San Jose State University in 1975, I volunteered my time as a docent for the new San Jose Historical Museum. This became a place to relocate original buildings of 100 years old: schools, firehouses—even the Dashaway Livery Shop. The museum's goal at that time was to build a replica of the Great San Jose Light Tower that provided the city with a main source of light 1888–1915. My grandfather's claim to fame was that he saw the great light tower collapse on a winter day in 1915. A model of the tower now stands in the park.

Another influence on me was Clyde Arbuckle, the official historian of San Jose. Though he lived to be around 90, no one ever talked to him about his half-brother, Roscoe "Fatty" Arbuckle. I developed a theory that he thought commercial movies were not the best way to portray people, history or the community. Which brings up a point: none of these historians ever seemed to discuss Vernon Dent. Did they know about him? Perhaps Arbuckle had no interest in questions about "picture people." They had, after all, used "Fatty" as an example and dirtied the very name of Arbuckle. He had no use for them. Clyde wasn't a politician — he was an educator. It is with humility that I submit this book as a missing page from the history of San Jose. May it awaken a newfound appreciation for one of her long-forgotten native sons.

Fortunately, there are film buffs who really care about the unheralded comedy film actors. It is from their knowledge and encouragement that I continued my research into the life of Vernon Dent. They include: Dave Allard, Richard W. Bann, Alex Bartosh, Kimm Benton, Robert S. Birchard, Randy Brown, Leo Brooks, Tommy Bupp, Jr., Mark Cantor, Bill Cappello, Phyllis Coates, Gary Cohen, Lon Davis, Jean Dresden, John Duff, Andy Edmonds, Mike Esslinger, Richard Finegan, Joan Fontaine, Paul E. Gierucki, Sam Gill, Richard Green, Ron Hall, Lois Laurel Hawes, Gregory Hilbrich, Colin Hilton, Gary Hammonds, Cole Johnson, David Kalat, David Kiehn, Marshall Korby, Gary Lassin, Gary Lesser, Paul Lisy, Leonard Maltin (the man who started it all with his book on two-reel comedies), Jim Maley, Steve Massa, Christina McKillip, Joe Mitch, James T. Mockoski, Ben Model, Jim Neibaur, Kit Parker, Scott H. Reboul, Richard M. Roberts, Bob Sattersfield, Randy Skretvedt, Alison and Dave Stevenson, Stan Taffel, Patricia Eliot Tobias, Mary May Vareen, Brent Walker, Jeffrey Weismann, David Wyatt, Bart Williams, and Bob and Duon Zeroun.

I also owe a debt of gratitude to the following libraries: the Margaret Herrick Library (Kristine Krueger, Faye Thompson, and Matt Stevens); Oakland City Library; the University of California at Los Angeles (Film and Archives); the University of Southern California (Ned Comstock of the Doheny Library); the Santa Cruz Public Library, the San Jose Main Library, and their California Room.

A special note of thanks to the two Vernon Dent family members who contributed to this project: Eunice (Dent) Friend and Ethel Pasques. Eunice, now past the century mark, continues to live a full and happy life.

I deeply appreciate artist Drew Friedman, whose image of Vernon Dent with the Stooges adorns the back cover of this book.

A sincere thank you to my friend, Edward Watz, who took special interest in this project. This book would not be complete without his generous input.

Thanks are also due to Comedy III Entertainment, Inc., Columbia Studios, and Ben Ohmart of BearManor Media. When Ben asked what I was working on and I told him "Vernon Dent," he replied, "Yes, yes, yes! I've been watching that mug of his my whole life!"

A youthful Vernon Dent gives Harry Langdon "The Look" in their very first screen appearance together. Picking Peaches *(Sennett, 1924).* COURTESY OF EDWARD WATZ

FOREWORD

I used to feel sorry for Vernon Dent. Through the years, in various tributes to the Golden Age of classic screen comedy, Vernon never received the recognition he deserved; film critic James Agee might have equated the Vernon Dent story to that of the "humblest journeyman" of movie comedy...toiling in near-obscurity, "sweating to obey the laws of his craft." And yet, like most kids growing up in the 1960s, I was enjoying the comedy genius of Vernon Dent nearly every day of my childhood. I first discovered him through his numerous appearances with those disgraceful vagabonds, those moronic imbeciles, The Three Stooges, who were on daily display back then in all their unedited, violence-prone glory, on local television. In his two-reel comedies with the Boys, Vernon Dent excelled at playing hotheads with a temper so quick that Moe Howard appeared almost angelic in comparison. The upsetting of dignity (and authority) was the foundation of every Three Stooges comedy. With his imposing frame and commanding demeanor, no slapstick straight-man was better equipped to tangle with Moe, Larry, Curly, and Shemp than the formidable Mr. Dent, and almost always with hilarious consequences. What impressed me most was Vernon's skill as a comic feed; his characterizations would quickly establish that he had no time for nonsense and no tolerance for tomfoolery. This literally set the scene so that the Stooges' antics actually became that much funnier. There were other fine performers in the Three Stooges stock company — Christine McIntyre, Bud Jamison, Emil Sitka, among others — but none were better equipped for two-reel comedy fare than Vernon Dent.

While we knew his screen character, we knew almost nothing about the man. In a time when Laurel & Hardy, W.C. Fields, and The Marx Brothers were written about and revered as reigning Comedy Kings, there was very little in print about the Three Stooges. Which meant nothing was ever written about Vernon Dent.

This situation actually worsened. Because of their comic violence content, the Stooges were banned from New York television in 1971 by what Moe Howard sarcastically referred to as the "neurotic mothers of America," effectively cutting off my TV exposure to the Stooges and to Vernon Dent. By coincidence, a major revival of Harry Langdon's silent comedies took place that same year in New York City. All of Langdon's existing silent films were shown, including ten delightful Mack Sennett shorts that paired Harry with Vernon Dent. Again I was impressed with Vernon's deft characterizations, but now realizing that he didn't need dialogue to be funny — he also excelled at subtle pantomime.

Late in the 1970s I went to work for the film archivist Raymond Rohauer, doing research for an intended biography of Harry Langdon. I soon learned that Harry Langdon and Vernon Dent were best friends in real life; Vernon appears in Harry Langdon's first Sennett release, *Picking Peaches*, and worked with Langdon through the years up to Langdon's last film, *Pistol Packin' Nitwits*, over 20 years later. By happy coincidence, Harry's widow Mabel, and Vernon's widow Eunice, still kept in touch. (I got to meet and interview both Mabel and Eunice; the stories they shared about their husbands are recounted in this book.) When my friend and fellow comedy buff Ted Okuda and I set off to write a book about Columbia Pictures' comedy short subjects, Eunice was one of our key supporters. She told us everything that she could remember about those days, and upon its publication in 1986, we were pleased to have captured at least a little piece of Vernon Dent's story.

But now, my dear pal Bill Cassara, the same man who wrote a superb book detailing the life of Edgar Kennedy, has done the seemingly impossible: he has written an equally magnificent book about the life, films and times of Vernon Dent. We are all indebted to Bill for uncovering the fascinating back-story behind this long-neglected and great comedian. There's much hilarity, as well as much sadness, in Vernon Dent's saga, but through it all is an indomitable American spirit that inspires newfound admiration and respect for a man whom up to now many of us only identified as "the angry grouch from the Three Stooges!" Thanks to Bill Cassara, the orchestra is tuned up, the spotlight is turned on, and the curtains are pulled back: Vernon Dent steps out to center stage…

Edward Watz
Morganville, New Jersey

Vernon Dent (as a harried director) tries to explain a scenario to a distracted Mack Sennett. The Hollywood Kid *(Sennett, 1924).* COURTESY OF EDWARD WATZ

PROLOGUE

It is possible that the first time Vernon Dent entered my consciousness was in 1958, when my dad took me to San Jose's downtown Studio Theater to see *The Golden Age of Comedy*. This Robert Youngson-produced compilation featured rarely seen clips from the silent film era. After the introductory credits, the opening shot is of an office, in which "an unsmiling king presides over his loony domain." Vernon Dent (as a bespectacled director) manically pitches an idea to the king himself — Mack Sennett. Bathing beauties line up to audition, comics chase each other with loaded rifles, and a lion — a *real* lion — walks in unannounced. Sennett may be used to this type of four-footed visitor, but Vernon and his cohorts are obviously not; they promptly dive out the nearest window to safety.

I looked around and noticed that all of my fellow audience members — grandfathers, fathers, and kids like me — were howling with laughter. One graybeard in the audience, in sheer exuberance, thumped the floor with his cane to coincide with every visual punchline. To the oldsters, it was a nostalgic look into their entertainment past; to me — a seven-year-old — it was an introduction to something new and wonderful. Here was fast-paced physical humor in its purest form. Narration, peppy ragtime music and sound effects were dubbed in, but the abstract visual images were even better than cartoons, an art form that knew no physical boundaries.

As I grew, my interest in physical comedy grew with me. After completing my paper route for the day, I would race to get home before five p.m. to watch Laurel & Hardy, The Little Rascals, and The Three Stooges (although not necessarily in that order). I was part of the Baby Boomer generation that reveled in television's backlog of Columbia and Hal Roach short comedies. The 18- to 22-minute two-reel format was perfect for TV. With constant viewing, I became familiar with the titles of the films and the names and faces of the supporting cast members: people like Edgar Kennedy, James Finlayson, Billy Gilbert, Andy Clyde, Charley Chase, Bud Jamison, James C. Morton, Christine (insert "wolf-whistle" here) McIntyre, Dudley Dickerson, and, of course, Vernon Dent.

To the casual observer, Vernon Dent was "the guy in the suit," the Stooges' bellicose authority figure; he co-starred in more of their films than any other supporting actor. Vernon was to the Stooges what James Finlayson was to Laurel & Hardy: a highly identifiable and confrontational comedy contrast. Standing five-foot-nine and weighing in at 250 pounds, Vernon fit the part of the comic "heavy" — and an angry one at that. You could be assured that the Stooges were "really going to get it" if his name was in the opening credits. When provoked, his disposition could go from genteel to all-out vengeance in three seconds flat. If Edgar Kennedy was "Master of the Slow Burn," then Vernon Dent was "Master of the Short Fuse." He'd just as soon clunk the Stooges' heads together to show them that he meant business. The resulting sound effects resonated like a lovely bunch of coconuts — hollow ones, of course.

Although Vernon was being seen daily on TV, nothing contemporary had been written about him. It wasn't until 1970, when Kalton C. Lahue and Sam Gill wrote a groundbreaking book, *Clown Princes and Court Jesters*, that Vernon was first given a semblance of the recognition he deserved. Out of the 50 deserving subjects in the book, he was crowned "King of Character Comics." More amazing to me was that this career profile was limited to the 1920s, long before he ever met Moe, Larry, and Curly.

It wasn't until 1976 that I learned that this veteran comic had actually been born in San Jose. An article celebrating the man was published in *Classic Film Collector* (later known as *Classic Images*). The authors, Ted Okuda and Edward Watz, actually interviewed Vernon's widow, Eunice, who identified his city of birth. This disclosure was of no small importance to me.

Subsequent articles or short bios about Vernon Dent usually made mention of the fact that he was "born in San Jose and attended schools there and in Oakland," but I wanted to know more. Where did he go to school, for instance? Who were his relatives? What were his show business roots? Just who *is* this guy anyway? Unfortunately, there were no family scrapbooks to pore over. My curiosity about the subject was placed on hold, indefinitely.

It wasn't until after a 30-year career in law enforcement that I decided to reopen this "cold case." Not too many people are still alive who could claim they followed Vernon Dent's ascending film career. In fact, most people *only* recognize Vernon Dent because of his association with The Three Stooges. Even though I was delighted to identify him in other Columbia comedy shorts of the sound era, I too worked backwards in years, tracing the impact he made in his 400+ film appearances.

It is clear that behind the scenes, personal tragedy was a common theme in Vernon's life. Achieving success in show business came slowly, but his optimistic approach helped him weather the lean times, and his endless curiosity about people allowed him to create many interesting characters. These skills held him in good stead in the motion picture industry for 35 years.

This tribute to Vernon Dent, Stooge Heavy, is overdue by more than half a century.

Bill Cassara
Salinas, California

CHAPTER 1

THE DENT FAMILY IN SAN JOSE

Vernon Bruce Dent was born February 16, 1895, in the city of San Jose, to William E. Dent and the former Fanny B. Mossman. At that time, San Jose had a population of approximately 20,000, with seven square miles within her borders. One hundred and five years later, this vibrant city boasts a population of one million within the city limits. Located in Santa Clara Valley, she is now known as the "Capital of Silicon Valley" (representing the high-tech computer industry). San Jose is the largest city in Northern California and the tenth largest in the country. During Vernon's time, it was a nice, small town compared to its bigger sister cities to the north: San Francisco, Oakland, and Sacramento.

San Jose had a prominent history while under Spanish and Mexican reign. This modest little pueblo was situated between the military presidios of San Francisco and the state capital of Monterey, some 75 miles southwest. The Santa Clara Valley was a significant crop producer, providing much-needed food for the missions and presidios.

Life in the valley changed when the great state of California was established in 1850; San Jose became the first state capital. This lasted only for a short period, and Sacramento ultimately won that distinction.

Vernon Dent was born at a residence at 80 E. St. John Street (now, regrettably, a parking garage). The Dent home was just north of the downtown area and overlooked the beautiful St. James Park, which was established in 1868. This tree-lined area was surrounded by imposing government buildings, stately courthouses, churches, and fraternal organizations. In 1901, when Vernon was only six years old, President James McKinley made a visit to San Jose to make a great speech from this public land. St. James Park held wonderful public events, and was the common meeting place for all of San Jose's populace. Political gatherings and bandstand music were mainstays on every weekend.

San Jose was only 48 miles southeast of San Francisco and easily accessible by train during Vernon's time. The town had wonderful theatres and a vast park in the east foothills, called Alum Rock Park. Just a few miles south, on Mt. Hamilton, was the Lick Observatory. By the time Vernon was born, this observatory boasted the world's largest telescope, and was a major tourist attraction. The Hotels Vendome and St. James provided the best of the overnight stays.

Though San Jose was the county seat of government in Santa Clara County, there was a time when the city might have been more famous for its ten-story-high Electric Light Tower. This massive structure was anchored at the corner of Market and Santa Clara Streets. An engineering marvel erected in 1888, the 207-foot tower provided a flood of illumination over the downtown area. There were horse-drawn cars and trolleys that connected the city and its far-reaching townships throughout the valley.

The rural valley was spread out to the west and included Los Gatos, Cupertino, and Saratoga. It served as the gateway to the Santa Cruz Mountains and the Pacific Ocean, only 35 miles away. The north region reached the south of the San Francisco Bay and included Alviso. Northwest was the mission town of Santa Clara on the El Camino Real. This was the road to San Francisco. Northeast toward Oakland included the Berryessa District and the township of Milpitas. Four hundred miles due south on the El Camino Real is Los Angeles. Just southwest of San Jose's city limits was rural Willow Glen. For many years it was simply called The Willows, literally named because of the wild growth of willow trees in the region.

The Willows were first described by pioneer William Lewis Manly. This noted explorer authored a book about his life, *Death Valley in '49*, after he settled in San Jose. Not only did Manly write about his experiences surviving the trek through the desert, he also wrote of his first impressions of what became known as Willow Glen. It was described as swampland fed by the Coyote and Guadalupe Rivers. Manly noticed that the "wild mustard greens were so thick that chattering squirrels sat atop [them]."

Developers saw some potential in this area, if only it could be tamed. Here was an area with cheap land and a moderate climate. The solution was made by draining the marshland via a manually made channel at the closest link between the two rivers. Once this successful engineering feat was accomplished, the next step was removing the willow trees as needed. As trees were torn out and the stumps removed, it exposed the rich sedimentary soil.

By the 1880s great ranches of land in the Willows were subdivided. It was a vibrant rural little community that continued to grow. In 1927 Willow Glen became a chartered city; in 1936, she was annexed to San Jose.

Under different circumstances, Vernon Dent might have been born in Willow Glen. His mother and father lived at the 15-acre ranch home during 1894 when Rawley E. Dent suddenly died. He had been such a colorful part of the history of the Santa Clara Valley that a mini-biography was written about him in 1888.

RAWLEY E. DENT

The name Rawley E. Dent once loomed large in the fruit industry of Santa Clara Valley. His biographical profile includes a first-hand account of his family heritage.

He was born to Enoch and Julia Dent (originally from Virginia) in the state of Indiana in 1821. Dent claimed the decision to move to California was primarily for his health. He passed through various locations in the Golden State before settling in San Jose. There he built his palatial home on Willow Street; the nearest cross street at that time was Cherry Avenue in The Willows. Dent cultivated the land into orchards of various fruit trees and ultimately reaped considerable profits. At that time Dent also owned ten acres of land on Curtner Avenue, between Lincoln Avenue and Booksin Road. In addition, this land baron owned 45 acres in Saratoga and 32 acres in Los Gatos. Nestled in the west side of Santa Clara Valley (in the foothills of the Santa Cruz Mountains), Saratoga and Los Gatos are now heavily populated communities, albeit with a charming village atmosphere.

Rawley Dent was married three times. His first marriage was in 1844 to Rebecca McCollum of Pennsylvania. When she died, he married Frances Burbank of Portland, Maine. It was from this marriage that Vernon's father and aunts Lena and Mabel were born. At the time of the article, W. E. Dent was attending school in The Willows. It was later renamed Willow Glen School.

On June 6, 1894 Rawley Dent died at his home on Willow Street at the age of 73; the cause of death was said to be consumption. The *San Jose Evening News* cited his success as an orchardist and the fact that he had maintained his residence locally for 25 years. He was survived by his third wife, the former Laura Chandler, originally from Yuba City, California. Dent is buried at the historical Oak Hills Cemetery in San Jose where many prominent citizens from the days of early California were laid to rest.

Looking at a property map of "The Willows," circa 1890, one can view the R. E. Dent orchard layout. His 15 acres of land faced Willow Street,

The Dent family house at 1305 Willow Street. PHOTO BY DIANA CASSARA

and was primed for growing fruit. As part of the land boundary, the Los Gatos Creek cuts through the rear portion, giving the acreage a ready water source. With trolley cars later providing service through Willow Street to downtown and points west and east, this was one of the most productive and exquisite lands in Willow Glen.

Rawley E. Dent, Sr. was survived by his namesake, an offspring of his second wife. Rawley, Jr. later lived on the ten acres of land on Curtner Avenue and continued as an orchardist. Rawley, Jr. died from natural causes in 1915, at age 60. He was a half-brother to William E. Dent, Vernon's father.

The Dents' palatial home still stands at 1305 Willow Street. Across the way, a former orchard area was turned over to the city in the late 1940s. Originally named Willow Street Park, the name was officially changed to Bramhall Park to posthumously honor the city planner who designed it.

This graceful public land of 13 acres features a baseball diamond and a natural amphitheater, made from an old dried-out river bottom, the original route of the Los Gatos Creek. Redwood trees still line the old river bank. It is not hard to imagine Vernon frolicking in the old creekside woods, like so many have done since.

FANNIE (FAY) B. MOSSMAN

Vernon's mother, Fannie, was born in August of 1873, in Kansas. The 1880 census indicates that she was living at the family house at 356 St. John Street in San Jose. Fannie's mother's name was Frances M. Mossman; Fannie had two siblings, Gertrude and Jessie. There were nine other people living at the residence, including Frank F. Jewell, who later became a clergyman. Little did he foresee the time when the opportunity came to bond in marriage Fannie to William E. Dent, on July 19, 1892. The groom was 19 years old, and the bride was 18. W. Dent was listed as a resident in Willow Glen at the time of his marriage. The marriage certificate specifies that the union had the approval of Rawley Dent, Sr.

WILLIAM E. DENT

Born in May of 1874 in what is now considered San Jose, Vernon's father must have been a spirited youngster. He attended the local school and helped his father with the never-ending work on the vast fruit orchards. After William married Fannie, he was listed in the city directory as an "orchardist," and resided at the family ranch home on Willow Street.

When Rawley Dent died in June of 1894, it had a major impact on the family. Fannie was pregnant with her first child. It is unknown if the new parents-to-be ever had the chance to inform Rawley that he was soon to be a grandfather. The newly expectant Dent family moved to 80 E. St. John to welcome their newborn son, Vernon Bruce Dent. On December 16, 1897, Vernon had a new brother, Melville E. Dent. The family called him "Mel."

William E. Dent went into the tavern business after the affairs of his father's estate had been settled. The opening was announced in the *San Jose Evening News* on September 18, 1899:

> The firm of Smith & Dent as proprietors of the Dash Saloon, 28 and 30 North First Street, has been dissolved, Mr. Dent having purchased his partner's interest. Next Saturday evening a fine lunch

will be served by Mr. Dent to all his friends. He is a native of San Jose, and has a legion of friends. He will always keep on hand the finest liquors and wines. The patronage of the public is solicited.

During the census of 1900, the Dent family still resided at 80 East St. John Street. It was a house full of people, including Fannie Dent's mother, who had since remarried and was listed as Francis Holley. There

Vernon Dent poses for a publicity still for Nob Hill *(20th Century-Fox, 1945), a Technicolor drama about the Barbary Coast in the 1890s. Could this be what Vernon's saloon-keeper father looked like?* COURTESY OF EDWARD WATZ

is no evidence that Mr. Holley was living there amongst the 15 other inhabitants.

FRATERNAL ORDER OF THE EAGLES

Vernon's father was involved in many community events and causes. He was a charter member of the Eagles when they incorporated in 1899. It was a big occasion when 300 Eagle representatives from San Francisco and Oakland came to town on a special excursion train to celebrate the organization of the new lodge. The original fraternal organization had its beginnings in Seattle, Washington. Grand Organizer Mitchell of Seattle City participated in the ceremony, making San Jose the eighth Ariel in the nation.

The out-of-town organizers were met at the train depot by a band and escorted to MacCabee Temple, on South First Street, where the grand affair took place.

Eagles Hall was built a few years later and was a huge structure that revived Greek architecture in its design. It was one of the most impressive buildings in the city and faced St. James Park.

According to the *San Jose Mercury* of April 3, 1899, there were 70 charter members received into the San Jose Lodge, "among them many of the most prominent and influential residents of this city." Appointed as "Inside Guardian," William E. Dent served as one of the officers.

On March 17, 1907 the Sunday *San Jose Mercury Herald* offered their weekly updates regarding the local fraternal organizations. Vernon's father made the papers as he had been complicit in a practical joke. There was a prominent citizen who became a member of the Eagles and "talked it up to William E. Dent." Dent claimed that he didn't have the funds for an initiation fee, so the gentleman agreed to sponsor him. It was arranged for Dent to play along for the entertainment of his brother Eagles. He was ushered in to take the initiation when he announced that he was, in fact, a charter member. Everyone had a great laugh at the expense of the generous soul who was convinced that Dent would make a great Eagle. A motion was made and approved that William Dent be made a "Double Eagle."

LOCAL BETTING

The presidential election between incumbent William McKinley and William Jennings Bryan was highly anticipated at the turn of the twentieth century. According to an item in the *San Jose News*, on November 7, 1900, this led to some spirited wagering:

Many Dollars Changing Hands — Betting upon the result of yesterday's election was very brisk, and inquiries at Bercovich's cigar store, served as a station for the sporting men, over $10,000 had changed hands with the announcement of McKinley's election. W. Evans Dent, proprietor of the Dash Saloon, won about $250.00 in bets with odds of 5 to 1 and 3 to 1. Betting was weak until yesterday, when rumors from the east encouraged the short spenders to place a few bets which were eagerly snapped up by the Republicans who have been seeking a place for their coin for some days.

The people of San Jose were enthralled in 1901 when President McKinley arrived to make a speech, right there in St. James Park. Historic photos of the occasion show American flags draped over every building façade, and a mass of humanity taking up every square inch of lawn. For the event, a temporary stage was built for the president to address the throng. A commemorative statue now stands where the president once stood.

THE BIG ONE

What became known as "The San Francisco Earthquake," on April 18, 1906, actually had far-reaching damage to towns north and south. From Santa Rosa to Salinas, the earthquake impacted the entire area along the San Andreas Fault. Being near the epicenter, San Jose lost many of its downtown buildings. The Hall of Records and the Hall of Justice, both at the edge of St. James Park, were destroyed. In San Jose proper, 20 people lost there lives, and there was over three million dollars of property damage reported. Just northwest of San Jose, the community of Agnews suffered the loss of 150 people when the state hospital collapsed.

San Francisco, with its condensed population, suffered the most in terms of property damage and loss of lives. People of San Jose were cut off from telegraphic communication as well. Rumors were rampant: one had the entire population of homeless San Franciscans heading south; it was feared that they would expunge all of the town's available resources. San Jose city officials had to hold a public conference to address the issue. Through the efforts of officials of the Santa Clara streetcar line, the *San Jose News* office was supplied with power, making it possible to receive wire communication and print editions of the newspaper. Gasoline burners were used for typesetting machines. The *San Jose News* reported on April 19, 1906 that the mayor, G. D. Worswick, issued a proclamation for all people to remain in their homes during the coming night. He warned citizens to stay away in particular from the business section of the city. Mayor Worswick said in part: "All lawlessness will be repressed with a heavy hand." Those without homes were encouraged to sleep in the parks (it was fortuitous that the Dents lived right across the street from one).

According to one historical account, *San Jose — California's First City*, "Recovery came quickly to the city [after the earthquake]. By April 19, water was back in service. On the twenty-fifth, the streets were clean, and by the thirtieth of April, it could be said that San Jose was back to normal — the saloons had re-opened."

CHAPTER 2

SHOW BUSINESS DEBUT

Many actors and actresses tend to exaggerate the events surrounding their show-business debuts. If it wasn't glamorous or notable, press agents or studios tended to invent a better story. No one seems to have asked Vernon Dent how he started in the business, but if someone had; his answer would have made for great copy.

As part of the downtown revitalization after the earthquake, the new Empire Theatre opened its doors on November 11, 1906. Built to accommodate both stage productions and film showings, it was located at 23 North Second Street, near St. John. William Weston, the proprietor, had built another Empire Theatre in San Francisco earlier that year.

Vernon successfully obtained a part-time position at the Empire. It acquainted him with show business, starting at the bottom of the rung of the entertainment ladder. He swept floors, sold tickets, and ran errands for the actors. Then, on January 6, 1907, the *San Jose Mercury* published a small news article on page nine about an accident:

BOY FALLS TO SEAT FROM THEATRE BALCONY

The young son of William E. Dent, employed at the Empire Theatre, fell over the railing from the balcony and landed in a sitting posture in the pit below. While the youth suffered no impending fatal injuries, he received a badly discolored face and his leg was broken.

During the performance, Vernon Dent, who was employed in the theatre, leaned against the railing in the balcony. This gave way and the boy was precipitated to the floor below. He turned somersaults in the air in his descent and landed in the only vacant seat in the audience. The sudden fall of the lad for a moment created a sensation, but when the little fellow loudly announced that he was "all right," a cheer responded to his bravery.

If this story had first surfaced years after the fact, then one would be justified in suspecting some sort of publicity stunt. But because this incident was covered as a sensational accident of an eleven-year-old boy, it raised concerns, sympathy, and scorn about the unsafe conditions of the new showplace. The fact that Vernon sustained a serious injury in front of an audience could have very well stopped the show. Instead, the young trouper reassured the crowd with a jovial "show-must-go-on" attitude. The crowd was put back into a good mood, and then settled in to enjoy the rest of the performance.

Vernon kept on working at the theatre in various capacities. Learning all that was involved with each show provided the foundation and confidence for him to learn his craft.

VICTORY THEATRE

On June 4, 1904, Vernon's name was mentioned in association with a children's stage production at San Jose's Victory Theatre. Only nine years old at the time, Vernon Dent was credited along with a hundred other children. The title of the play was *The House That Jack Built*, and it was a children's opera based on Mother Goose stories and songs. The newspaper listed the names of every child who participated and, judging by the numbers, it seems that every kid in town took part in the show.

The Victory Theatre was built in 1899 to celebrate the outcome of the Spanish-American war. It was a place not only for stage productions, but also for the eventual showing of moving pictures.

UNIQUE THEATRE

This grand family theatre first opened its doors on February 7, 1903; this is important to note, because the theatre is credited with showing not only vaudeville acts, but also movies. It is more than likely that Vernon Dent saw his first moving pictures on the screen at this San Jose theatre on Santa Clara Street, just east of First Street. As was the custom of the day, the theatre was designed along the lines of a grand palace.

The Unique Theatre was opened by the well-known entrepreneur Sid Grauman. One of the theatre's employees was Roscoe Arbuckle, a local lad who was hired to perform janitorial duties and an occasional song.

Years later, Roscoe (now known the world over as movie comedian "Fatty" Arbuckle) told the *San Jose Evening Herald*: "My first real professional engagement was in 1904, and singing illustrated songs for Sid Grauman at the Unique Theatre, San Jose, at $17.50 a week."

The San Francisco Earthquake shook the Unique Theatre to bricks and dust. This three-year-old building subsequently lay in ruin for many years, though there were constant rumors of a new Unique Theatre to be built in its place. It was never to be.

THE GREAT RACE

Downtown San Jose must have been an extraordinarily exciting place to live during Vernon's time. There were multiple theatres all within walking distance and some had amateur nights, which were always a welcome treat for locals, and a place to hone one's singing skills before an appreciative audience. The bustle of people coming and going from downtown would have been constant; the various modes of transportation took passengers all over the valley. The train was especially efficient — it could provide a ride to San Francisco in a mere two hours.

San Jose and her Tower turned out to be a destination for some of the drivers participating in what became known as "The Great Race" of 1908. Starting in New York's Times Square in February, the finish line was in Paris, France.

Different routes were taken by each driver, but all headed west on unpaved roads. The trip must have been grueling. The immediate goal was to reach San Francisco, where the drivers were allowed to travel by boat to Alaska to continue the race across the Bering Straits. The only road north to San Francisco passed through San Jose.

Some of the cars never made it to their destination, and some went indirectly through to Seattle. The ultimate winner — the American Thomas Flyer car — led the way and made an overnight stay in San Jose on March 24, 1908. This was followed shortly thereafter by the French and Italian vehicles, which were also welcomed and cheered on as the international celebrities they had become.

LIONESS GETS OUT OF CAGE AT THE EMPIRE THEATER TODAY

In what sounds like the premise of a later Henry "Suicide" Lehrman silent comedy, or maybe Sennett's *The Hollywood Kid*, there was a mishap of major proportions at the Empire Theatre (where Vernon was employed at the time), reported by the *San Jose Evening News* on March 27, 1908.

> During the transferring of a couple of lions from wagon to wagon, a feat [was performed] that required all extra stage hands to lift the cages and tilt the wagon. As the second cage was being lowered to the ground, someone's foot slipped and it went down sideways.
>
> There was a scramble with the cage and it broke the pin that is run through a staple at the door. As the cage reached the ground, the lioness, seeing the door ajar, pushed her head out and grabbed someone's leg.
>
> With a yell that was calculated to frighten several lions, the animal backed inside. The bolt was slipped through the staple in a second. The incident caused great excitement, and there was a scattering of quite a crowd that had gathered. Some of the crowd may be running yet.

SEPARATION AND DIVORCE

The marriage of William E. Dent to Fanny Dent seemed to be a cloudy one — at least it had become so by 1906. In the latter part of the year, William E. Dent succumbed to "gold fever" and went to Nevada for a time with his half-brother, Gale Dent. They became proprietors of a saloon in the town of Goldfield, Nevada. The *San Jose Evening News* reported on November 10, 1906 that Gale Dent had died of typhoid pneumonia and "he was sick but a short time." The paper also reported, "Gale Dent was a resident of San Jose nearly all his life and was very well known here. He was a native of Illinois and was thirty-three years of age. He was a member of the local lodges of Eagles and Foresters and of the Brotherhood of Railroad Trainmen."

By 1907, the city directory indicated that William E. Dent had returned to San Jose and was living at 33 South 13th Street, a part of San Jose that was one of the first upscale neighborhoods carved out of the original grounds that belonged to Henry Morris Naglee, a former Union general in the Civil War. Only the elite of San Jose could afford the expensive houses in this area east of downtown.

HORACE MANN SCHOOL

San Jose's oldest public school, Horace Mann, was built in 1868 at the corner of Seventh and Santa Clara Streets.

Vernon attended this school during his elementary education. The principal during Vernon's time was Professor John Munzer. Vernon publically acknowledged the educator when he returned to San Jose for some location filming in 1922. The professor apparently encouraged Vernon's theatrical pursuits while he was a student.

THESPIAN BEGINNINGS

Without any first-hand accounts, it would be difficult at best to identify what inspired young Vernon Dent to go the road of show business. There are several possibilities: the fact that his father was a saloonkeeper may have been one of his incentives. Churches, organizations, and civic-minded people wanted to rid the town of alcohol to save mankind from evil. Saloons, taverns, bars, and the like were so-called "dens of vice." Where there was alcohol, there were gamblers, slot machines and cards, and these vices were said to lead some married men to the red-light districts. The local Anti-Saloon League and the national temperance movement were in full swing. They put political pressure, in the form of ordinances, on the citizenry to try to banish such establishments from their neighborhoods.

To counter the strategy, most saloons argued that they served food and provided entertainment. What could be more charming than a street urchin to sing the popular songs of the day? Undoubtedly prompted by his father, Vernon sang his heart out, receiving adulation, applause and (most importantly) tips. Some might consider this parental encouragement to be merely exploitation, but William E. Dent did not view it as such; he considered the environment a wholesome training ground for the aspiring entertainer.

Vernon did his share of performing, all the while learning the tricks of engaging an audience's attention. He was encouraged by his family and trained musically to enhance his natural talent. This aptitude may have come from his mother, the former Fannie Mossman. Newspapers of the period show that Mrs. William E. Dent was actively involved in many local shows as an amateur actress. On December 8, 1905, Mrs. Dent was included in the cast of *The Mandarin* at the local Elks Club. She was also credited as part of the cast of *El Capitan* for the Oratorio Society on March 19, 1908.

On December 17, 1908, the *San Jose Mercury* announced: "Delightful Operetta is Presented by Tots." The "tots" referred to were the students of Horace Mann School, and the "delightful operetta" was a new version of the classic folk tale *Cinderella*. Thirteen-year-old Vernon Dent played the part of Cinderella's stepfather. It was a juicy part for Vernon, the first of his many "heavy" roles.

There was another school play reported by the *San Jose Sunday Mercury and Herald*. The January 9, 1910 newspaper edition reported on a Horace Mann reception, sponsored by the faculty members. Vernon Dent received mention for his vocal solos, which were described as "well-rendered."

Vernon was not only active in drama; he was a standout in sports as well. He represented Horace Mann elementary school and competed against other athletes from the Longfellow, Lincoln, Lowell, Washington, and Grant grammar schools in a contest of various running events. On June 6, 1909, the *San Jose Mercury* reported the results of the races: In the 100-yard dash, Vernon Dent finished second with a time of twelve seconds flat. At fourteen, Vernon was a skinny kid, several meals away from the portly gentleman we know from his later films.

All seemed well with the Dent family in that spring of 1909. Little did they realize that their world was about to be thrown off its axis.

CHAPTER 3

THE DEATH OF WILLIAM E. DENT

On the evening of June 23, 1909, W. E. Dent and divorcee Ida Schley returned to Schley's apartment after visiting a local dancehall. Cleveland Urlin, Schley's ex-lover, was awaiting the couple's return, hiding — and armed with a gun — in a bedroom closet. Urlin had broken into Schley's apartment in a jealous rage after seeing Dent and Schley together at the dancehall.

As Dent and Schley retreated into bed, Urlin burst from the closet, shoved the gun into Dent's chest, and pulled the trigger. Before Dent could react, the bullet had ruptured the trunk of his body and killed him.

Ida Schley jumped from the bed and lunged at Urlin. Following a brief scuffle, Urlin fired at Schley's back as she struggled to escape. The bullet penetrated Schley's hand and continued into her right shoulder blade. Urlin then turned the gun on himself and fired the pistol, point blank, at his head. He died instantly.

Schley attempted to leave the scene, but collapsed in the hallway. Her moans for help were answered by her neighbors, who enlisted the aid of police to transport her to the hospital. She ultimately recovered.

The two local newspapers presented opposing perspectives on who was to blame for the deaths. The headline of the *San Jose Evening News* proclaimed, "MURDER!"

In stark contrast, the *San Jose Mercury* presented two headlines which seemed to point the finger at both parties:

MRS. IDA SCHLEY, FAIR DIVORCEE, IS CAUSE
OF SHOCKING CRIME
and
VICTIM OF DEAD MAN'S WRATH WAS
WELL-KNOWN SALOONKEEPER HERE.

The less-incriminating attitude of the *San Jose Mercury* was almost certainly due to the newspaper's relationship with Urlin, who was a solicitor for the paper at the time of his death. At the height of the scandal's coverage (on June 25, 1909), the *Mercury* printed a vituperative editorial, one that scorned the victims and not the murderer.

> William Evans Dent has lived his chosen life in this community and has come at length to the tragic and pitiful ending toward which the courses of all such lives inevitably end. A saloonkeeper and gambler by choice; a friend and active supporter of every form of civic and social energy which makes for evil; a tempter and corruptor of youth in an alluring form of vice and wrong: a willing investor of his rather attractive personality, and of considerable means, in those various agencies which are the opposing forces of upright and honest ways of living and of earning a livelihood; a boast[ful] panderer to lust and scoffer at virtue and purity in either sex, he has come to an untimely end by violence while in the company of a woman who had better never to have been born than to live and grow to be the paramour of sin and the inciting cause of murder.
>
> William Evans Dent had not the excuse for evil living that some men might offer in the presence of this obituary. He is reputed to have been a member of a family that has, during all his life, stood high in public estimation and in opportunities for honorable service and distinction. He had education, personal graces and qualities for making friends, of no mean order. He had the material means and the business ability to have commanded success and prosperity in almost any honorable occupation or calling. He lived in a community that is as ready and generous as any in according honor and reward to those who are worthy of its esteem. With all of these advantages and inducements to a life of honest and productive worth he has willfully chosen to go the ways of sin which lead to death. As to his connection with the Grant family it is to be hoped for his own sake and not for the sake of that distinguished name that the actual relationship did not exist. There is much mitigation for the faults and vices of those whose tendencies to evil are inherited or whose family origin and environment are unfertile for the growth of good. But if William Evans Dent was in fact a scion of the family of Grant, he can plead no such excuse for a worthless and wasted life.

De Mortuis nil nisi Ronum is the cloak that it is often charitable to cast over the frailties of those whose lives have come to naught. But there are lives and deaths about which the truth should be told to the end that they may serve as a solemn warning to those who may be entering upon courses of living, which however attended at the outset with the gilded allurements of evil, have nothing but a sordid tragedy for their inevitable end. The worthless and wasted life and sordid and tragic death of William Evans Dent is such a one about which the plain truth should be told for the sake of its warning lesson to men, and especially to the young men of the community in which Dent has ignobly lived and died.

By no means did the murder of W. E. Dent remain a local story. Several regional newspapers paraded the headlines because of Dent's famous name and the fact that he was a cousin of Mrs. General U. S. Grant. The Portland Oregon newspaper, the *Oregonian*, for example, had a column that shouted:

NEPHEW OF GRANT [sic] KILLED — EVANS DENT SHOT DOWN IN BRAWL OVER SAN JOSE WOMAN.

On June 24, 1909, the *San Jose Mercury* presented a more objective view of the altercation as information from the coroner's inquest became available. Highlights of the inquest, as summarized in the *Mercury*, included the statements: "Dent came to his death from a gunshot wound inflicted by Cleveland Urlin," and "Urlin came to his death from a gunshot wound self-inflicted with suicidal intent."

Not surprisingly, the rival paper highlighted the murderer's connection to the *Mercury*. On June 26, 1909, the *San Jose Evening News* reported:

> The remains of Cleveland Urlin, the man who shot and killed William Evans Dent, wounded Mrs. Schley, and ultimately committed suicide, was shipped to the home of his relatives in Montana this afternoon. Urlin was twenty-five years of age and had worked on several newspapers in the state and was working at the Mercury at the time of the tragedy.

News of Dent's murder continued for days, until the public had their fill of the same details being rehashed.

W. E. Dent's murder and the sensational media coverage associated with it surely had a profound impact on young Vernon, who was just thirteen years old at the time. That it encouraged him to choose a profession allowing escape from the real world is a likely possibility.

CHAPTER 4

MOVE TO OAKLAND

Between the town gossips and anti-saloon leagues, it was no wonder that Fannie Dent moved her children north to the cosmopolitan city of Oakland. It would have been brutal to continue living in the same town that condemned an innocent victim by social consciousness. The move north offered an opportunity for a fresh start.

The effects of the incident remained vivid in Fannie's mind, however. As a witness to alcohol's negative impact on her husband, she admonished her children to remain temperate. In later years Vernon said that his mother made him "swear on his father's grave" that he would never drink. Vernon upheld this oath the rest of his life.

In 1910 the population of Oakland, California was 150,000, which made San Jose appear to be a small town in comparison. Just ten years earlier, before the earthquake, Oakland had a population of only 67,000. It was a sophisticated community, with nearby Berkeley, and was just a ferry boat ride away from San Francisco, the most populous and cultured city in the west.

Fay Dent (as she was referred to in the census of 1910) moved her two boys into a boarding house at 589 22nd Street, where eight other people resided. Oakland is approximately 45 miles north of San Jose, on the east side of the San Francisco Bay, which was far enough away to assure some anonymity for the scandalized family. Vernon and his brother, Melville, were spared the agony of defending their father in this new environment. However, there is no doubt that Mrs. Dent suffered severe monetary difficulties without her divorced husband's support.

Fourteen-year-old Vernon found work, singing in a saloon in Oakland. He felt comfortable in such establishments (due to his upbringing) and no doubt was financially dependent on his performing skills. Vernon would not have been the first downtrodden kid, though, to sing for peanuts and pennies. As part of his job description, he was required to clean the bar and shine the spittoons that were sometimes ill-targeted on the sawdust-covered floors. Unlike his father's bar, this kind of "show business" was for sheer sustenance. Vernon learned the art of being diplomatic and engaging, no doubt from his ability to assist drunks and disorderly persons with aplomb. This gregariousness helped draw people to him throughout his life.

Instead of liquor, Vernon's had an insatiable appetite for sweets. It was his one true vice and helps to explain his future weight gain.

MUSIC & SCHOOL

Vernon immersed himself in the entertainment opportunities that were hardly glamorous; they were, in fact, merely seedy ocean port bars. On the other hand, Oakland was also a venue for some of the best live entertainment on the west coast.

The Idora Park was one of those venues. A mainstay in Oakland since 1904, the park offered everything from opera to John Philip Sousa concerts and comedy operettas. After the earthquake, Ferris Hartman (the former entrepreneur of the Tivoli Theatre in San Francisco) took his troupe and set up shop at Idora Park. He was the star and he hired and fired supporting acts accordingly. Mr. Hartman specialized in many comedy operettas over the years, and at one time or another employed hundreds of people for the stage.

Vernon continued his education at Oakland's Fremont High School, one of two public high schools in the city. He was prominently mentioned in the *Oakland Tribune* on two occasions, both times for his thespian pursuits.

SHOW BUSINESS RETURN TO SAN JOSE

Fifteen years old now, Vernon Dent was cast in a charity show put on by the Philotros Club. According to the *San Jose News*, on January 13, 1910, this was a program of sketches with vocal selections. One of the acts was entitled, "A Day at the Vendome Hotel," named after one of the most famous hotels in San Jose at the time. According to the paper, "Mr. Vernon Dent, who recently made such a hit in [the musical-comedy] 'The Jeffersons,' will take the principal part, that of the colored bell-boy." Minstrel singers were a staple of vaudeville and amateur acts during this era. It is probable that Vernon performed in saloons and onstage in "blackface" makeup throughout his teenage years.

"WON BY WIRELESS" TO BE PRESENTED

On September 7, 1911, there was a mention in the *Oakland Tribune* about the Clover Leaf Dramatic Society, performing a play at the Armory Hall. The article also listed the officers of the society, including sixteen-year-old Vernon Dent, who served as secretary. In the society's latest offering, *Won By Wireless*, he was cast in the plum role of Count di Lucco, an Italian nobleman. It is clear that, even at a very young age, Vernon had a flair for dialects.

THE SINCEREST FORM OF FLATTERY

Vaudeville was in its prime and patron support guaranteed a draw of the best talent. Early in 1913 a highly anticipated act came to the city of Oakland. It was called "The New Leader" and starred Sam Mann. The actor, only nine years older than Vernon, developed his dialect humor into a comedy sketch that had just enjoyed a successful run on Broadway; Mann then took his act on the road. One of the stops was The Orpheum Theatre in Oakland, a top vaudeville circuit destination.

Mann represented the American stage tradition of the typical "Dutch" comic. The characterization included an exaggerated German accent with paintbrush whiskers. It seems as though no vaudeville program was complete without a comic specializing in dialect humor. Other big names (e.g., Weber and Fields, Kolb and Dill) built their whole show around their characters. Even during the early Keystone comedies for Mack Sennett, Ford Sterling employed the Dutch comic "look" for the movies.

VERNON MEETS HIS IDOL

When the Mann show arrived at Oakland's Orpheum Theatre on 12th Street, between Clay and Jefferson Streets, Vernon was employed as a theatre usher. Vernon had a chance to watch the show as often as he could and absorb the comedic portrayals.

At some point during the show's run, Vernon met and interacted with the star of the show. It's apparent that Mann greeted Vernon not as a fan, or a lowly employee, but as a peer. Vernon gave his own interpretation of Mann's character, and with the confidence of a seasoned trouper. The headliner was impressed. Sam Mann mentioned this meeting to a reporter for the *Oakland Tribune*, calling the spontaneous performance "the best impersonation of himself that he had ever seen." Such comments no doubt contributed to Vernon's belief that show business was his destiny. He would never forget Sam Mann's kind endorsement.

The entertainers' friendship was cemented when Sam Mann consented to loan Vernon the script of "The New Leader." Arrangements were made for Vernon's high school thespians to reprise the show before their own school audience, on one condition: Vernon had to take the lead comic role. A handshake later, the deal was done.

Mann had a long career on stage and specialized in ethnic humor; German, Irish, and Jewish dialects were his specialty. Actually a Russian immigrant, he perfected a routine in which his character gulped down several beers of assorted sizes and smashed his prop fiddles.

According to the *Oakland Tribune*, March 22, 1913 was a gala day: "Upon the remodeled stage at the John C. Fremont High School, the senior students of that institution will impersonate the celebrities of the Vaudeville world in their annual show which will be held. The young performers who have been selected for the entertainment were successful in securing manuscripts of various sketches which were recently presented on the Orpheum Stage."

Vernon Dent must have brought the house down with his version of "The New Leader." It was such a memorable character that he refined it as his own over the years. During the same evening, Vernon was also part of a singing act called The Midway Quintet; the *Tribune* referred to it as "A Rhapsody of Ragtime."

In a February 27, 1913 article entitled, "Music Enlivens Banquet," a reporter for the *Oakland Tribune* noted that Vernon Dent, Miss Helen Mason, and Bobbie and Charles Bowen made up a quartet called The Gladstone Entertainers. Rounding out the program was Geo. Oscar Young, Vernon's future collaborator.

Vernon was again mentioned by the *Oakland Tribune* in an October 19, 1913 article entitled, "Fremont High Awaits Big Show." This play was performed by fellow senior thespians. The article read, "Vernon Dent, Leslie Fletcher, Howard Vose and Miss Angelina Petty will handle the various roles in the act, described as an operatic 'Punch and Judy.'" The column also promised "an entertaining sketch by Jay Roberts and Vernon Dent in a singing, dancing and piano playing act." This is the type of act that came to be a cornerstone of Vernon's later stage routines and early sound film comedies.

Seventeen-year-old Vernon Dent graces the cover of a song sheet for his joint composition, "Rythmatic Rag," circa 1912. COURTESY OF EDWARD WATZ

CHAPTER 5

COMING OF AGE

Vernon's mother, Fannie M. Dent, died on March 31, 1915, at the age of 41. Her obituary appeared in the *San Jose Evening News* three days later. It announced that the funeral would be held at the residence of her mother, Mrs. F. M. Holley — 114 South 16th Street, in San Jose.*

Nineteen-fifteen was a pivotal year for Vernon. He was a professional musician playing every day at the Panama-Pacific International Exposition in San Francisco. Some say this was the greatest celebration of the arts ever exhibited in the world. There were planning stages for a number of years before the famous earthquake struck. After the fire and earthquake of 1906, the goal of having the world's fair in 1915 seemed unachievable. Virtually the entire city had been destroyed. It was considered an upscale community and a regional magnet to attract people to the Pacific Coast. From the rubble came the determination not only to rebuild the city, but to showcase it in time for the 1915 exposition. Officially, this was a celebration of the completion of the Panama Canal, combined with the discovering of the Pacific Ocean by the explorer, Balboa. The opening of the Panama Canal was timed to celebrate "man's greatest engineering achievement."

Since 1911, other cities formally competed for the honor of hosting this event. New Orleans and San Diego were the primary competition. San Francisco, "The City that Knows How," took great pride when Congress awarded the World's Fair to the city. President William Howard Taft signed legislation to that effect on February 15, 1911. A deciding factor, according to author Dr. William Lipsky, was "the City's promise to accept no federal tax dollars to build the exposition, a pledge no other city could make."

---

*Both of Vernon's parents are buried with elaborate markers at San Jose's historical Oak Hill Cemetery at Curtner Avenue and the Monterey Highway. Rawley E. Dent is also buried there; curiously, his grave is unmarked.

The 635-acre fair was located on a large amount of landfill between Van Ness and the Presidio, its southern border extending to Chestnut Street and stretching north to the San Francisco Bay.

When Vernon Dent was only 17, his name was printed in the paper in association with promoting the San Francisco Exposition. On June 19, 1912, three years before the event, the *Oakland Tribune* ran the following column:

> The moving picture staff of the San Francisco exposition tour company will entertain the directors of the Chamber of Commerce, Merchants' Exchange and other civic bodies tonight at 8 o'clock with an illustrated talk on the cities about the bay. The lecture is one to be repeated throughout the Eastern states to interest visitors to California in its attractions and the features promised in connection with the Fair of 1915. In addition to the pictures, a musical and vaudeville program will be given by the company's staff of entertainers, including George Oscar Young, Miss Celia Terweanor and Vernon Dent.

One of the promotional strategies was to write songs, and the parent company would have them published and circulated nationwide. The songwriting team of Young and Dent was extraordinarily talented, with youthful exuberance. Music sheets were published and distributed all over America in an attempt to draw excitement, money and crowds for this showcase in San Francisco. Two examples of sheet music of this collaboration are still extant. One is "Rhythmatic Drag," which includes a cheery illustration of a couple dancing. The cover also features the credits "Words by Vernon Dent and Music by Geo. Oscar Young," accompanied by photos of the boys.

Messrs. Young and Dent were being recognized as up-and-coming talent. The *Oakland Tribune*, of November 17, 1914, was already calling Young "The Rag Time King" as he had just completed an engagement at Hammerstein's in New York City.

Dent and Young collaborated on another song — "1915 Rag" — to build interest in the fair. Both music sheets were printed by the Pacific Coast Motion Picture Co. of San Francisco. A sample of the lyrics penned by 17-year-old Vernon:

> *Everybody's heard a bout the great big fair,*
> *They're goin' to San Francisco just to see it there,*
> *Folks, we hope to meet you, greet you at the fair,*
> *Bring along your mothers-in-law if you dare!*

When the fair finally opened its gates on February 20, 1915, Mayor Jim Rolph led the way with a grand parade. The attendance swelled to 250,000 people the first day.

It was a standout fair, and some say has never been equaled artistically. The tallest and most recognized exhibit was the "Tower of Jewels." Symbolically lit by President Taft, the edifice boasted more than 100,000 colored glass jewels that shimmered in the night. The court yards, foreign buildings and "Toyland Grows Up" (a nostalgic reference to Victor Herbert's operetta, *Babes in Toyland*) were major attractions. Music was everywhere. Hundreds of concerts were performed.

You can bet that Vernon Dent the "song-pitcher" was there every day. It is unclear if Vernon was simply meeting and greeting people or by then was appearing onstage. A daily duty of interacting with fresh crowds honed his skills as an entertainer. It also drew the attention of Mr. Frank Burt, who was in charge of all concessions.

Stunning as they were, most of the exhibit buildings were constructed of temporary material, meant to last for the duration of the exposition. The exception was the Palace of Fine Arts. It was made of fine heavy duty material to house the most expensive artifacts. It stands to this day as a proud monument.

The San Francisco-Panama Exposition ran from February 20 until December 4, 1915. The imminence of a world war was a concern and hindered commitments. Some countries did not even participate in sending representatives or facsimile landmarks of their own land. Transportation was another barrier from overseas.

In this year of 1915, the exposition's display of electric lights was on the cutting edge of technology. There were actually people who were very nervous with multiple lights reaching far out into the sky during the night. Would such powerful illumination attract Martians like the science fiction novels H. G. Wells suggested? That theory was actually discussed by concerned citizens of the day.

THE KEYSTONE INVASION

Mack Sennett did his part to celebrate the exposition in San Francisco. In April of 1915 he brought a skeleton crew to shoot footage of Roscoe Arbuckle and Mabel Normand. They were shown with Mayor James Rolph, the future governor of California.

During that first week of April 1915, the Sennett crew filmed *Fatty and Mabel Viewing the World's Fair in San Francisco*. While they were in the city, they also took the opportunity to shoot a comedy at San Francisco's Golden Gate Park, *Wished on Mabel*. This one-reeler featured Fatty and Mabel, of course, but also had a juicy role for Edgar Kennedy, who had been raised in San Francisco.

Another film production was scheduled within a week's time while they were in Northern California. Both Oakland and San Jose vied for the honor of having the film shot in their respective cities. This also must have been of great interest to Vernon Dent. Which city would win? On April 6, 1915 leaders of the city of San Jose invited the crew down for a couple of days. They were wined, dined and escorted all through town. It looked so certain, in fact, that the following article appeared in the *San Jose Mercury Herald*:

KEYSTONE COMEDY STARS HERE FOR PICTURE WORK

Roscoe Arbuckle, a former resident of San Jose, and Miss Mabel Normand, of the Keystone Comedy Co. known throughout the United States and many foreign countries as "Fat and Mabel," arrived in this city yesterday with several other members of the same company for the purpose of taking motion pictures in various sections of the valley.

It was just a few years ago that Mr. Arbuckle was singing illustrated songs at the old Unique picture house in this city. Today he is one of the most widely known motion picture actors in the country.

With Mr. Arbuckle and Miss Normand are other members of the company who came down by train: Edgar Kennedy, Glen Cavender, William Gilbert, Joseph Bordeaux and Elgin Leslie, Cameraman.

Yesterday afternoon was spent in looking about the valley and selecting locations for settings. The company is greatly pleased with Alum Rock Park, where several films will be taken this morning. A comedy will probably be staged on Market Street or Santa Clara Street with a chase and a fight half way up the Tower. Pictures will also be taken at Mount Hamilton. The films will show that they were taken in Santa Clara County.

Mr. James Beatty, Manager of the Liberty Theatre, has made arrangements with the two comedy stars to appear in person at the Liberty [on Market Street] Wednesday evening.

As it turned out, the Keystone Company was lured to Oakland's Idora Park to make their comedy. It was called *Mabel's Willful Way*, and was shot in April of 1915, in a few days' time. This time Edgar Kennedy played Roscoe Arbuckle's competitor for Mabel Normand's love. The movie showcased the many feature attractions of Idora Park. One of the most stunning scenes was Arbuckle feeding a bear an ice cream cone while holding the cone in his mouth.

As wonderful as the scenes are of Idora Park's setting, it is regrettable that such a comedy was not shot in San Jose — the chase up the famous San Jose Electric Tower would have been stupendous. Time had run out on this great landmark; the great San Jose Tower collapsed during a wind storm later that year in 1915. The twisted iron carnage blocked the major intersection of San Jose and photographs of the demise made newspapers editions around the country.

On June 6, 1915 Vernon took a day off from the San Francisco Exposition; he traveled south the 45 miles for a family reunion. The *San Jose Mercury* reported the event:

Mr. and Mrs. Chas. Warren entertained about sixty friends at a picnic at their ranch on Stevens Creek. The occasion was in honor of their nephew, Vernon Dent. A bountiful lunch was spread under the trees on the bank of the creek. Mr. Dent added much to the pleasure of the guests by giving a number of comic recitations. Fred Bell sang two beautiful solos, and the trio composed of Miss Call, Mr. Dent and Mr. Bell was much enjoyed.

MINNIE CALL

On July 1, 1915 an advertisement appeared in the *Oakland Tribune* promoting a cabaret show at the Forum Café. The featured performers would be Geo. Oscar Young and Miss Minnie Call. Miss Call, who played piano, accompanied Mr. Young for the cabaret dance act.

Vernon's friends included a small group of entertainers. It was a matter of time before he and Minnie Call struck up an interest in each other. They were married later that year.

Minnie Elizabeth Call was born in 1896, in California. The daughter of William and Maggie Call, the family (including two siblings) is shown in the 1900 census as living in Stockton, California. In 1910 Minnie and her family were living in Grass Valley, in the California gold country. By then Minnie had four additional brothers and sisters. Minnie was an accomplished pianist.

HIS FIRST MARRIAGE

With the exposition concluded and his mother's death behind him, Vernon took another big step in his life: he proposed to Minnie Call. They were married on December 27, 1915, at the courthouse in the city of San Francisco. The best man was Harry Highsmith and the matron of honor was Mrs. F. C. Bell (Fred Bell's wife). It was the trio of Highsmith, Bell and Dent that went on to Seal Beach, California, to resume their cabaret act.

On October 6, 1917 the *San Jose Mercury Herald* reported a benefit bazaar at the ranch of Vernon's aunt off Homestead Avenue in Cupertino, northwest of San Jose.

> Mr. and Mrs. Vernon Dent of Los Angeles were the guests of Mr. and Mrs. Chas. E. Warren this week. As part of the entertainment, Mr. Vernon Dent gracefully favored the assemblage with a splendid and versatile program of humor dialect impersonations and songs, his hearers clamoring for more. All enjoyed a treat of generous portions of ice cream and cake through the hospitality of Mr. and Mrs. Chas. E. Warren.

Postcard shot of Gus Mann's Jewel City Café, circa 1917. AUTHOR'S COLLECTION

CHAPTER 6

JEWEL CITY

After the steady employment of the San Francisco Panama-Exposition and with the enchantment of matrimony, Vernon was feeling his oats. No reason to stay in the San Francisco Bay Area; he had built up goodwill and business contacts elsewhere. One such contact was Frank Burt, who had handled the concessions at the exposition.

Burt moved to Seal Beach, California, formed the Jewel City Amusement Company, and sold investment shares. Seal Beach was in Southern California, between Long Beach and Huntington Beach on the Anaheim Bay, some 500 miles directly south of San Francisco. This area previously had no real attraction other than the beach. With great foresight, the city and county of Los Angeles approved the "Red Cars," part of a mass-transit plan to transport beachgoers to what was then known as "Bay City." Land was cheap, but there were other beaches close by.

Frank Burt took advantage of the potential business opportunities and built a landmark facility on the beach; the nightclub was called Jewel City. (It is a point of speculation if it was marketed in recent reference to the Tower of Jewels, the main exhibit at the San Francisco exposition.) To add more pizzazz, Mr. Burt built an adjoining amusement park and called it The Joy Zone (another identifier from San Francisco). It featured what became known as "The Derby." In actuality, it was the rollercoaster from the exposition, dismantled and shipped south.

At the entrance to the pier was the famed Jewel City Café, which included a dance floor that could accommodate 500 patrons. This being so far out in the "sticks," it was a place where wild jazz music would play and the liquor flowed at night; there was also gambling and prostitution. The daytime hours brought out the families looking for the more wholesome attractions at the beach and boardwalk.

In an article by Sarah L. Sawyer ("Seal Beach: City with a Past and Future"), Frank Burt was described as "the finest amusement man in the world." Burt heavily advertised and promoted the resort as the "Coney Island of the Pacific." Seal Beach was only 45 minutes from Broadway in Los Angeles, and in 1916 one million people visited the resort. Legend has it that some movies were made at the beach.

With the recent success of playing to the San Francisco crowds, Frank Burt hired Vernon as part of a cabaret act that included his pals Harry Highsmith and Fred Bell. Jewel City Café kept Vernon permanently employed and gave him the opportunity to sing and use his talent for dialects. His act included eccentric dancing and interactive routines with the audience. The Jewel City Café was the spot that Mabel Normand, Fatty Arbuckle, Harold Lloyd, and Bebe Daniels competed for the nightly dance prizes. The proprietor of the Jewel City Café was Gus Mann. As Vernon later recalled to a reporter, "I found myself at the popular Jewel City Café in Seal Beach in a trio. There was Harry Highsmith and Fred Bell, both names to remember, and I sang baritone." (It is of interest that Vernon sang baritone; in most of his movie singing opportunities, he displayed a marvelous tenor pitch.)

UNCLE SAM WANTS YOU!

With war looming in Europe, legislation was enacted to register all males between the ages of 18 to 50 for the purpose of compiling a draft list. Vernon registered for the draft on June 5, 1917. He identified his occupation as a "Musician at the Jewel City Café." When Vernon filled out the papers, he listed his height at five-seven, his eye color as blue, and his weight as a relatively slight 206 pounds. His wife was identified as Minnie Elizabeth Dent, and his permanent residence at 48 South 5th Street in San Jose. During The Great War, Minnie and her sister-in-law lived at this address, which was a boarding house.

Of interest in the news in 1917, there was a new fighting ship that had been launched by the U.S. Navy: *Battleship Dent*, named after Captain John Dent, born in 1782 and died, in Maryland, on March 16, 1823. He was Vernon's great-great grandfather. It stands to reason that Vernon chose to enlist in the U.S. Navy, and he did so on May 24, 1918. He went to the Recruiting Station at San Diego, most likely hoping to land on the destroyer. This was not to be, however; he stayed stateside, working as a paymaster for the duration of the conflict overseas.

After signing up, Vernon's ranking was that of "Enlisted Man" after going through training; he graduated to Yeo-3c on July 22, 1918, and was assigned as paymaster for $32.60 a month. (There was a compulsory monthly allotment to his wife of $17.50.) Vernon was in the capable hands of Uncle Sam and had free room, board, and medical care. Petty Officer Dent never went overseas. Once the war wound down, he was honorably discharged on December 6, 1918, in San Diego, California. As for *Battleship Dent*, she served 27.2 years through two wars and was decommissioned on December 4, 1945.

THE GIRL OF MY DREAMS

In 1919 another Vernon Dent song, "The Girl of My Dreams," was published. His music collaborator this time was Ben Light. Who was the mysterious girl on the cover of the song sheet for "The Girl of My Dreams"? She was Beatriz Michelena, known to moviegoers at the time as the star of various productions of The California Motion Picture Corporation. A former opera star, Beatriz Michelena won acclaim for her movies, which were produced in San Rafael, California. These films were based on writings of Bret Harte (1836–1902), who had written stories and poems celebrating the California Forty-niners. Some of Beatriz Michelena's films include *Salomy Jane* (1914), *The Lily of Poverty Flat* (1914), *A Phyllis of the Sierra's* (1915), and *The Flame of Hellgate* (1920).

Song sheet for "Girl of My Dreams."
AUTHOR'S COLLECTION

In addition to songwriting, Vernon continued to work as an entertainer, as this item in the *Los Angeles Times* of December 17, 1919 attests:

Creditmen Entertain —
Four Hundred Members and Friends Attend Annual Affair

The Annual high jinks of the Associated Retail Creditmen of Los Angeles were held last night in the Broadway Dept. Store Café. Film comedian Charles Murray presided over the evening's festivities. Others on the program were James J. Corbett,

Vernon Dent and others. Christmas presents for everyone were distributed.

Vernon's brother, Melvin, was a big part of the Creditmen organization, being in the retail business. According to the 1920 census, the Dents shared a common house with his brother, wife, and sister-in-law Doris. They lived on a farm in then-rural Alhambra, California, in the Township of San Gabriel, near Los Angeles. Vernon's occupation was listed as "Actor–moving pictures." Vernon was also listed in the Los Angeles city directory. The entry included his address (1839 S. Main), his occupation ("Photoplayer") and his telephone number (H[ollywood]-1839).

Vernon photo and ad in Hollywood Blue Book *for agents, circa 1919.*
COURTESY OF MARGARET HERRICK LIBRARY

CHAPTER 7

VERNON IN THE MOVIES

Hank Mann (born David Willie Lieberman on May 28, 1887, in New York City), was an important contributor to the history of silent film comedy. According to Mack Sennett's autobiography, Mann had been one of the seven original Keystone Cops. He also has the distinction of introducing Vernon Dent to the moviegoing masses.

On January 6, 1917, the *Moving Picture World* announced: "HANK MANN HAS OWN COMPANY." This new company was actually under the banner of Foxfilm comedies, the director being Charles Parrott (Charley Chase). When war was declared, Hank Mann enlisted; when the war ended he returned to the States and was given the opportunity to star for the Arrow Film Corporation. Mann put together a supporting cast, and needed someone versatile enough to play any kind of role, from villains to juvenile leads. He found him in Vernon Dent. Vernon gave his all in such one- and two-reelers as *An Auto Nut*, *A Harem Hero*, *The Dentist*, *The Janitor*, *The Messenger*, *In Hock*, *The Bill Poster*, *The Bell Hop*, *When Spirits Move*, *A Gum Riot*, *Broken Bubbles*, *Naughty Nurses*, *The Paper Hanger*, *Roaming Romeo*, *Mystic Mush*, and *Way Out West*.

On August 7, 1920, a photo appeared in the *Exhibitor's Herald* from Hank Mann's newest comedy, *Don't Change Your Mrs.* (a parody of Cecil B. DeMille's 1919 five-reeler, *Don't Change Your Husband*). The caption reads, "Hank Mann, Vernon Dent and Director Charlie [*sic*] Parrott try out a new melody between takes of Mann's latest Arrow Comedy, while Marge Kirby, leading lady, listens attentively for a sour note."

ANOTHER HOLLYWOOD CASUALTY

On January 6, 1921, after six years and ten days of marriage, Minnie Dent sought a complaint of divorce. The only community property listed was "one Nash Sedan automobile and an unknown sum of money under the control and in the possession of the defendant." Mrs. Dent alleged that she was abandoned and without the necessities of life.

In the complaint Minnie Dent claimed that Vernon "is a motion picture director and is capable of earning $250.00 a week and is a strong and capable man." They were legally divorced on July 19, 1924. There were no children from this marriage.

VERNON GETS HIS OWN SERIES

On February 20, 1921 the *Los Angeles Times* reported that the Pacific Film Company "has taken possession of its studios at Culver City. Production for the present is confined to one-reel George Ovey comedies, the schedule calling for one release a week." Release dates would be inconsistent because of "states rights market."

Vernon, wearing hat (à la Roscoe "Fatty" Arbuckle), shares his dinner with a dog in an unidentified Folly Comedy, circa 1921. COURTESY OF SAM GILL

Vernon did support George Ovey in one of the comedies, *Mummy's Nightmare*, in 1922. However, it appears that the studio eyed Vernon with just as much potential to be a star for them. The *Film Daily* trade journal announced about this time that Pacific was putting out 26 comedies for the year, 13 with Vernon Dent and 13 with George Ovey.

The Vernon Dent titles included *Fat and Sassy, Coming and Going, Get the Hook, High and Mighty, In at the Finish, Now or Never, On the Jump, Sleeping Sickness, Slow But Sure, They're Off,* and *Up and at 'Em.*

According to the August 7, 1921 *Salt Lake Telegram*:

> The one Southern California motion pictures studio in which visitors are made welcome and are given an opportunity of witnessing real stars at work is that of the Pacific Film Company, where each week Manager John J. Hayes entertains hundreds of tourists. They see George Ovey, Vernon Dent and their White Cap comedians in action, filming single-reels in an ambitious program that schedules fifty-two releases during the next twelve months.

In the September 25, 1921 *Oregonian*...

> Add the name of another Oregon man to the list of those who have made good in filmdom. A. Guy Frum is Secretary and Treasurer of the White Cap Productions, Inc., at Culver City, California.
>
> The White Cap Production Company is a subsidiary organization of the Pacific Film Co. and was organized for the purpose of producing "Folly" Comedies, featuring George Ovey and Vernon Dent.
>
> Frum is acknowledged to be the busiest man on the lot for he is in charge of properties and acts as assistant to Milton H. Fahrney, veteran Director of the company.

And in an issue of *Camera* magazine (Vol. 4. no. 33)...

> "Folly" Unit Resumes Program — After a vacation of a few weeks, one of the "Folly" comedy units of the Pacific Film Company has resumed operations and it is expected that production will be steady from this time forward. Vernon Dent and Violet Joy are the featured players.

Very little of the Pacific Film Company's output still exists. In some films, Vernon plays a character known as "The Boob," a country bumpkin. Other roles have him playing a virtual imitation of Roscoe "Fatty" Arbuckle's screen persona. Like Roscoe, Vernon wore a too-small derby, four-in-hand tie, trousers that didn't reach his ankles, and large canalboat shoes. With his physical stature and comic prowess, it must have

Coming and Going *(Folly Comedies, 1922)*. COURTESY OF EDWARD WATZ

seemed like a logical choice. (In several of the shorts, Vernon was referred to as "Babe" — the same nickname given to Oliver Hardy in his solo film days, both on and offscreen.) Arbuckle was truly a giant in the industry and anyone who could similarly entertain the masses (at a cheaper salary) had a chance to make fame and fortune. But his popularity would end abruptly when he was charged with manslaughter in the Virginia Rappe case in 1921. By the following year, some distributors were calling for the banishment of Arbuckle movies. The "Fatty" persona that Vernon was using came to a screeching halt.*

---

*There are several books pertaining to the Arbuckle scandal; one of the best is Andy Edmonds's *Frame-Up! The Shocking Scandal That Destroyed Hollywood's Biggest Comedy Star, Roscoe "Fatty" Arbuckle* (New York: Avon Books, 1991).

A DRAMATIC CHANGE

Vernon was hired by the Thomas Ince Company, this time for a part in *Hail the Woman*, a contemporary drama about women's rights. It was produced immediately after the Nineteenth Amendment was ratified in 1920. This film was praised for its gripping realism. Vernon was cast as

Vernon Dent portrait (Sennett, circa 1923) COURTESY OF THE MARGARET HERRICK LIBRARY

comic relief — a good-hearted country boy who comes-a-courtin' Florence Vidor. Vidor, the star of the film, played a modern woman fighting for her rights. At one point, a scandalized Vernon exclaims about Vidor: "I caught her smokin' cigaroots!"

Director John Griffith Wray had grown up in Oakland and directed stage performances in Oakland. According to *The Silver Sheet*, the in-house periodical produced by the Ince Studios, Ince signed Vernon in 1920 to make pictures. Had Wray and Vernon worked together before in Oakland? There is nothing in print to confirm this, but it is likely that they knew of each other. Another person in Vernon's corner might have been Ince himself, a former associate with Mack Sennett and his Triangle Pictures (along with D.W. Griffith).

On January 22, 1922, the *San Jose Mercury* had this to say about *Hail the Woman:*

> The triumph of "Hail the Woman" continues at the T & D [the initials of the owners, Turner & Dahnken]. The great Thomas H. Ince picture will close tomorrow night, and those who have seen it are advising their friends not to miss the extraordinary screen epic. Grandeur is the keynote of "Hail the Woman." Mr. Ince has laid it on with a lavish hand. The story itself is a mighty one. In fact, "Hail the Woman" is certain to stand out as one of the milestones in the history of the screen.

Three days later, *Hail the Woman* had a screening in Los Angeles at the Mission Theatre. According to the *Los Angeles Times*, the gala event was attended by the producer, director and the cast, including Vernon. This fact garnered considerable attention in the actor's hometown. The following article appeared in the *San Jose Evening Mercury* on January 7, 1922:

> San Jose Boy is Ince Star
>
> San Jose has added another name to its already list of celebrities, both on the stars and on the screen Vernon Dent who is very well known in San Jose, having been born, raised and educated here, is now a star in his own right. He is being featured in a series of comedies which are being made in Los Angeles and is very fast working himself to the front. He graduated from the Horace Mann grammar school, and later went to the Oakland

high school. He then took up singing as a profession and gradually got into pictures. He is a nephew of Mr. and Mrs. Charles Warren of Cupertino.

Thomas Ince in looking about for an all star cast for *Hail the Woman* saw Mr. Dent's work, and immediately borrowed him to appear in his current masterpiece. He was the type and had the capability which Mr. Ince immediately recognized. *Hail the Woman* has real stars and Mr. Dent is highly elated over the fact that Ince selected him over so many others who are better known in pictures. In *Hail the Woman* he has established a reputation which will lead to a brilliant future, as his work will show when his San Jose friends see the picture. He has been home visiting his parents [*sic*] for the holidays and has just returned to Los Angeles to resume production of his own comedies. Mr. Dent stated in an interview that production will resume after the first of the year and a bigger year and bigger and better picture that's ever before offered will be given to the American public. *Hail the Woman* is a fore-runner of what the picture producers will offer during the coming year and Thomas Ince has produced a picture which will live forever in the minds of those who see it.

"It was a great pleasure to work with Mr. Ince for he is considerate and an all around good fellow and one of the most capable masters of the silent drama," [Vernon apparently told a reporter].

Mr. Dent was accompanied to San Jose by his leading lady, dainty little Violet Joy who was the guest of his relatives during the holidays. *Hail the Woman* will be show at the T & D all next week.

It is interesting that Vernon was accompanied with Violet Joy/Duane Thompson during this trip. His marriage was clearly on the rocks, with his divorce proceedings already underway. Vernon's aunt and uncle accepted the circumstances and welcomed the new couple.

Vernon's co-star was later one of the thirteen WAMPAS Baby Stars of 1925. This "baby" was twenty-two years old, and a petite five-one. She was born July 28, 1903, in Red Oak, Iowa. Little Violet's first film role was to support Vernon Dent in *Up and at 'Em*. By 1923 the actress was using the name Duane Thompson. She made four other films in 1923, and continued to play leading roles until 1929. Some speculate that it was the "talkies" that held her back, although she did appear along with other silent comedy veterans in the 1937 film, *Hollywood Hotel*.

In a press sheet for the Christie comedy *Plumb Crazy* (released June 3, 1923), there was advance publicity. Entitled "New Christie Star with Bobby Vernon," the item attempts to clarify the name change.

Duane Thompson, the new leading lady with Educational-Christie Comedies, who makes her bow with Bobby Vernon in

Violet Joy a.k.a. Duane Thompson a.k.a. Duane Maloney. COURTESY OF COLE JOHNSON

"Plumb Crazy," has had a lot of trouble with her name. Duane Thompson happens to be her real name, but she used to be known in comedy pictures as Violet Joy. The latter name was wished on her some time ago when she was first featured in pictures, no one knows why. We've often wondered who thinks up some of the fancy names for movie people. At any rate, Miss Thompson likes her own name and isn't ashamed of it, so she went back to her real "nom de movie" as soon as she had the opportunity.

Violet Joy, who "confessed" that her real name was Duane Thompson, in reality, was born with the name Duane Maloney, according to the United States Census. Why all the subterfuge? No one knows.

BACK TO SAN JOSE

On April 25, 1922, the *San Jose Evening News* announced the arrival in San Jose of Howe's Great London Circus. On May 3rd a movie company with several well-known screen stars would be filmed in a feature picture for the Thomas H. Ince studios. The paper promised that "many San Jose residents will have the opportunity to appear in scenes of this motion picture production."

The next day, there was a small item in one of the San Jose papers. It pertained to the coming of Howe's Great London Circus. This particular circus was an annual event dating back many years. As part of the standard entertainment, the circus featured trained wild animals, including an elephant that was soon to get the Hollywood "treatment" and become a movie star overnight. On April 26, 1922, the *San Jose Mercury* had this to say about the forthcoming spectacle:

Howe's Circus to Show in San Jose

Coming of Howe's Great London Circus with Van Amberg's trained wild animals to San Jose, afternoon and evening on Wed. May 1st is being thoroughly exploited throughout the city and surrounding rural districts. Today an advertising car arrived and in no time at all 20 billposters, programmers and lithographers were busy hanging colored posters for The Howe-Van Amberg, The World's Wonder Show.

The *San Jose Mercury* also noted the return of its native son. Vernon was visiting his aunt and uncle and was present when the above Howe's Circus was performing its act. The fact that a Hollywood camera crew and cast was in San Jose made it all the more newsworthy. It must have been a proud homecoming for the local lad who made good.

CHAPTER 8

TRIUMPHANT RETURN TO SAN JOSE

The following article, which appeared in the San Jose Mercury during Vernon's visit to his hometown (on May 3, 1922), is the only one in which he identified his exact place of birth and the school he attended. For all the wonderful disclosures, there were still some mighty silly explanations pertaining to Vernon's "coincidental" inclusion in his current movie project.

>   Hale, heavy and hearty, with a broad smile on his face, Vernon Dent, one of the prominent motion picture stars of the Thomas H. Ince Co., visited his "home town," San Jose yesterday, while his company is taking a feature picture at the circus here.
>   "It is the strangest coincidence, how I am here in this picture," Vernon told the reporter. "I finished a picture down in Los Angeles just recently and came up to visit my aunt and uncle, Mr. and Mrs. Charles Warren, at their ranch in Cupertino. We were taking a weekend trip to Carmel last Saturday and on the road down we ran right into a motion picture outfit. Not knowing they were a part of the Ince Company, we stopped and the first thing I knew, the director welcomed me with 'Hello, Dent, you are just the man I am looking for, sent a letter to Los Angeles to get you, but you had gone. How did you happen to know I wanted you?'"
>   "So today I am visiting all the pawnshops in San Jose to find just the costume I want for my part," Vernon continued. "I am to be a country hick who is just visiting the circus for the first time with my best clothes all pressed out of shape for having been packed away for a long time. That is the scene I have to play here."

"Sure is great to get back to the old city again," chortled Dent yesterday, as he dropped in at the office of the T & D theatre. Dent was born here about thirty years ago at the corner of Third and St. John Streets. He attended the Horace Mann grammar school under John Munzer and later completed his education in Oakland schools.

With beautiful Violet Joy, accompanying him yesterday when he talked with The News, he is playing a comedy part in the picture "Someone to Love." The picture is bringing many famous movie stars to this city, most of them took part in the recent picture, "Hail the Woman," in which Dent scored such a great success as the villain. Among the stars that are in San Jose are Madge Bellamy, Cullen Landis and Noah Beery.

The following column from the *San Jose Evening News*, also dated May 3, 1922, gives some fascinating background on the making of the film.

Circus in Town

The circus is here, and so are the "movies." Twenty-eight screen folk including stars, directors, camera men and "extras" from the Thomas H. Ince studios at Culver City, are in San Jose today with Howe's Great London circus and animal show. The screen players joined the circus here to "troupe" with it to film a screen feature that has a circus for the background.

Many San Jose residents will be "shot" in the scenes to be taken tonight in the main show tent before the conclusion of the performance. Daylight scenes of the circus crowds and performances are being made this afternoon. The circus is showing on The Alameda near the West San Jose depot.

The screen players include Madge Bellamy, one of the stars in "Hail the Woman," Cullen Landis, Vernon Dent, former resident of San Jose, along with others [including] Clarke W. Thomas, Ince General Manager. The circus is a California corporation with winter quarters at Redwood City. It includes many wild acts not found with any other circus.

The main attraction for the movie was the exploits of their tamed elephant named Anna May. This talented creature did tricks on command and was one of the most popular draws of the circus. A plot had been developed around the elephant to co-star with Madge Bellamy. The working title was "Someone to Love."

Here's some interesting gossip found in the *San Francisco Chronicle*, dated May 21, 1922:

Screen Stars Fail to Mix with the Circus Folk

When Thomas H. Ince starts to make a picture he stops at nothing in the way of expense, even to buy a circus for a week so that real "atmosphere" goes into the work. John Griffith Wray is directing the picture and Cullen Landis, Madge Bellamy and Noah Beery are its stars. Ince bought Howe's Great London Circus for a week playing San Jose. The cast joined the circus at San Jose taking with them forty or fifty "types" and carrying their own animals and their own freaks for the side-shows.

It is just as well this was done because for the circus people grew very temperamental, performers, animals and attendees and held aloof from the mere picture actors.

When Wray offered to take the crowd into the eating tent for breakfast, 30 to 40 [of those seated individuals] got up from the long tables to leave hungry rather than join the screen actors.

Frank A. Cassidy and Charles T. Boulware, owners of Howe's gave themselves whole-heartedly in helping the movie people. Howe's is an animal show, with troupes of real tigers, lions, pigs, and a goat act. The story requires a small town atmosphere.

The *Santa Cruz Evening News* closely followed the progress of this production since certain actors and the star elephant made the trek west through Santa Clara Valley, through to the redwoods of Santa Cruz County.

March 26, 1922, *Santa Cruz Evening News:*

Movie People Arrive

Greeting the newcomers, who arrived on the noon train today from Los Angeles were the movie people, about forty in number, who for the next several weeks will be engaged in the production of a film under the direction of Mr. Wray, of the Thomas. H. Ince

Motion Picture Producers. Two special coaches were needed for the players and their baggage and their arrival created quite a little excitement in this village. And many exclamations of delight were uttered by the women visitors at the beautiful mountain scenery, on every side in evidence, as they emerged from the train. The several hotels and rooming houses have ample accommodations for the visitors who have been given a glad welcome.

March 29, 1922, *Santa Cruz Evening News:*

Boulder Creek Harbors Many Movie Actors

At the present time Boulder Creek is harboring in its midst the largest company of movie players ever assembled at one time in Santa Cruz County, the total number aggregating sixty, which includes actors and others necessary to film the production, *Some One To Love.* The company represents the players of the Thomas H. Ince concern, with headquarters at Culver City.

Some of the stars that are engaged in the production of the play are Cullen Landis and Madge Bellamy, who are assuming leads.

The Director, John Griffith Wray, is a brother-in-law of B.F. Brissac of the Mission garage of this city. It is the present intention of the company to remain in Boulder Creek for a month. Many of the settings for the play will be filmed on the old site which marked the place for a large number of the scenic features of "Poverty Flat."

Poverty Flat was a local name for an area in the Santa Cruz mountains near Boulder Creek. It had been used through the years by many movie companies on location; but the one name stuck because *The Lily of Poverty Flat* was shot there in 1915 by the California Motion Picture Corporation. It was financially based in San Francisco, but had studio headquarters in San Rafael, in Marin County, just north of San Francisco.

There were many important film pioneers using the Santa Cruz Mountains to obtain a sense of authentic western backdrops. Gilbert M. Anderson of the Essanay Film Manufacturing Company shot some of his popular "Broncho Billy" Westerns between Felton, Boulder Creek and Ben Lomond. G.M. Anderson later added a western studio extended the Essanay Studios westward in Niles, California, where his "Broncho Billy"

Westerns would thrive. Anderson and George K. Spoor had formed Essanay in Chicago in 1907.*

April 8, 1922, *Santa Cruz Evening News:*

Boulder Creek

Tuesday was one of the big days at the movie village since a large part of the population of Boulder Creek and Brookdale were employed for the day to assist in the make up of some of the scenes to be produced. The village — consisting of one long street — represents a typical village in northwest Canada in pioneer days. The log cabins and the buildings were ablaze with colored streamers and other decorations, while large flags of Canada and England were in evidence on the street. Under the direction of Fred Moody, farmers from the mountain regions and the San Lorenzo Valley had gathered with saddle horses, buggies, and spring wagons to play their roles. And when all was ready Mr. Wray, the director, gave the signal for action, and then began the parade through the village.

Among the more noticeable figures seen was Deputy Sheriff Horstman on prancing steed, while the crowd of young and old joined in the procession. It was an animated scene as they marched, laughing and greeting each other as though they met for the first time in many years.

Then there was the dance on the village green to the concertina music and the old-time mirth and hilarity abounding. The movie people mingled with the local people, the stars playing their respective parts more effectively than the amateurs, who had to be repeatedly coached by the director, whose labors called for much patience and ability. Several hundred dollars were paid to the local people by the company for the day's performance, which was the day when the circus came to town.

---

*Niles was actually in Alameda County and is now part of Fremont, California. It is located between Oakland and San Jose. It is interesting that the Essanay Company was located in Alameda County instead of in the Santa Cruz Mountains. There was a great deal of money and influence behind building a motion picture studio near Santa Cruz. The most prominent of these notables was Fred Swanton, the builder of the Santa Cruz Beach Boardwalk, in 1904.

April 12, 1922, *Santa Cruz Evening News:*

At the noon hour yesterday, it became apparent to the persons who happened to be on Main Street that something out of the ordinary had occurred; children excitedly pointed and ran in the same direction as they pointed, dogs barked and horses shied and vainly endeavored to break loose from their hitching posts — all of which commotion was caused by the arrival of a strange looking quadruped — an elephant. It arrived on the freight train, the man in charge saying that it was the first ride on the railway cars that the elephant had experienced. The trip seemed to have brought on an attack of malaise, which is akin to seasickness, so the mammal was led into the large garage of Moody and Cress for a period of rest. It will be used for several days in the production of a film by the movie company — the San Lorenzo River at its confluence with the waters of Boulder Creek being the place selected for the production.

April 20, 1922, *Santa Cruz Evening News:*

Boulder Creek Folks See Themselves in Film

At Sweeney's Hall Monday evening one of the reels shown at the picture show was the street carnival scene, recently played on "Poverty Flat" by the movie people, assisted by a large number of local citizens. As was to be expected, the picture created an unusual amount of interest. Anna May, the elephant, has been very busy the past week at the movie colony and is playing her parts in the film production with skill and aptitude.

April 21, 1922, *Santa Cruz Evening News:*

Boulder Creek Notes

Anna May was the attraction, along with the movie folks at a beautiful part of the creek and some good pictures were taken of a scene in which Madge Bellamy was the heroine. Anna May is a most intelligent animal.

The Ince Co. is still here. They expect to remain two weeks longer. They have been busy working some of the time until midnight. The name of the production is "Some One to Love." Anna May, the queen of trained elephants, arrived several days ago and has been kept very busy acting her several parts. She can be made to do anything but talk.

April 24, 1922, *Santa Cruz Evening News:*

Much merriment was caused on Thursday on Central Ave., the main business street, when Anna May, the movie colony elephant, paraded the avenue with four passengers on her back; Mr. and Mrs. G. A. Cress and Mr. and Mrs. A. W. Gibbs being the daring riders. Later, Mr. and Mrs. L. Steers rode in the saddle, and Mrs. Gibbs on the elephant's head, while the cameras clicked, taking pictures of the unusual scene, amid the applause of a crowd of onlookers. The elephant is docile and intelligent and responds to both signs and words from her trainer, H. Johnson.

April 28, 1922, *Santa Cruz Evening News:*

Movie Players Come to Felton

The Thomas Ince Film Company of players at present filming scenes for the new play, "Some One to Love" at Boulder Creek are now engaged in taking scenes in the neighborhood of Felton. While in the latter place, they will make the trip back and forth to Boulder Creek by auto.

The *Santa Cruz Sentinel* noted that the movie star colony had left the area by May 2, 1922. Filming continued at the Ince Studios in Culver City. *Soul of the Beast* was released on May 7, 1923, a full year after the scenes were shot on location. (That was an unusually long time for a film to be held back or still in production. No studio could afford to have an asset tied up so long without money coming in.) Many changes had been made on the original script. The title, for example, had been changed from "Someone to Love" to *Soul of the Beast*. That happens frequently enough, but the most astonishing change from filming to release, was the elephant's name. Originally, the newspaper articles in Santa Cruz referred to the elephant as Anna May. Then upon release of the finished product, they changed the elephant's name to "Oscar."

What happened here? The elephant was so engaging in its interaction with the star Madge Bellamy, the Ince studio was apparently unsure how to best promote the characters. Did the gender of the elephant really matter in the plot line? Apparently it did. It is likely preview audiences saw different versions, specifically to see if the emotional attachment was keener for an Anna May or an Oscar.

As late as February 4, 1923, the *Los Angeles Times* wrote a story about the imminent release of the film, with a new twist. The article, "Anna May's Ten-Ton Love," stated that the "lady elephant had a strange affection for the movie actress whose life she saved in a circus picture."

The story goes that a drunken keeper gave an incorrect order for the pachyderm to roll over the actress. She would have been crushed to death, but the intelligent animal (not the keeper) was able to foresee the potential peril, and averted doom. There was a photo of Madge Bellamy visiting Anna May at the Selig Zoo in appreciation.

The attempt to have the audience bond with the elephant and actor for saving her life seemed a little bit of a stretch, even by Hollywood standards. The Ince Company needed a hit that would capture the hearts of their movie customers. They decided to reach for the widest general audience. Now they needed to get the picture into theaters.

Newspaper ad for Soul of the Beast *(Ince, 1923)*. COURTESY OF RANDY BROWN

A little over a month had passed and a new publicity strategy was developed: "Change Everything." On May 5, 1923 the *Moving Picture World* announced that the maternal relationship would have been a different cinema expression altogether. The trick was in the editing. In the scenes with Madge Bellamy and Oscar, it appeared that the elephant had a protective crush on his human co-star. The studio decided that was more palatable.

The Ince Studio poured out the publicity on pre-release. *Soul of the Beast* was celebrated as a special movie with an all-star cast. The Ince movie trade paper, *The Silver Sheet*, made the false claim that the film was shot "in the Canadian Woods." The completed film eventually made its way to the new Santa Cruz Theatre on July 4, 1923.

This circus movie with an abused runaway girl and an adoring elephant charmed critics and audiences of the time. In a groundbreaking technique for its time, this silent feature film actually showed close-ups of animals with subtitles indicating dialogue. The editing made it appear that the various creatures of the woods were literally *talking* with one another. Those scenes look a bit antiquated to modern audiences, but it apparently worked in 1923. In any case, it was a noteworthy credit in Vernon Dent's burgeoning career.

COMEDY HEAVYWEIGHTS

Vernon got a break later in 1922, when Vitagraph film comedian Larry Semon hired him for two of his comedies: *A Pair of Kings* and *Golf*. There was another young "fat" supporting comic working in these films: Oliver "Babe" Hardy. Interestingly, Vernon plays his country-boy "Babe" characterization one last time in *Golf* while *A Pair of Kings* looks forward to his suave and subtle late-silent appearances, with Vernon here as the king's loyal prime minister.

On July 23, 1922, Semon, Hardy, and Dent volunteered their time for a gala event on behalf of "World War" veterans and their "less fortunate brothers." It was held at the Overseas Club, located at First and Spring Street. During the musical portion of the program, Oliver Hardy and Vernon Dent led a sing-along of the World War I hit, "*Mademoiselle from Armentières*."

Vernon appeared at many of these charity fundraisers. On one memorable occasion he and Charles Parrott (later known as comedian/director Charley Chase) entertained the Los Angeles Letter Carrier's Band. This 60-piece band performed at the Philharmonic Auditorium. An article in the *Los Angeles Times*, on May 6, 1923, stated that "a special dancing feature will be presented by members of the motion-picture colony." Comic dancing was a specialty of Vernon's repertoire.

CHAPTER 9

MACK SENNETT STUDIOS

Vernon was hired for another feature film, this time for Mack Sennett. Amazingly, it was not a pure comedy, which made *The Extra Girl* an unusual departure for the studio known exclusively for creating laughter.

The production started on September 26, 1922 as "Millie of the Movies," and was originally to star actress Phyllis Haver, a graduate of the Mack Sennett Bathing Beauties. With a working title of "The Phyllis Haver Story," production came to a halt. Haver was inexplicably replaced by Mabel Normand. It might have seemed a strange choice at the time; Normand's name briefly surfaced as a link with the William Desmond Taylor scandal.* Nevertheless, Mabel had been a proven star for Sennett in short comedies and features during the mid-to-late teens.

The script went through many changes and included the dismissal of the original director, William Seiter. Sennett assigned his director-general, F. Richard Jones, to help the picture. He knew how to handle the excitable Mabel and had done so in many past film assignments. Although some actors were replaced from the original cast, production stills from the beginning verify Vernon Dent's presence. It took nearly a year to complete the feature and get it to the distributors; it was finally released under the title *The Extra Girl* on September 24, 1923.

Vernon's character was Aaron Applejohn, a sinister and overbearing suitor of the naïve Sue Graham (Normand). Applejohn is a dark and intense man who has come for his arranged marriage. Vernon did not overact in the melodramatic style, which was still the vogue to some extent. Instead, he personified an unspeakable and disturbing reality about

---

* Director William Desmond Taylor was murdered on February 1, 1922; the case remains a notorious Hollywood "unsolved" crime.

his character. Perhaps it was in his deliberate gait, or in the way he moved his eyes. Whatever it was, females in the audience knew instinctively not to trust this shady character.

While this movie went through editing and production transformations, Vernon was allowed to work elsewhere. An opportunity presented itself back up the coast, 400 miles away, in the community of Santa Cruz. A brief write-up in *Santa Cruz Evening News*, on August 14, 1923, provides some insight:

> Tracy Productions, a newly formed moving picture producing company, has chosen Santa Cruz as the ideal background for their busy activities.
>
> The chief comedian, and for whom the company is named, is Bert Tracy, an inimitable funster. Vernon Dent, a popular and well-known member of the Hollywood film colony, was engaged especially for the comedy heavy in the first "Lightning" release. The rotund comedian has appeared in a variety of highly successful comedies as well as in many heavier features. Among the latter, he has been in "Hail the Woman," and "Soul of the Beast," and others. Just previous to coming to Santa Cruz, Dent finished an important engagement with Mack Sennett, having appeared opposite Mabel Normand in "The Extra Girl," not yet released. Glen Lambert is directing the local comedies.

On August 25, 1923, the same newspaper reported a local screening of the film for members of the cast and critics at the new Santa Cruz Theater. There were familiar settings of beach scenes; the Arch Rock and the Casa Del Rey Hotel were just across the street from the boardwalk.*

It is unknown if this two-reeler was widely distributed or even released. There is no trace of the movie reviewed in any of the trade journals. Of note, there are two photographs that survive of the production. Both feature Bert Tracy, a slim, mustachioed comedian, posed with the hulking Vernon Dent. They are enclosed within the arched frame of Natural Bridges, a formation of rocks at a nearby beach. Frolicking among them are slender pixies, dancing women in thin and delicate outfits. These aren't knock-offs of the famed Sennett Bathing Beauties; they are more reminiscent of the water nymphs associated with Greek mythology.

Randy Brown, a Santa Cruz historian, explains that the Tracy production was a last-gasp effort to convince local support for subsidizing a real

---

* Arch Rock is now better known as Natural Bridges.

motion picture studio in Santa Cruz. Ugly rumors persist that Tracy left the investors "high and dry" and skipped town. This might help explain the many aliases over the years of the mysterious little comedian.

BACK WITH SENNETT

After *The Extra Girl* was finally released, Mack Sennett re-signed Vernon, this time as a comedian. Vernon may have reminded the boss of another Roscoe Arbuckle, or even a John Bunny type.

Vernon Dent's best asset was his versatility. He could play a serious role, essay zany comic portrayals, or play it straight as a "reaction comic." No doubt about it, Vernon was now also "a type" — in this case, a "fat comic" — and one who could take a fall with the best of them.

The addition certainly augmented Sennett's current stable of talent: Ben Turpin, Billy Bevan, Andy Clyde, Edgar Kennedy, Harry Gribbon, James Finlayson, Sid Smith, Louise Carver, Dot Farley, and Ruth Hiatt, to name a few.

Some say the Mack Sennett studios were in their heyday during this period of the Roaring Twenties. Two-reel comedies were in demand and Sennett had the name and talent to produce them. He was, in fact, the self-proclaimed "King of Comedy."

In service at 1712 Alessandro Avenue in Glendale, California, for over ten years, the studio went through many name changes. It actually started as Bison Studios until 1912 when Sennett and his financial backers formed the Keystone Company. Stars came and went: Charlie Chaplin, Syd Chaplin, Fred Mace, Ford Sterling, Charles Murray, Slim Summerville, Walter Beery, and many others. The females also climbed the slippery ladder of success: Mabel Normand, Mae Busch, Louise Fazenda, Gloria Swanson, Madeline Hurlock, and Dot Farley were some of the first ladies of film comedy.

HARRY ENTERS THE SCENE

In late 1923 Mack Sennett signed a popular vaudeville comic named Harry Langdon. For nearly 20 years, Langdon and his wife, Rose Frances Musolff, toured America with their signature sketch, "Johnny's New Car."

The Sennett studios cranked out press releases which were printed in newspapers across the country. The following article, printed in the Iowa newspaper, the *Davenport Democrat and Leader* on November 25, 1923, led off with a grand announcement:

Sennett Claims another Chaplin in Harry Langdon

Mack Sennett, that discoverer of pulchritude and talent, claims he has found a second Chaplin. In view of the cold reception accorded second Mary Pickfords, second Jackie Coogans, et al, we wonder at his temerity in making such an announcement.

Harry Langdon inscribed this portrait to his good friend Vernon. COURTESY OF EDWARD WATZ

Harry Langdon, former vaudeville comedian, is Sennett's so-called "find." Langdon is under contract with Principal Pictures Corporation for a series of comedies, the third of having been finished. The comedian was loaned to Sennett by Sol Lesser.

So impressed with Langdon's screen personality and new brand of comedy antics that he comes forth with the interesting announcement that Langdon can capably fill the gap left by the world's greatest comedian who went in for drama.

As part of the Sennett stock company, Vernon inevitably shared screen time with the studio's latest acquisition. Vernon could not have anticipated how much this little clown would impact his life, both personally and professionally.

For the debut release of Harry Langdon's *Picking Peaches*, Vernon was cast as the arrogant boss to Harry's shy shoe salesman role, and provided a nice comedy contrast. For the first time, we see Harry's introverted screen character to Vernon's domineering "short fuse" personality. It was standard stooge-heavy stuff, but a pleasant little entry nonetheless. Highlights included supporting players Dot Farley and Irene Lentz as customers. Harry contributed a thrill gag when he dangles out of a window at the end of a ladder.

Langdon, however, proved to be a unique entry of comic expression; he had subtle gestures and slow facial reactions. In comparison, a typical Sennett comedy of the era seemingly went 100 miles an hour. There was usually a kick-in-the-pants action, reaction, retaliation, cops, knocks, pratfalls, bathing beauties, thighs and pies, bees and knees, double takes, a chase and a "topper" of a sight gag — all as part of the slapstick formula. If it wasn't funny, speed it up and add a lion.

Comedies featuring Langdon intentionally slowed down this familiar tempo. If the "Old Man" (as the 40-something Sennett was called by his employees) thought Chaplin was slow in 1914, Langdon must have seemed like molasses in 1924.

After the release of *Picking Peaches*, Langdon continued in his own unit while Vernon appeared in other Sennett comedy productions as needed. He was cast in a Harry Gribbon comedy, *The Half-Back of Notre Dame*, for which the director was none other than slapstick specialist Del Lord. It was the first of many screen associations between the two that lasted through the years at Sennett and Columbia Studios.

Sennett gave Vernon Dent some opportunities to shine, *The Hollywood Kid* being one of them. Cast as the onscreen director, Claude Climax,

Vernon wore horn-rimmed glasses, replicating the then-famous look of New York theatre critic Alexander Woollcott. In a scene involving an escaped lion, Vernon registered an expression of genuine panic and displayed physical agility by diving out an open window. It was just another day's work at the Mack Sennett studios.

As on any film production, the cast had to endure long hours of wait-

A candid shot of Harry Langdon and Vernon Dent on the set of The Hollywood Kid *(Sennett, 1924).* COURTESY OF HARRY LANGDON, JR.

ing between takes while the director and crew set up the next scene. The actors would have to stay in costume and be available at a moment's notice. Some folks amused themselves by talking, playing cards, gambling, or finding a shady spot. The musically inclined passed the time by singing or playing instruments.

During the making of *Hollywood Kid*, a still camera caught a candid shot off the set. There is Harry Langdon, playing his portable peddled piano, with Vernon, who is obviously singing. Vernon was in his costume for the next scene. Harry was not in the film *Hollywood Kid;* he was between takes for his own movie. Though Langdon and Dent would not be working together again for a period of months, a Brownie camera moment recorded the budding friendship and commonality of the two comedians.

Vernon's next role was in the Sid Smith comedy, *Black Oxfords*. Vernon was clean shaven for this one. *Black Oxfords* contains a gag that would be much duplicated in later comedies and cartoons. Vernon and Sid hide out successfully inside a barn and don a handy cow costume, with Vernon bringing up the rear. Not suspecting a thing, the farmer attempts to milk the cow. Seeing the development, the boys put an inflated glove through an opening where the udder would be. The confused farmer pulls on the fingers but can't figure out why his cow won't "give." Beating a hasty retreat through the field, the "cow" is spotted by a bull, which runs after her. The boys run in different directions, splitting the cow costume in half. The perplexed bull is left with its tail curving to form a question mark at this sight.

In an article printed in the *Los Angeles Times* on April 4, 1924, Mack Sennett stated that he was so impressed with Smith and Dent that he left them each an envelope marked, "For a good boy." It contained a bonus of an undisclosed amount of money. This unsolicited financial tip seems to contradict the reports of Sennett's stinginess with his employees. (Or was this bit of information merely hype from the publicity boys?)

For his next assignment, Vernon reprised his Alexander Woollcott character. *The Lion and the Souse* was a golf comedy with plenty of pratfalls and dunks in the drink. Vernon made the biggest splash in this comedy, which also featured Sid Smith, Andy Clyde, and Numa the Lion.

Seeing that Vernon had made the grade as a stock comedian with occasional featured characters, Sennett groomed him for more opportunities to shine. The portly comedian was re-signed to a contract on July 18, 1924. In the first six months he made $150 a week. The signing was announced in a press release. The resulting article in the *Los Angeles Times* on August 15, 1924 documented Vernon's assignment of playing the "heavy" in Harry Langdon's new comedy, *All Night Long*.

One of the obligations for each new contract player was to work with the promotional staff to come up with a biographical press sheet. The usual details of birthplace and education reveal no surprises. However, one aspect about Vernon's career was exaggerated somewhat. His bio sheet indicated he "started as a cabaret entertainer in Chicago [sic], singing and dancing, thence to vaudeville." This minor detail, meant to enhance his background, popped up every now and then in future references.

Also mentioned was that Vernon's favorite pastime was golf; that he was the second cousin to Ulysses S. Grant [he was actually the *third* cousin of Grant's *wife*]; and that Vernon's favorite author was Gene Stratton Porter [a writer of romantic novels and nature books]. Vernon's published songwriting credits included the titles, "I Tried to Say it With Flowers, but the Flowers Died" [unconfirmed], "What Have I Done (to Make you Stop Loving Me)," and "Girl of My Dreams." The little biography said Vernon signed a two-year contract as a featured comedian and that his highest ambition was to reach "The Top."

During this time in Vernon's life, his permanent residence was at the Washington Hotel in Culver City. As an actor, he was all over the Sen-

Elsie Tarron, Sid Smith, Numa the Lion, Vernon Dent, Andy Clyde, Leo Sulky, and Virginia Fox in Lion and the Souse *(Sennett, 1924).* COURTESY OF COLE JOHNSON

nett lot. He was directed by Edgar Kennedy in *Love's Sweet Piffle*, and then appeared with Kennedy in *Wall Street Blues*. The latter was directed by Del Lord, and was actually a Billy Bevan comedy. Little Billy was supported by Sid Smith and Andy Clyde, while Vernon continued his Alexander Woollcott character. The most amusing moment was "stolen" by Edgar Kennedy. Big Ed is a no-nonsense robber holding everyone up with a large caliber handgun.

Vernon finished off the year of 1924 with a number of roles: *Romeo and Juliet* (a Ben Turpin vehicle), *East of the Water Plug, Little Robinson Corkscrew, Riders of the Purple Cows,* and *Bull and Sand,* another Sid Smith comedy. He was also assigned to two Harry Langdon shorts. Vernon invented characters as needed for each film. When he wasn't featured, he was co-featured or in a supporting role. Sometimes he was in scenes without calling attention to himself at all. Nevertheless, he was noticed. Sennett took note of Vernon's development into a first-rate comic straight man.

Meanwhile, the experiment with Harry Langdon was playing out with only so-so results. In hindsight, the hype Sennett spewed out about "the next Chaplin" placed an undue burden on the new screen comedian. After Langdon's first released film with Sennett, he starred in nine more comedies, none of which co-starred Vernon.

With so much at stake, Sennett devoted all of his creative resources to the project of making Langdon a screen success. According to Frank Capra, a committee of sorts was assembled: Harry Edwards, Arthur Ripley, and Capra himself worked with Langdon to come up with a distinctive character. This included a consistent garb and a sense that God Himself looked out for this vulnerable "Little Elf." This story (which appeared in Capra's autobiography, *The Name Above the Title*) does not hold up under closer examination. Langdon had already created his innocent baby character years earlier on the stage. Sennett had to let Harry take his time and move at a much slower pace than any Sennett comedies had ever done before. Capra was not even part of the Langdon unit's staff until November 1924, a full year after Langdon started with Sennett (and Langdon had made seven hit comedies without Capra's assist).

There was a conscious decision to have Vernon Dent play off the evolving characterization of Harry Langdon. Of the remaining 13 shorts Langdon made for Sennett, Vernon was in 12 of them. They were all shot late in the year 1924 and throughout 1925. Mack Sennett withheld some of the later titles for specially timed releases.

While the Langdon unit was in production, Vernon continued his stooge-heavy support to seven additional comedies, mostly in Ralph Graves and Alice Day vehicles. Despite Vernon's work with the other comedians, it became clear that he and Langdon had a special chemistry, even though they were not a comedy team in the traditional sense. Langdon was the star, and Vernon knew his responsibilities. He had done it before with Hank Mann; that is, *he let the star get the laughs*. No matter what role Vernon played (a rival, a lunatic, a rogue, a crook), it all helped to enhance Langdon as a major comic force.

As a body of work, it might be helpful if we examine some of the last appearances Langdon and Dent made at Sennett's. Their efforts together made screen magic and evolved into an enduring friendship.

All Night Long was a turning point in the Langdon series. First introduced into the plot as a safecracker, Vernon meets Harry and reminisces (via flashback) about their initial rivalry when stationed together during the Great War. Vernon especially recalls the time he took Harry with him to his French girlfriend's home for dinner. It had been a mistake. The sexual allure of the Little Elf proved too much of a temptation for

Billy Bevan plays an obnoxious pest annoying Vernon in *The Beach Club (1928).* AUTHOR'S COLLECTION

the lovely hostess. This is an odd (but hilarious) element of Langdon's character: he seems to cast a magic spell over women. He tries not to be noticed, but Vernon's girlfriend can't resist kissing Harry repeatedly. This both confounds and angers Vernon.

Vernon's supporting characters in Langdon's *Feet of Mud* (a football coach) and *Boobs in the Wood* (a rugged woodsman) also offer adversarial figures with whom Harry must contend.

If one were to select a favorite Langdon/Dent collaboration, it would likely be *His Marriage Wow*. In this comedy, it appears that Langdon is a supporting straight man for Vernon. The titles introduce Vernon as a "pessimist," and his strange features and demeanor are of great concern to Harry. Vernon's character is Professor Looney McGlumm. The professor is bald with long locks of hair in the back. He looks "mad as a hatter," and proves it when he has the opportunity to drive a car with poor, terrified Harry as passenger. Displaying a host of diabolical expressions, Vernon looks like a combination of John Barrymore's Mr. Hyde and Lon Chaney's Phantom of the Opera. The professor was just as spooky as these icons of horror, cackling with glee as he tears the steering wheel off its cylinder. Eventually, Harry learns that Professor McGlumm is an escaped lunatic.

Next up for release was *Plain Clothes*, a modest little comedy in which most of the humor derived from Vernon (this time as a crook) who sadistically toys with Harry, in his role as a detective.

Frank Capra had recently been contributing gags for the Langdon unit, but for *Plain Clothes*, Mack Sennett elevated him with writer credits alongside Arthur Ripley. The infusion of this creative influence helped the Langdon storylines and solidified the Elf's consistent screen personality. Vernon Dent's steady support was recognized to be an important ingredient.

The next-released film from the Langdon Unit was *Remember When?* The main plot was simple: in flashback, it tells the story of six-year-old Harry Hudson (Langdon) running away from his orphanage. This was a result of seeing a girl (on whom he had developed a crush) being taken away for adoption. Cut to contemporary times. We now see an adult Harry wandering without aim or ambition into hobo camps and onto train tracks. Enter Vernon Dent's character, Mack, a circus proprietor. While travelling on the top of his circus carriage, Vernon notices Harry standing on the side of the road. Little Harry is being victimized by some wild bees that crawled down his neck. (This scene is beautifully done: First there is a close-up of the bees scurrying about on Harry's collar, and then a slow reaction shot. Uncharacteristically, Harry goes into a fit of physical flips that would surpass any acrobat. In actuality, this sped-up scene benefited from the use of a stunt double.) The "performance" raises a smile on Vernon's mustachioed features. He is impressed enough to offer Harry a job with his show. Although Vernon's character was Harry's boss, there is some camaraderie shown to the Little Elf. After all, they are part of a show business family.

Remember When? has an almost Chaplinesque feeling to it, with moments of pathos throughout. Harry later discovers that the disguised "bearded" lady (a member of the troupe) is the same girl with whom he had been smitten at the orphanage. It's a wonderful reunion.

While hardly in the same league as Chaplin's *The Circus* or *City Lights*, *Remember When?* is, nevertheless, a compelling entry in the Langdon oeuvre. Its offbeat spin seems to be a specialty of Arthur Ripley, who co-wrote the screenplay with the inimitable Clyde Bruckman.*

The following release, *His First Flame*, was considered to be Harry's first starring feature-length film. Mack Sennett had past success in this

Harry Langdon, Vernon Dent with Anna May the Elephant in Remember When? *(Sennett, 1925).* COURTESY OF EDWARD WATZ

field (his production of *Tillie's Punctured Romance*, the very first feature-length comedy, was released in 1914); so did Chaplin, Lloyd, and Keaton. Their features were well received by critics and audiences alike. If one became a star, there was more money to be made. There were risks as well. Some — like Larry Semon — failed miserably. Langdon made the list of successes, if only briefly.

Filmed in 1925, *His First Flame* was not released until May 28, 1927, well past the time Harry was actually at the Sennett Studios. Sennett

---

* Clyde Bruckman contributed his talents as writer or director to the films of Buster Keaton, Laurel & Hardy, Harold Lloyd, W.C. Fields, The Three Stooges, and Abbott and Costello.

knew he was going to lose Langdon to a competitor, so he rigged the release schedule and then sat on the finished product. *His First Flame* was a pip of a yarn; the Langdon brain trust built a strong storyline, with believable characters and great comedy support. This time, Vernon played Harry's uncle, Amos McCarthy. Amos is captain of the city fire department, something for which Harry has no aptitude or apparent physical skill. Captain McCarthy is a veteran of the world, and had seen women come and go out of his life (mostly go), leaving him with a cynical view of romantic love.

Uncle's number-one priority is to look out for his naïve nephew when dealing with women. He tells him that he had married three times and had been "burned" on them all — and "on a fireman's salary." As Captain McCarthy, Vernon registers the ache of a man who knows what it's like to pay alimony. He appears to have all the qualifications for potential membership in the "Woman Haters Club."*

Despite his uncle's warnings, Harry is in love with a woman he could never obtain — a selfish "gold-digger." Fortunately, however, she has a younger sister of strong virtues, who professes that she would be happy with Harry as he is. The older sister is the type of girl Uncle Amos warned him about. She goes to extremes to actually stage a fire at her apartment so Harry can dramatically save her. Smoke, circumstances, and ineptitude bring about the predictable results. The fire escalates and takes over the whole apartment complex. Now both girls are in peril, and Harry is unable to help.

Called to action under the emergency conditions, Captain McCarthy climbs the ladder and saves the first victim, who turns out to be the older sister. The girl is nearly unconscious from smoke inhalation, but the captain dutifully carries her down the ladder and transports her to a waiting ambulance. Meanwhile, Harry hasn't done so badly, either. He reaches the second-story window and inadvertently finds the girl who harbors a crush for him. He awkwardly carries her down the ladder, but doesn't quite know what to do with her, so he keeps her in his arms. He retreats when his uncle sees what has transpired. Harry tentatively backs away, one hesitant foot at a time. He is not about to let his uncle interfere. Uncle Amos was just watching to see if it was the real thing, for he had more important things to do, namely smooch this latest conquest as they are driven off in the ambulance. It looks as if they were made for each other.

---

*This is a reference to the fictional fraternal organization The Three Stooges joined in their first two-reeler for Columbia Pictures, *Woman Haters* (1934).

Frank Capra received credit with writing the story, which proved to be a good vehicle for Langdon.

Lucky Stars was the next entry in the series. Harry is on familiar ground in a traveling medicine man show theme. He meets up with Vernon as Dr. Hiram Healy, a quack if there ever was one. After fleecing Harry of all his money, Dr. Healy convinces Harry he has what it takes to become a fine doctor and offers to teach him. They hit the road to San Tabasco, across the border. Harry is made an assistant to the con artist, even getting duped into concocting contents of phony bottles of medicine.

Harry remembers that, according to his "Lucky Star," he will meet a dark, beautiful girl. He does so in San Tabasco, and it looks again like the woman cannot resist Harry's character. In reality, she is the pharmacist's daughter who is trying to lure him close enough to stab him. Harry escapes unscathed (naturally) while Dr. Healy gets tarred and feathered.

Langdon's and Dent's interaction in this comedy is that of a seasoned comedy team. Each moment together there is genuine chemistry between the two players; they seem to anticipate each other's actions. Working off Vernon Dent also helped to speed up Langdon's occasionally laborious timing.

Unfortunately, the next released Langdon/Dent/Edwards/Ripley/Capra collaboration, *There He Goes*, only exists in brief fragments from its last reel, and cannot be properly assessed. But the one after that, *Saturday Afternoon*, is readily available — and it is now considered a minor classic. Filmed during September of 1925 and held back for release until January 31, 1926, allegedly for Sennett's strategic marketing purposes. In *Saturday Afternoon*, Vernon and Harry are pals. It's a classic case of boys pursuing girls. Complications are immediately established in that Harry has a shrewish wife who won't let him go one moment without accounting for his whereabouts. Vernon's character has no respect for Harry's marital status. And as any "pal" would do, he tries to help him out by arranging a date for him. As an enticement Vernon tells Harry, "A girl with a swell pair of lamps is dying to meet you." Harry, new to the idea of infidelity, covertly rehearses his confrontation with his wife: "From now on you can wind the clock and fix the cat," he says emphatically to no one. "And I have a date with a pair of beautiful lamps."

Naturally, his wife can hear every word and slips into the room to hear the rest of his tirade. Realizing he has been discovered, Harry turns back into the mouse he is. Instead of being outraged, she is condescendingly sympathetic, even to the point of giving Harry some coins for "his date."

Harry is stunned momentarily until he accepts the situation on face value, then catches up to Vernon. After all, what could go wrong?

After a near mix-up with "the wrong girls," Harry, Vernon, and their dates pile into Vernon's roadster, with Harry relegated to the rumble seat. Vernon — his mustache as lush as the carnation in his lapel — is at his confident best as he sits in the front seat with a couple of pretty girls

Harry Langdon and Vernon Dent in Plain Clothes *(Sennett, 1925)*. This was taken two years before Stan Laurel and Oliver Hardy became a team.
COURTESY OF EDWARD WATZ

next to him. Harry is happy enough to exchange finger waves through the back window slot.

And whom do they pass while traveling along the road? Why — the wife, of course! Harry panics, and even Vernon is concerned for everyone's safety. The short wraps up on an original note. Instead of dishes being thrown, Harry's wife realizes the error of her ways and makes up for it by being more appreciative and loving of her husband. (A fantasy ending, to be sure; perhaps it was wish fulfillment for Langdon, whose personal life was in chaos at the time.) Harry's character has no idea what happened, but happily accepts the turn of events. Maybe someone really *was* looking out for the Elf.

Saturday Afternoon is seen by some aficionados as a precursor to such Laurel & Hardy comedies as *We Faw Down* and *Sons of the Desert*, in that the boys are pitted against their wives through their own ineptitude. Although these scenarios had been borrowed and enhanced since silent comedies were made, *Saturday Afternoon* stands out in its originality. It was filmed a full two years before Stan Laurel & Oliver Hardy were officially teamed. The physical characteristics of Langdon and Dent (one small and helpless; the other large and imposing) seemed to prefigure the legendary Stan and Ollie. But Langdon, it seems, was not going in that direction, and he and Vernon Dent were not a team.

Soldier Man was held back by Sennett for three years and finally released on September 30, 1928 as a three-reeler. The comedy opens with Harry still in the trenches (on a strict diet of beans) on Armistice Day.* Blissfully unaware of the lack of activity, he finds a countryman who tries to convince him the war has been over for some time. Harry is suspicious.

A turn of events has Harry discovered to be a spitting image of the current "King Strudel of Bomania." Vernon plays the prime minister to the king and advances the plot to switch places of the drunken king with the mild-mannered Harry. The bogus king cannot remember the prime minister's name or title, so he simply addresses him as "Hey, mustache!" (Vernon played the role with the type of mustache worn by Kaiser Wilhelm.)

In a part take-off from *A Prisoner of Zenda* and *A Connecticut Yankee in King Arthur's Court*, Harry awakens to find that he had dreamed the preceding situations. Spoofs of popular plays, novels, and features were comic fodder for short comedies. This entry was not a particular standout, but it had some inspirational moments.

The last product for Sennett was *Fiddlesticks,* shot in November and early-December 1925 but released before *Soldier Man*, on November 27, 1927. *Fiddlesticks* is Langdon's film all the way with a nod to Vernon Dent's more-than-capable support. This time Vernon plays two roles to the support of Harry: Professor Von Tempo, and Penrod the junk dealer. One needs a good eye to spot the difference, as the characters look so different.

Professor Von Tempo is a role Vernon seemed to enjoy, that of a music teacher. For this he has long hair in the back, a frock coat, a bushy mustache, and spectacles that give the appearance of an educated man. Though

---

* A similar plot device would be elaborated upon by Laurel & Hardy in their 1938 feature, *Block-Heads*. It was not a coincidence: Harry Langdon was a co-writer of the script.

this is a silent film, one can just imagine Vernon's affected German dialect when he speaks. His old-country mannerisms and pride in his profession reinforce that image.

Little Harry has ambitions to be a musician and even has his own bass fiddle on which to practice. His style of playing confounds everyone but his mother. The professor tolerates it strictly for monetary reasons, but

Harry Langdon and Vernon Dent in Fiddlesticks *(Sennett, 1927).*
COURTESY OF EDWARD WATZ

even that incentive wears thin after a short time. He prematurely gives Harry a certificate of music and proclaims he "is now a musician." It works; Harry thinks the piece of paper qualifies him, and then proudly shows his degree to his family. Mom is proud, although the rest of the family has had enough of the unproductive runt sawing back and forth on his bass while singing, "My Wild Irish Rose." (An illustrated title shows an alley cat yowling to the lyrics.) Harry is banished from the house to go out and make a living. He meets up with a stereotypical Jewish junkman who scores a bonanza of discards when Harry plays his oversized fiddle.

"There's a lot of money in music," Harry triumphantly tells his family upon his return.

In late 1925 Langdon left Sennett to star in his own feature comedies at First National. It has been well documented that Langdon brought his new brain-trust with him — namely Harry Edwards, Arthur Ripley, and Frank Capra — with hefty raises and new responsibilities. Harry was now the boss.

Though there was a crest of innovation and commercial success at the initial releases, creative in-fighting and its fallout doomed Langdon. After a few flops, some considered him a "has-been." Of course, there were many reasons; one of the most discussed was Capra's firing after only three films and Langdon's own attempts to direct. Could the fall from stardom also be at least partially explained by the fact that Vernon Dent was not a part of the new team?

Press release for The Talkies *(Educational, 1929).* COURTESY RICH FINEGAN

CHAPTER 10

THE TALKIES

By 1925 Vernon had married again; his new bride was Grace M. Rousseau, the daughter of Benjamin F. Rousseau and the former Clara M. Currier. Grace was born in Fort Wayne, Indiana, on May 6, 1896. Not much is known about Grace, but when Vernon met her, she was working as a studio seamstress and was said to be a very skillful one. In the census year of 1930, Mr. and Mrs. Dent were residing at 3622 Empire Drive, in Los Angeles.

VERNON IN PERSON

An article in the June 30, 1926 issue of the *Los Angeles Times* — "Mack Sennett Night to be Observed at Million Dollar Theatre" — reported that the King of Comedy and members of his stock company were to appear locally on stage.

> The evening was in honor of Mr. Sennett's latest comedy, "Hoboken to Hollywood." Those who appeared were Billy Bevan, Vernon Dent, Thelma Hill, Johnny Burke, Ruth Hiatt, Alice Day, Madeline Hurlock, Eddie Quillan, Andy Clyde, and even Baby Mary Ann Jackson.

It's worth noting that Vernon's contract with Sennett was not exclusive; he also appeared in a comedy for Hal Roach: *A One-Man Mama*, which was released on March 6, 1927. In this silent two-reeler, Vernon plays the rival to Charley Chase and shares a hilarious scene in which the two comics trade haymaking punches. Chase had requested the services of his old friend from the Hank Mann Arrow Comedy days. Seeing the finished film, one wishes that Chase had been allowed to make more.

Vernon Dent's Roach appearance may have convinced Mack Sennett to hold onto his comedian — it wouldn't have been the first time Roach had stolen one of his valuable properties. By June of 1927, Sennett had re-signed Vernon to a contract at the salary of $250 a week. This amount was raised every three months, peaking in December of 1928 at $400, a generous salary for a supporting comic. Sennett proved he had big plans for the comedian, a chance to be featured. The contract also allowed Vernon the freedom to freelance.

The *Los Angeles Times* released this curious item from the Sennett publicity machine; it was printed on November 27, 1927:

> When a story is "adapted" for the screen, it frequently means just that. Vernon Dent and Billy Bevan were in the midst of a Sennett comedy in which they were being co-starred when Dent (thoughtlessly) went to his walnut ranch for a week-end and spent a whole day picking walnuts. When they returned to the studio on Monday, his hands were so badly stained that a new sequence calling for him to appear as a Negro chef had to be written into the script to "adapt" the picture to the fact that walnut stain takes weeks to wear off.

Sometimes these press releases were no more than a weekly attempt to get Sennett's comedians in the public eye. This little anecdote, though, has a grain of truth; Vernon *did* have a walnut grove in Alhambra, Ca. and he *had* donned black-face make-up for *Motorboat Mamas*, which was in production at the time of the press release. In that domestic comedy two-reeler (released on September 28, 1928), Vernon and Billy Bevan frolic with some girls aboard Billy's boat. The conflict arrives in the form of Vernon's wife and mother-in-law. To avoid a confrontation with these unwelcome visitors, Vernon disguises himself as a black cook. According to a Sennett press release,

> Vernon Dent, the suave comedian who is featured in Mack Sennett Comedies with the boisterous Billy Bevan, has just signed on the dotted line for another two years with the comedy producer.
>
> For the past four years Dent has been with Mack Sennett and has appeared in the All-Star Comedies, his smooth comicalities and droll behavior providing a perfect foil for Bevan. During the time that Harry Langdon was under contract with Sennett, Dent was featured in the Langdon pictures.

But all was not rosy on the Sennett lot. "The Old Man" was making big investments in a new facility with recording equipment, and the public's taste was changing. And unbeknownst to anyone, a world-wide depression was looming.

To make matters even worse, Pathé was in the process of dissolving as a film distributor. Sennett therefore made a deal with Educational Pictures (a low-budget film company that advertised its output as "The Spice of the Program") to release his comedy shorts. Educational was also the film distributor to Sennett's rivals Al Christie and Jack White.

The Hal Roach Studio was facing a similar problem; in the film industry, Roach and Sennett were just little guys making short comedies; however when Pathé morphed into FBO, and then RKO, Roach found Metro-Goldwyn-Mayer willing to distribute his shorts. By this time Roach was decidedly winning the comedy crown by virtue of his talented stable of performers, including Stan Laurel & Oliver Hardy, Charley Chase, and the kids from Our Gang. Roach had a knack for finding the top talents in the comedy field. Director F. Richard Jones went from Sennett to Roach along with Mary Ann Jackson, a child actor used in Sennett's "Smith Family" Series. She was promptly integrated into Our Gang. Other Sennett veterans who found employment at the Roach Studios were Mabel Normand, Mae Busch, and gagman/director Gus Meins.

Lobby card for Hubby's Quiet Little Game *(Sennett, 1926).*
AUTHOR'S COLLECTION

As with every other studio in town, voice tests were made before actors were signed to new contracts. Those with unsuitable voices, or actors not proficient in memorizing dialogue, were in jeopardy. No one needed to worry about Vernon during this transitional period, however. With his extensive stage training, he knew how to use his voice to suit each of his characters. Vernon must have been quietly comfortable with this new technological advance in movies. Maybe now he could actually sing, or develop a character with a distinctive speech pattern. The world could be *his* if he only had the right opportunity. Would he be a star or support player? No one could predict his future, mainly because Vernon had no one character. His strength continued to be his versatility.

VERNON'S FIRST TALKIE

Naturally, Vernon participated in the very first Sennett talking comedy, *The Lion's Roar* (released on December 9, 1928), starring vaudevillian Johnny Burke. In this two-reeler, Vernon was cast as the "Music Professor." His co-stars were Billy Bevan and Daphne Pollard.

The Educational press sheet touted the fact that pie-throwing would not only be *seen* in this sound offering, it would actually be *heard*: "You will hear just what a man says after being smacked with a juicy blackberry pie. That is, all of it that the censors will let you hear."

Sound effects were promised in such mundane activities as "clanging of street car bells, the honk of auto horns, the singing of birds," and as suggested in the title, "the audience will get to hear a real lion roar." The novelty of sound must have been a thrilling sense of reality for cinemagoers in 1928.

Not every comedy company, though, was equipped for sound. The Jack White comedies, among others, were behind in the trend of talking pictures. It took them almost a year to realize that sound was not a novelty.

During the same month (December 1928), Jack White produced a Cameo Comedy that promoted Vernon Dent as the comedy star. Titled *Murder Will Out*, this one-reeler was directed by Jack's brother, Jules. The one-page press release elaborated: "Vernon Dent is a new type of funster who is sure to make your audiences roar with laughter. He is aided and abetted by such favorites as Al Thompson, Jackie Levine, and Georgia O'Dell. There is plenty of action and fast comedy in this one."

In this silent comedy, Vernon receives a phone call from a friend inviting him to go to a baseball game. His wife, however, wants him to accompany her on a walk. As a ruse, Vernon has to pretend he is sick. Not surprisingly, his plan backfires.

On December 30, Vernon was again touted as the star of a Cameo comedy, this time bearing the title *In the Morning*. The Educational press sheet said that Vernon had appeared in numerous two-reelers and recently "scored" in a Cameo comedy in which he was featured. "Vernon Dent chalks up another laugh treat in this novel fun film," the press release trumpeted. "This ponderous comic is surrounded by a cast of males that nearly equal him in weight and laugh-producing proclivities."

THE WHOOPIE BOYS

After the successful *The Lion's Roar*, Jack White had an idea to team Vernon Dent with Monty Collins. Although the two comics had shared screen time in *Social Prestige*, a one-reeler released late in 1928, this time they were being marketed as a team.

A portrait of Vernon for The Whoopie Boys *(Jack White Comedies, 1929).*
COURTESY OF EDWARD WATZ

A press release was issued to coincide with the unveiling of *The Whoopie Boys* on February 10, 1929. The press sheet had full-cover caricatures of Collins and Dent. Inside were typical promotional ads and articles to establish the team. One of the "catch-lines" was: "Monty Collins and Vernon Dent, that laughable team, in their latest Educational-Mermaid Comedy, *Whoopie Boys* — Good For Twenty Minutes of Solid Laughter."

The publicity materials encouraged the use of creating a "Whoopee Essay Contest." This was standard fare for the pressbooks of the time. The "essay lure" was a marketing scheme to promote the film, and in this case, "to describe the origin of the expression 'Whoopie.'"

The Whoopie Boys casts the team as detectives sent to guard the presents at a fashionable wedding. The pressbook claims, "The boys are somewhat rusty on social usages, and their rough but playful ways form the basis for a lot of fast and funny comedy."

Press sheet for Parlor Pests *(Jack White, 1929).* COURTESY OF RICH FINEGAN

Parlor Pests (March 24, 1929) was the title of the fledgling team's next offering. The Educational press sheet ballyhooed the pair as follows.

Real Bargain in Laughs from Collins and Dent

One comedian is generally enough in a Jack White Mermaid Comedy. You can imagine the bargain in laugh making material when two funsters are in the leading and featured roles.

There are two experts in the art of mirth-manufacturing in *Parlor Pests*. The two laugh producers are Monty Collins and Vernon Dent, the latest comedy team in the short feature end of the business. The two boys are seen as radio mechanics that are sent to install a receiving set at a millionaire's home. They are disguised as guests.

Monty Collins and Vernon Dent have definitely clinched their claim to fame as one of the few top-notch laugh making teams in short comedies. Mating comedy teams is one of the most difficult accomplishments in the picture business. Individual comedians who are successful alone are not always effective when members of a team. Monty Collins and Vernon Dent, however, are ideally suited to each other. They are entirely different physical types but both have had the same training. Both are former vaudeville players.

Vernon has had more screen training than Monty. He has been a featured player with Mack Sennett and other comedy producers for a number of years. Collins has played comedy roles in feature productions and was only "discovered" as possible stellar material by Jack White. He is considered one of the most rapidly rising funny men in the short laugh makers.

Jack White followed up with another pairing of Collins and Dent. The film was released on May 5, 1929, along with the following promise to distributors: "Both Collins and Dent are crackerjack comics and together they form a comedy pair hard to beat. In *Those Two Boys* they are seen as a couple of newly established millionaires who become members of an exclusive men's club. They are a couple of diamonds in the rough."

The highlight of this silent comedy is reached after an argument with the club manager escalates into a kicking match with all members joining in. (This climactic ending was similar to the build-up and payoff of Laurel & Hardy's *You're Darn Tootin'*, released a full year earlier.) *Motion Picture News*, on March 30, 1929, asserted, in part: "[*Those Two Boys* is] a very good comedy, easily one of the best of the Collins-Dent team. It clearly defines the influence of Hal Roach upon other comedy producers. The gags are excellently detailed."

Another Collins-Dent effort was *Household Blues*, released on June 6, 1929. This one-reeler was directed by Jules White and featured the type of fast action, slapstick and general mayhem that the director would come to employ with The Three Stooges.

The Collins-Dent teaming continued with *What a Day*, released on June 16, 1929. The director on this late silent effort was Stephen Roberts.

Monty Collins and Vernon Dent were finally getting ready to break into the talkies. A huge newspaper press sheet accompanied the release of their sound debut on August 25, 1929. Much publicity was gained starting with an illustrated image on the cover of the two boys.

Ticklish Business
(Educational, August 25, 1929)

Educational Pictures teamed friends Vernon Dent and Monty Collins in a series of silent comedies in the late 1920's and *Ticklish Business* was the first sound short in their series. In this one Vernon and Monty play a pair of aspiring but inept songwriters and so naturally at a few points in the story we need to hear some of their compositions. Their songs are not very good, in keeping with the story, but are funny and enjoyable, and as an extra treat, they are composed by Vernon Dent and Monty Collins themselves! The first song they sing is called "In the Mountains of Missouri" (lyrics by Dent and Collins, music by Stephen Roberts, the film's director). Later they do a comedy number, "Laughing Song" ("Don't Tickle Me"), lyrics and music by Dent and Collins.

The boys are the authors of the principal song, actually a "laughing" song which they sing for a hard-boiled producer. Unfortunately, the song was never recorded for separate release, but it was the hit of the film.

According to the *Motion Picture News* of August 24, 1929, "Opinions on Pictures" were offered from the trade. One of the remarks seems most insightful:

Collins and Dent demonstrate that they are in the front rank of comedy teams in the talkies; keeping company with such names as Laurel & Hardy or Clark & McCullough. If they are given as good material in the future as they have here, then everything is jake [slang for satisfactory] for them because they are certainly there.

Collins and Dent were again teamed in *Hot Sports*, another one-reeler from Jules White. According to a press release, Monty and Vernon are two plumbers headed for the Plumber's Ball. After wrecking their flivver, they find themselves in front of a mansion where a formal party is being held. They decide to "crash the gate." However, inside they find their manners don't fit in with their clothes and soon they are in trouble. As a practical joke, Monty rips a window shade, and rips the curtains to make the male guests think they split their trousers when bowing. Eventually, their antics result in a pretty young socialite accidentally having her dress ripped off — a bit that later became a signature gag of director Jules White.

In October of 1929, Educational Pictures actually released a comedy with the title, *The Talkies*. Who better to showcase the new medium than Monty Collins and Vernon Dent? The text below is from the original Educational Press Sheet:

Jack White Shows Funny Side of Making Talkies

Monty Collins and Vernon Dent, teamed together in several successful comedies last season under the supervision of Jack White, are proving to be one of the most successful screen teams in talking pictures. Both players are products of the vaudeville and musical comedy stage. When talking pictures took Hollywood by storm, the team of Collins and Dent was a "natural," for the boys were more at home in the new medium than they had been in silent comedies.

And from the same press sheet:

In this innovative "behind the scenes" look at talking picture production, Monty Collins and Vernon Dent are cast as a couple of dumb sound engineers whose errors in making unwanted sounds prove costly to a director.

There is little doubt that Jack White was hoping to cash in big with the team of Collins & Dent. In reality, comedy teams came and went in the movies. Many series of fat and skinny comedians were explored over the years. Once Laurel & Hardy took center stage, they were incredibly well received by the public. Other teams seemed sub-par in comparison.

It is fair to say that Jack White and (for that matter) Collins & Dent did not achieve the demand to further the series. It was an interesting pairing of comic talents, and it was innovative in that there was no "straight-man" supporting the star. They were *both* the funnyman, albeit with completely different styles. Collins & Dent were experts at pantomime and pratfalls, but when sound came in vogue, Educational was behind in technology. It affected their distribution opportunities and, ultimately, their production values. Collins & Dent were doomed from the start.

Vernon Dent and Blanche Gilmore in Vernon's Aunt *(Universal, 1930).*
COURTESY OF COLE JOHNSON

CHAPTER 11

IN TRANSITION

Vernon Dent was not just a film comedian specializing in pantomime. He had all the tools to be a star in the new medium of sound motion pictures. After all, his first show business successes were as a singer on the stage.

Even before the experiment of the Collins & Dent team had run its course, Universal Studios lured Vernon to co-star in a series of shorts with vaudeville comedian Lou Archer. Originally named Louis Archambeau, he was born on October 7, 1892, in Detroit, Michigan. Although primarily a stage performer, Archer had some experience on film, beginning with an appearance in *Creeps*, a 1926 Jack White comedy.*

Teaming the two men seemed like a good idea at the time. A study in contrasts, Archer was as thin as Vernon was husky. In a three-month period between late 1929 and early 1930, Archer and Dent doubled up for Universal's *Sunday Morning, Up and Down Stairs, Watch Your Friends*, and *Vernon's Aunt*. Harry Edwards, an old hand from the Sennett studio, handled the directing duties. Unfortunately, not one of the films has survived the passage of time. There is, however, a brief write-up from a February 1, 1930 edition of *Motion Picture News*. In announcing *Vernon's Aunt*, the editors of the trade magazine asserted: "Clever gags provide many laugh-provoking situations concerning the efforts of Vernon Dent and Lou Archer, posing as a pair of nuts in an attempt to discourage a visiting aunt from prolonging her stay."

A press release of the time offered a rare insight into Vernon's offscreen activities:

> Raising Strawberries Hobby for This Actor: Vernon Dent, for eight years a featured player in Mack Sennett Comedies, will be

---

* Of interest to Three Stooges fans, Lou Archer would achieve screen immortality as Charlie, the soldier who walks with a limp, in the 1935 short, *Uncivil Warriors*.

seen as Charlotte Greenwood's principal supporting comedian in the star's latest laugh maker.

The comedian is a rancher, horticulturist, business man and sportsman who owns a large ranch near Los Angeles, where his hobby and specialty are raising strawberries. He has improved his fruit until it is eagerly sought by confectioners in Southern California.

Dent is also invested in a chain of candy stores in Los Angeles and Hollywood and is the owner of several miniature golf courses.

On January 24, 1931 the *Motion Picture Herald* announced: "*Girls Will Be Boys* is a domestic comedy in which Vernon is married to his co-star, Charlotte Greenwood." The journal complained that "this particular story is a long way from new. The wife changes places with her husband, a piano mover. Her antics are amusing enough in delivering a piano, and of course he blows himself into the hospital and the stove into junk. They awake in adjoining beds in the hospital and swear off each other's jobs." A long way from new was right. Audiences saw variations of this plot repeated endlessly in film comedies and, later, in television sitcoms.

EDGAR KENNEDY AND VERNON DENT

It was just another two-reel comedy for producer Al Christie, but *Don't Divorce Him* (May 31, 1931), starring Clyde Cook, featured both Edgar Kennedy *and* Vernon Dent in supporting roles. The press release issued through Educational touted the fact that Vernon and Edgar were "original natives of California," and that "Dent was born and educated in San Jose, while Kennedy claims San Rafael [*sic*] as the town of his nativity. Both entered the motion picture business through the stage and both have similar experience in light opera, musical comedy and vaudeville. Each is a heavyweight, Dent scaling nearly three hundred, while Kennedy runs him a close second, with two hundred and fifty as his tonnage."

It's a shame that this press release compared the two comedians in such a superficial manner. Both had fascinating careers up to this point, but supporting comedians simply did not get much publicity.

Famous or not, Vernon was working at studios all over town. He made a memorable appearance in RKO's *The Iceman's Ball*, supporting the comedy team of Bobby Clark and Paul McCullough, in August of 1932. Even with mugs like James Finlayson, Fred Kelsey and Walter Brennan in the short, Vernon tops them all at the ending by intercepting a flying pie with his face.*

Vernon continued to shine even in his smaller roles. A good example can be found in the Mack Sennett-directed short, *Fainting Lover* (August 16, 1931). The star was Andy Clyde, a comic actor who specialized in playing befuddled old men and other eccentrics. Vernon plays Professor Ludwig Schmidt, an educated and talented musician with an enchanting Viennese accent.** Professor Schmidt is smitten with someone else's bride-to-be, and makes an impression. It seems that Vernon's character can play *any* musical instrument. Humbly, but with clear intent, he uses the piano and saxophone to achieve an impossible range of musical scales. *Fainting Lover* also gives us a clear idea of Vernon's talents as he performs a ballroom dance (at waltz tempo) with a lady partner. As this is a sound comedy, we also get to hear Vernon sing "The Waning Honeymoon."*** This short features Vernon at his musical best as he pretends to play *The Hungarian Rhapsody No. 2*, "The Prisoner's Song," and "Elephant's Parade."

Vernon proved he had the range to play *any* funny character, but he seemed to excel as professors and European dignitaries. In *The Girl Rush* (October 25, 1931), the Al Christie/Educational press sheet claimed that "Vernon Dent, funny fat man, is superb as a janitor with a Swedish accent and Helen Mann is one of the most gorgeous examples of eye-filling pulchritude to be found on the screen."

A definite highlight of this period was another Andy Clyde short, *Sunkissed Sweeties* (October 30, 1932), with Vernon as Mayor Vosberg, "an outraged public servant." Andy is hired as the "Beach Censor," and is on the trail of "zippy (much too zippy) bathing suits." Vernon would go on to support Andy Clyde all through their careers with Sennett, Educational, and later, Columbia studios.

---

* During a rare theatrical screening of this short in the 1980s the audience shrieked with laughter and applauded when Vernon took off his coat and prepared to beat the scrawny Finlayson to a pulp!

** Vernon reprised his role of Professor Ludwig Schmidt in Sennett's *For the Love of Ludwig* (July 24, 1932).

*** "The Waning Honeymoon" was first introduced in a musical comedy called *The Time, The Place, and The Girl*, in 1907. Written by Joseph E. Howard, the song was usually referred to as "The Honeymoon Song." Howard (1878–1961) was a prolific songwriter in his day and composed the music for the 1909 Broadway play, *A Stubborn Cinderella*. His most popular songs are the standards, "I Wonder Who's Kissing Her Now" (with Harold Orlob) and "Hello! Ma Baby" (with his wife, Ida Emerson).

SINGING WITH BING

By 1932 a crooner named Harry Lillis "Bing" Crosby was performing his way into the nation's consciousness with a regular live, 15-minute radio spot. He had worked his way up from being part of a trio (The Rhythm Boys), supporting bandleader Paul Whiteman, also known as The King of Jazz. Aside from Bing's radio time, he was ushering in his own style of music. He was certainly different than the higher-pitched tenors of the day. Bing's baritone voice resonated well with the advancing broadcasting and recording technology. During the evenings, Bing also performed at the Cocoanut Grove, a hot Hollywood night spot. He was a draw for the celebrities, executives, and big spenders of the day. Bing also had an easygoing personality that lent itself well to live performances.

Mack Sennett decided to try this singing sensation out for movies to see if he could capitalize on his name, and more importantly, his voice. The formula was essentially the same for each of Bing's five Sennett shorts: the crooner played himself, and no one recognized him until he sang. The objective for Bing was to be recognized *visually*. Was he movie star material? Could he be taken seriously? Those ears alone suggested comedy material.

Sennett featured Bing in *Dream House*, using sight gag extraordinaire Del Lord as the director and Vernon Dent in an important role. A press release announced:

> *Dream House*, Mr. Exhibitor, is a B. O. [box-office] natural. The public these days want light, tuneful melody and are looking for new screen personalities. All of these and more are offered in Educational's latest Mack Sennett Featurette, *Dream House*, featuring the phenomenal singing comedian, Bing Crosby. The millions of radio fans will want to see the man who entertains them every night with his tuneful crooning.
>
> *Dream House* is the story of a young plumber whose sweetheart "goes Hollywood" and Bing's adventures as a motion picture extra, which culminate in a mix-up with the studio lion, are guaranteed to cure the bluest case of glooms.

Crosby never does look comfortable onscreen with this material — except when he sings. Sennett tried to make Bing a film comic by resorting to an old standby: he put the crooner in "blackface" and had a lion chase him in one scene. This gag produced laughs in the 1920s (in *The Extra Girl* and *The Hollywood Kid*), but by 1932 it had worn thin.

Vernon's character in *Dream House* was that of a film director. Playing an impatient European film transplant à la Fritz Lang or Erich von Stroheim, Vernon got the best line in the film. Frustrated when his "serious" movie-within-a movie was constantly interrupted by Bing ruining the takes, Vernon spits out: "Vat do you think, dis is a two-reeler comedy movie?"

Bing Crosby continued his day job and took film roles when the opportunity presented itself. Bing and Vernon would appear together again.

Vernon Dent with Nell O'Day and Harry Langdon, candid photo circa 1933. COURTESY OF EDWARD WATZ

CHAPTER 12

VERNON DENT, SECOND BANANA

By the early thirties, Harry Langdon's star had waned. Since leaving Sennett, Langdon went from being one of the highest-paid stars of feature comedies to the bottom of the entertainment ladder. Even his stint as a starring comedian at Hal Roach failed to jell. Harry was surrounded by the best creative minds in the business and talking comedies should have enhanced his appeal. It didn't. Roach gave up on him in less than a year. His next chance came from Educational Pictures.

Vernon was recruited to aid Harry, not as a comedy partner per se, but close to it. He was to provide support and receive second billing. Harry knew he could trust Vernon and allowed him writing opportunities for a new series of shorts, to be directed by Arvid E. Gillstrom. The objective was to get Harry into the public eye once again.

The Langdon series included *The Big Flash*, *Tired Feet*, *The Hitchhiker*, *Knight Duty*, *Tied for Life*, and *Hooks and Jabs*. The shorts were shot and released beginning in late 1932 and continued until August 18, 1933. Although not great comedies, many fine moments do stand out. In *The Hitchhiker*, for instance, Harry reprises "the cold scene" from his 1926 feature, *The Strong Man*. Brooks Benedict was Harry's nemesis in the original sequence. This time the man seated next to him is the aggravated Vernon Dent, and the remake scene immediately improves upon the original because of it. Shot virtually silent (except for a simulated constant airplane motor hum), Vernon is stuck next to this germ-spreading wimp who has his head resting on Vernon's shoulder. The audience could almost smell the foul odor of the limburger cheese that Harry thinks is cold medicine.

In *Tied for Life* (Mermaid Comedies, December 15, 1933), Harry is a victorious suitor, who has won the hand of Nell O'Day against rival Vernon Dent. The press release offers a catch line: "Harry was a good fellow…he took his mother-in-law, his worst rival, and his bride along on his honeymoon. See the season's maddest, merriest comedy, *Tied for Life*."

In *Hooks and Jabs*, Vernon wrote a role for himself, that of a bartender in a saloon. Here we are rewarded with one of the very best Vernon Dent vocal performances on film. In a heartfelt, beautiful tenor, he sings the old standard, "When You and I Were Young, Maggie," with lyrics by George W. Johnson and music by James Austin Butterfield. The song wasn't necessary to further the plot, but it did help to break Langdon's pacing, and captured the aura of an old-time saloon — the kind that Vernon's father might have run.

By August 18, 1933 the Harry Langdon series remained almost intact as Paramount took over distribution. The five titles included *Marriage Humor, On Ice, Roaming Romeo, Circus Hoodoo*, and *Petting Preferred*. Unfortunately, none of these titles are believed to be extant. The association of Arvid Gillstrom served Langdon and Vernon well as they continued their collaboration with Paramount.

Gillstrom was assigned directorial duties for another two-reeler in late 1933, this time to Bing Crosby. Vernon was prevailed upon to write the story and provide the comic relief. The result was *Please* (December 1933), the title song of which was a huge hit for Bing.*

Paramount threw some money into this production. They actually took a film crew to Yosemite National Park to take advantage of its scenic beauty. Paramount published a synopsis, which gives us an indication as to the plot.

Please

While driving along a beautiful road, Bing Crosby meets Mary Kornman who is having trouble with her car. Bing fixes the tire and is about to make a date with Mary when Vernon Dent, her boyfriend, sticks his head out of the car and flips Bing a coin for his troubles. Bing finds out that Mary is a music teacher in that town and decides to take vocal lessons. Mary arranges a recital at which her two protégés, Bing and Vernon, are to compete for a prize. Vernon does his number first, but is interrupted by a

---

*The song "Please" inspired John Lennon to write one of the Beatles' earliest hits, "Please, Please Me," in 1963. Lennon was intrigued by the double meaning of "Please" in Bing's version: "Oh, Please, lend a little ear to my pleas."

pesky dog, much to Vernon's annoyance. Bing takes the house by storm and woos Mary by singing the title song "Please." Humiliated, Vernon goes back to a garage where Bing's car is stored and smashes it to pieces, until Bing informs him that the car he smashed was his own. Mary and Bing drive off in Bing's car as Vernon "crumbles."

Please was recently rediscovered in a private film collection. The production values are strong, but more importantly, Bing comes off as a comfortable actor with a flair for light comedy. His future was never brighter.

One highlight of *Please* occurs when Vernon competes with Bing by singing an antiquated ballad, "Dear Old Girl." Another memorable moment has Vernon walking from "the green-room" to go out onstage. Competitor Bing wishes Vernon an insincere, "Good luck!" (the preferred show business phrase is "Break a leg"). Vernon stops in his tracks and does a double-take at Bing.

While filming *Please*, the production crew shot scenes for another short, which also featured Bing and Vernon. *Just an Echo in the Valley* was another opportunity to put on film this popular record title. It is considered a "lost" film. Paramount Studios put out the following scenario.

Just An Echo In the Valley

Bing Crosby, a rookie ranger, patrols his post in the Yosemite Valley and accosts a pampered girl in a limousine, smoking in a forbidden spot. He pulls the cigarette out of her mouth several times when she starts off suddenly and frightens Bing's horse, which runs off without his master. Mary is the daughter of the Captain, Vernon Dent. Misunderstandings get Mary into physical danger when the hero rushes in to save her — and all is hunky-dory after that.

The *Motion Picture Herald* had the following observation:

For those among the motion picture audience who have a fondness for Bing Crosby, of the radio, this may be found reasonably effective as comedy with music. Rather unfortunately Mr. Crosby, in the role of a state trooper, is several times astride a horse. To say the least, he does not ride in a manner comparable to our better western stars. In fact, he is occasionally laughable.

While offering no competition to Bing Crosby's singing success, Vernon enjoyed vocalizing for the camera when the opportunity presented itself. One of these examples is *Good Morning, Eve* (Warner Bros., Vitaphone, September 27, 1934). In a time-travel look at music (starring Leon Errol as the Biblical Adam), he and Eve come across Vernon in the role of Nero. Vernon, dressed in a toga that could pass for a tent, sings again.

Author and film historian Rich Finegan reviewed this short for *The Three Stooges Journal* #114, summer, 2005:

> In the Technicolor short *Good Morning, Eve*, Vernon treats us to another especially fine performance. This time it's an upbeat number entitled "Rhythm in the Bow" (Cliff Hess). Vernon's great singing, along with the excellent sound of the Warner Bros. Orchestra at its best, make this number an absolute highlight in Vernon's entire film career. The song itself is wonderfully catchy, typical of the songs written by Cliff Hess for several Warner Bros. Vitaphone shorts of the period. Warner Bros. liked the song enough to produce a "Merrie Melodies" cartoon based upon it.

Vernon continued with his wonderful ethnic character roles, some in A-pictures, including *Manhattan Melodrama* (May 5, 1934). The film was directed by the renowned W. S. "Woody" Van Dyke and starred some of MGM's biggest stars: Clark Gable, William Powell, Myrna Loy, and Mickey Rooney. Vernon was in the first few scenes as a German immigrant, dancing with his girl on a Hudson River excursion boat.

It is always jolly to see Vernon, even in small roles, supporting major comedians. In the 1934 W.C. Fields Paramount vehicle, *You're Telling Me!*, Vernon has a brief scene (again, as a comic Dutchman, this time whistling "Ach, du lieber Augustine") in a train sequence. It wasn't the first time the two comic actors worked together; Vernon had also appeared with Fields in *Million Dollar Legs*, in 1932.

On the subject of memorable scenes, who could forget Vernon and Buster Keaton in *The Cameraman* (MGM, September 22, 1928)? In this late-silent feature, Buster steals Vernon's bathing suit from the locker so that he can swim in the public pool. Left behind with Buster's tiny bathing suit, Vernon must find a way to fit into it if he is to leave the locker even semi-clothed. When he finally emerges, the sight of the hefty (and angry) Vernon in the shrunken tank-topped swimwear never fails to make the viewer laugh.

Buster sought out Vernon again when he made *Tars and Stripes* (Educational, May 3, 1935). This two-reel sound comedy took place in San Diego at the Naval Facilities. Vernon was perfect as the second banana in this one, playing an overbearing officer. Officer Dent has a little blonde girlfriend who likes men in uniform. Buster, a lowly sailor, spends more time in the brig than out at sea. Vernon bullies Buster, who always seems to get tangled up with his girl.

Buster Keaton, Dorothea Kent, and Vernon Dent in Tars and Stripes *(Educational, 1935)*. COURTESY OF EDWARD WATZ

HAIL, COLUMBIA!

On May 21, 1935, 45-year-old Arvid Gillstrom died unexpectedly. It was Gillstrom who had been paving the way for Harry Langdon to loftier heights at Paramount. And both Gillstrom and Langdon were firm believers in Vernon Dent's talents. A promising potential career with Paramount died along with Gillstrom.

By the time of Gillstrom's death, many of Vernon's colleagues had joined the new Columbia Studios short subject department. Monty Collins was there; so was Bud Jamison. Both participated in a forbearer of the Three Stooges comedy unit in a *Musical Novelties* series entry called *Woman Haters*, released May 5, 1934. The unit was run by Jack White's kid brother, Jules. The White Brothers (along with another brother, Sam) had lived near the Sennett lot and learned the comedy film business from the ground up.

Other key members of the new unit were Del Lord (director) and Arthur Ripley (screenwriter and gagman). Ripley was an essential collaborator who worked closely on Langdon's screen image at Sennett's. During Edward Watz's 1979 interview with Jules White, the director recalled that he offered Harry a contract of $1,000 a picture to star in a series of Columbia shorts. His first title was *His Marriage Mix-up*. It was released in September of 1935 and was directed by none other than Jack White. (To avoid alimony payment to an ex-wife, Jack White used the pseudonym Preston Black.) *His Marriage Mix-Up* was also memorable for another reason: it re-teamed Vernon Dent and Harry Langdon. The duo continued the series with *I Don't Remember*, although Vernon was not signed exclusively for the Langdon unit; he was given a steady job as a stock player to support the other comedy units on the lot. Following the Langdon vehicles, Vernon was called on to support Andy Clyde in *Share the Wealth*.

Next up was a brief role with the biggest stars in the new unit, The Three Stooges — Moe Howard, Larry Fine, and Curley (later Curly) Howard. The comedy was entitled *Half-Shot Shooters*, and it served as the beginning of a collaboration that would last 18 years.

Half-shot Shooters *(Columbia, 1936)*. AUTHOR'S COLLECTION

CHAPTER 13

THE THREE STOOGES

As film comedy evolved through the early taking era, slapstick comedy was slowly being phased out. By the 1930s it was the storylines — not the sight gags — that carried the movie. Furthermore, the whole concept of two-reel comedies was being replaced by the Double Bill. A typical program at a neighborhood theater now consisted of an "A" movie, another lesser feature product, and selected short subjects, such as cartoons and newsreels. Such was the playing field when The Three Stooges hit the screen for their own series in 1934. As Curly said in *Three Little Beers* (1935), "We don't follow nobody!"

Most assuredly not! This madcap team played comedy the way they played golf: against the grain, and without rules. The humor of The Three Stooges was physical, low-brow and "vulgar." It was anything for a laugh. The Stooges were a curious combination of surrealism and exaggerated sound effects. Something was happening on the screen every second. They mocked Emily Post etiquette, authority figures, and a sense of fair play. They pursued food, liquor, and women with equal relish.

Brothers Moe and Curly Howard, along with Larry Fine, personified unique screen characters. Moe was the bulldog-faced enforcer; Curly the cherub man-child; and middleman Larry was the conduit of all this energy. Though many of their gags had been seen before in various silent film comedies, The Three Stooges came off as amazingly fresh. This can be attributed to the Stooges' training under Ted Healy, as well as to their physical appearance and innate comic timing. But the Three Stooges comedies were collaborative efforts, requiring the skills of first-rate directors, writers, and editors. When mixed thoroughly, the amped-up antics of Moe, Larry, and Curly created a new art form.

With the Columbia shorts department expanding, more talent was needed. Stock players were hired to work full-time on the many comedy units on the lot. Some of the men and women who populated the Stooge universe in the mid-thirties were Monty Collins, Bud Jamison, Elinor Vandivere, Grace Goodall, Jack Norton, Tiny Sanford, Hank Mann, Fred Kelsey, Leo White, James C. Morton, Billy Gilbert, and Stanley Blystone. By the late-thirties and throughout the forties and into the fifties, the most ubiquitous Stooge co-star of all would be Vernon Dent.

Vernon made his debut with the Stooges halfway through the 1936 two-reeler, *Half-Shot Shooters*, playing a man in a restaurant. With his prolific profile, he settles down to devour a veritable feast. He picks a table with a window view, but he doesn't count on having some vagrants staring at him like three hungry dogs. Actually, *four* hungry dogs: the Stooges send their canine pal inside to snare the Cornish-game hen and bring it back to them. Complications ensue when the dog refuses to turn over the grub, allowing Vernon enough time to punch the daylights out of them. The hapless victims attempt to appeal to the prosperous diner's sense of compassion. Vernon disingenuously offers sympathy and tricks them into joining the army. Vernon is so pleased at his own cleverness that we see him chortling to himself as he walks away.

A TOWN CALLED HOLLYWOOD

It would have been easy to miss this tidbit in Philip K. Scheuer's regular column in the August 23, 1936 edition of the *Los Angeles Times*. Scheuer wrote about a local radio broadcast on station KMTR (later KLAC), in Los Angeles. Former silent screen actress Louise Glaum hosted a Sunday evening program called *Stars of Yesteryear*. This particular episode featured Chester Conklin, Dot Farley, Minta Durfee (Arbuckle), and Vernon Dent. The columnist correctly identified them as "ex-Sennett comics all." Then Scheuer wrote, "It is the crowning irony, I think, that these disembodied voices, audible at last, are in many cases the sole means of expression left to those who in all their long screen careers never uttered a sound."

That last sentence must have seemed a poignant (albeit inaccurate) observation. During August of 1936, Dot Farley had a regular role in the cast of Edgar Kennedy's "Average Man" series for RKO, and Vernon was then working for Columbia Pictures. Chester Conklin, too, had spoken several lines of dialogue in early sound shorts.

A PERSONAL TRAGEDY

During the late 1930s Vernon's comfortable home life was shattered. His wife, Grace, had originally been diagnosed with a serious medical condition back in 1915 (believed to be complications from measles), but went on to lead a fulfilling life. As the decade of the 1930s progressed, however, she suffered a relapse. Grace was weakened with pain and became bedridden. On January 31, 1938, she was transported to the Norwalk, California State Hospital to receive intensive care.

Grace's medical condition only worsened at the hospital; there was nothing anyone could do. Her breathing became labored, and then, twenty days after admission, she died on February 19, 1938. The official cause of death was myocarditis (inflammation of the heart muscle). According to the death certificate (#1490), Dr. W. H. Wooley recorded her death at 9:50 a.m. No autopsy was necessary. Grace Dent, former seamstress for the studios, was laid to rest at Inglewood Cemetery. She was only 41 years old.

SOLDIERING ON

After Grace died, Vernon immersed himself in his work. Fortunately, there was plenty of it. He not only continued his stock work for Columbia (supporting all the comedy units), he also free-lanced at the other studios.

One of the most heartfelt performances Vernon ever gave was in a relatively obscure one-reeler for MGM, *Mendelssohn's Wedding March*. This musical novelty is a fictionalized story of the ceremonial piece that has become a tradition of marriage in Western culture. Vernon played the German-born composer to perfection. Considering his talent for dialect and love of music, this homage must have given the actor much satisfaction. The *Motion Picture Herald* gave a preview in its December 2, 1939 issue:

> An episode from the life of Felix Mendelssohn is brought to the screen in color and reveals how he came to write his Wedding March. Walking in his garden he heard a peasant playing the violin for his wife-to-be. The boy, offered an opportunity to study at one of the better European colleges, declined because it would interfere with his marriage. Mendelssohn agreed to finance the trip for both husband and wife. At the wedding ceremony his march is played.

As wonderful as Vernon's musical portrayals were, his bread-and-butter persona was as a comic heavy to the various comedians he supported. This took many forms; sometimes as a business man, sometimes as a dignitary, an authority figure — or simply a person in the wrong place and time.

When Vernon worked with the Stooges, his characters covered a wide range. After all, Vernon's years with the Sennett, White, and Christie comedies prepared him for just about any zany role that could be imagined. Vernon built a reputation in the business for projecting comedy contrast, a necessary ingredient for the stars to get the laughs. Onscreen it appeared that Vernon was offended at the mere sight of Moe, Larry, and Curly (and later, Shemp). Vernon could go through many stages of outrage, depending on his character.

THE LOOK

Even in the animal kingdom, the very basics of survival depend on "reading" a dangerous situation. One knows not to provoke an animal for fear it will retaliate. A cornered cat will arch its back and hiss to fend off a confrontation. A dog will bare its teeth and growl. A wife will tap her toe impatiently with her hands on her hips. Vernon Dent displayed his own dictionary of "Body Language." He projected it in different scenes and in various stages. The audience knew what was coming way before the Stooges did. And that was part of the fun.

When Vernon's personal space was violated, his scowl could warn any sane person to get out of his way. If the antagonism continued (and it always did), then Vernon added to the warning of "back off" with his piercing eyes. This expression became even more exaggerated, as though he were a carnivore honing in on his prey. His eyes became fixed like heat-seeking missiles. There was no telling what the next step might be; sometimes he telegraphed his subsequent move by lurching his shoulders back and bringing his hands up as though he were about to tear someone limb from limb. At other times, he would coil up and strike with his fists.

Vernon Dent appeared in more than 50 of The Three Stooges' shorts; he was by far the most ubiquitous member of their company of supporting players. Between the years 1936-1954, Vernon took on the Stooges in some of the best filmed comedy moments ever to be captured.

The following pages pertain to Vernon's interactive highlights with the team, arranged in order of Vernon's occupational titles. The listings are separated into categories; they are not in chronological order, nor is this meant to be comprehensive. After all, there are many funny moments in any interaction between Vernon and the Stooges. Since all humor is subjective, the list is offered merely as a "thought piece." The reader is encouraged to interject his (or her) favorite Vernon moments.

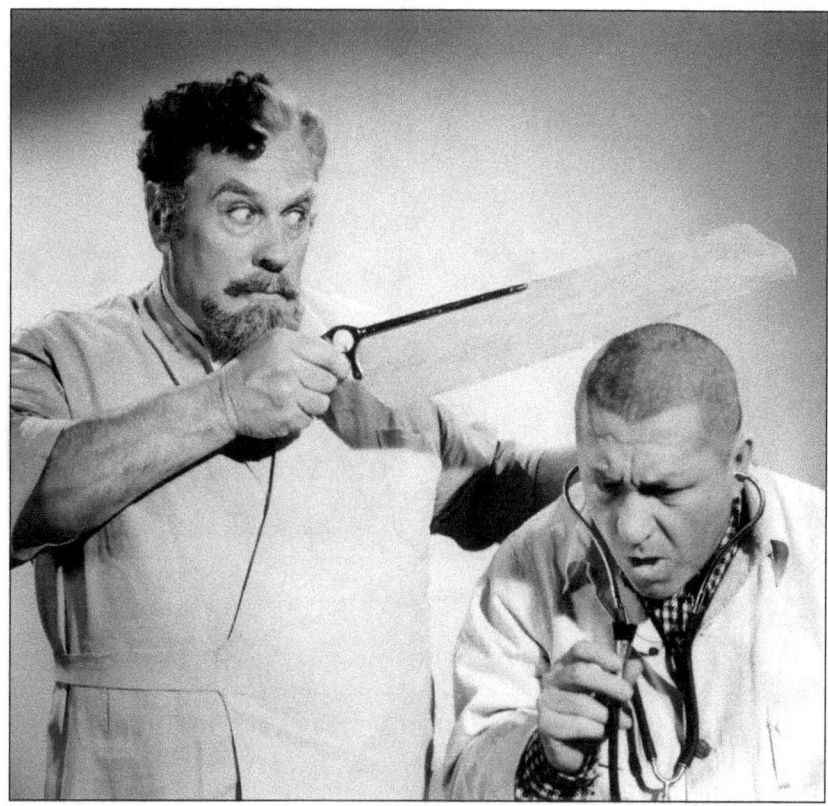

Mad scientist Vernon wants Curly's brain for his experiments in A Bird in the Head *(Columbia, 1946).* AUTHOR'S COLLECTION

VERNON'S FILM ROLES WITH THE STOOGES

Dr. D. Lerious, *From Nurse To Worse*
Best Line: "Prepare the patient for cerebral decapitation."
Highlight: Vernon takes a pratfall.

Dr. Harry Arms, *Dizzy Doctors*
Best Line: "If I ever catch you guys again, I'll tear you limb from limb."
Highlight: Vernon gets poked in the eyes by Moe.

Doctor, *Out West*
Best Line: "I've never seen a vain [vein] like that in my life."
Highlight: Vernon *(reading a chart),* makes the above remark as though he were a gold prospector looking at a surveyors map.

Matri-Phony *(Columbia, 1942)* COURTESY OF RICH FINEGAN

Doc Keefer, *The Tooth Will Out*
Best Line: Keefer: Gentlemen, you can have your diplomas [for dentistry] in only one week.
Stooges: We only have three dollars.
Keefer: I'll take it.
Highlight: Vernon wearing 1890s garb, complete with a handlebar mustache.

Professor Panzer, *A Bird in the Head*
Best Line: "Through Igor, I'm going to become famous. Igor the Beast of the Jungle will have a human brain. He'd have one tomorrow if I can find a brain small enough. What size hat do you wear?"
Highlight: Vernon with a machine gun.

Dr. Walters, *Nutty but Nice*
Best Line: "I'm going to ask you boys something that will save the life of a little girl: Will you do it?"
Highlight: Vernon plays it straight; a smiling, engaging professional doctor, with care and warmth.

Phil Van Zandt, the Stooges, Vernon Dent, and Christine McIntyre on the set of Knutzy Knights *(Columbia, 1954). This was the last Stooge short to offer new footage of Vernon Dent.* COURTESY OF THE MARGARET HERRICK LIBRARY

Prof. Quackenbush, *Half-Wits Holiday*
Best Line: "I'll take a man from the lowest strata of life and in two months, through environment, make him a gentleman" *(The Stooges enter on cue.)*
Highlight: Vernon gets a pie in the face.

Emperor Octopus Grabus, *Matri-Phony*
Best Line: "Who are these morons? Throw them to the lions!"
Highlight: Vernon, as a Greek emperor, can't see without his glasses.

King Ruttin' Tuttin, *Mummy's Dummies*
Best Line: "I have no time for trifles — throw them to the crocodiles!"
Highlight: Shemp crunches Vernon's nose with pliers while attempting to extract a tooth.

Three Little Pirates *(Columbia, 1946)* COURTESY OF COMEDY III ENTERTAINMENT, INC.

King Arthur, *Squareheads of the Round Table*
Best Line: "I'll have your heads for this!"
Highlight: In ancient knight's armor, the Stooges perform a dance routine to the music of "Swanee River" for the unsuspecting King.

Old King Cole, *Fiddler's Three*
Best Line: "And now for our daily laugh, there's nothing better, so good for the soul than a hearty laugh."
Highlight: Vernon's infectious guffawing, and the ending, in which he follows the trail of men whistling at the girl.

Governor, *Three Little Pirates*
Best Line: "They don't look like seafaring men to me." *(Off camera: wolf whistles.)* "They're sailors alright"
Highlight: Vernon tells the Stooges, "You may choose the manner in which you will die." Larry responds: "That's easy — old age."

Vernon, the Stooges, and George Lewis in Malice in the Palace *(Columbia, 1949).* COURTESY OF THE MARGARET HERRICK LIBRARY

Governor, *Back to the Woods*
Best Line: Vernon reassures the Indian Chief, "Peace, no more war."
       (Chief reacts as though he's heard that one before.)
Highlight: Vernon wearing a period wig.

Simitz, Arab Chief, *Wee Wee Monsieur*
Best Line: "Find them and throw them to the lions!"
Highlight: Vernon gets poked in the eyes by Curly; later, the Stooges
       (disguised as harem girls in a chorus line) kick him in the face.

Hassan Ben Sober, *Malice in the Palace*
Best Line: "I could have quit my job as doorman at the Oasis Hotel."
Highlight: Vernon's reactions to a feast of hot dog and rabbit.

Sheriff, *Yes, We Have No Bonanza*
Best Line: "Why, this is the money that was stolen from the First
       National Bank!"
Highlight: Stooges drive into the Sheriff's jail.

Heavenly Daze *(Columbia, 1948)*. COURTESY OF COMEDY III ENTERTAINMENT, INC.

Officer Sharp, *Sing a Song of Six Pants*
Best Line: "I don't want a coat… I don't want a coat… I DON'T WANT A COAT!!!"
Highlight: The Stooges try to fit Vernon with a pair of "slick slacks" while a bank robber gets away.

Warden, *Beer Barrel Polecats*
Best Line: "Oh, wise guys, huh? Send them to solitary!"
Highlight: Vernon and the boys are shown as they would appear "40 years later," when they are released from prison.

Capt. Mullins, *Shivering Sherlocks*
Best Line: When asked where *he* had been on the night in question, Vernon responds, "Why, I was at a lodge meeting."
Highlight: The lie detector goes haywire.

Back From the Front *(Columbia, 1943).* AUTHOR'S COLLECTION

Judge Henderson, *Listen, Judge*
Best Line: "I'm not going to make these poor unfortunates the victims of your prejudice and guess work. Case dismissed. You're free, boys."
Highlight: Chicken flies out from Shemp's coat and onto Vernon's face.

Judge, *Idiots Deluxe*
Best Line: "Were you ever indicted?"
Highlight: Vernon's reaction to Moe's answer, "Not since I was a baby, your honor."

Lawyer (I. Fleecem), *Heavenly Daze*
Best Line: "Any other lawyer would've taken the case for twenty dollars."
Highlight: Vernon chuckles as he says, "That's what I call easy pickings."

Capt. Casey, *Studio Stoops*
Best Line: "Look, Stoop, this is my day off. If you bother me anymore with your phony baloney, I'll punch you in the stomach, chuck you in the chin and knock your head in."
Highlight: Vernon demonstrates the above threats on Shemp.

Higher Than a Kite *(Columbia, 1943)* Larry, Curly, Moe, Vernon Dent, and Dick Curtis. COURTESY RICH FINEGAN

Desk Sergeant, *So Long, Mr. Chumps*
Best Line: "Yeah, so what'd you do, kill Cock Robin or start the San Francisco Earthquake?"
Highlight: The Stooges try to confess to a crime to hardboiled Vernon, the desk sergeant who's heard it all.

Mr. Ixnay, *I'll Never Heil Again*
Best Line: "I'm positive [they won't return], your majesty — look!"
Highlight: Cut to ending scene of mounted heads of Moe, Larry, and Curly.

Hans, *They Stooge to Conga*
Best Line: Vernon, with a convincing German accent, says, "Ven ve catch them, ve shoot them between the eyes!"
Highlight: Vernon does a parody of the Goosestep.

Hugo, *No Dough Boys*
Best Line: Moe, pointing at Vernon, doing the old Shnitzelbank routine; "Is this not a dirty rat, yah, dat is a dirty rat."
Highlight: Vernon wearing swastika-covered long underwear.

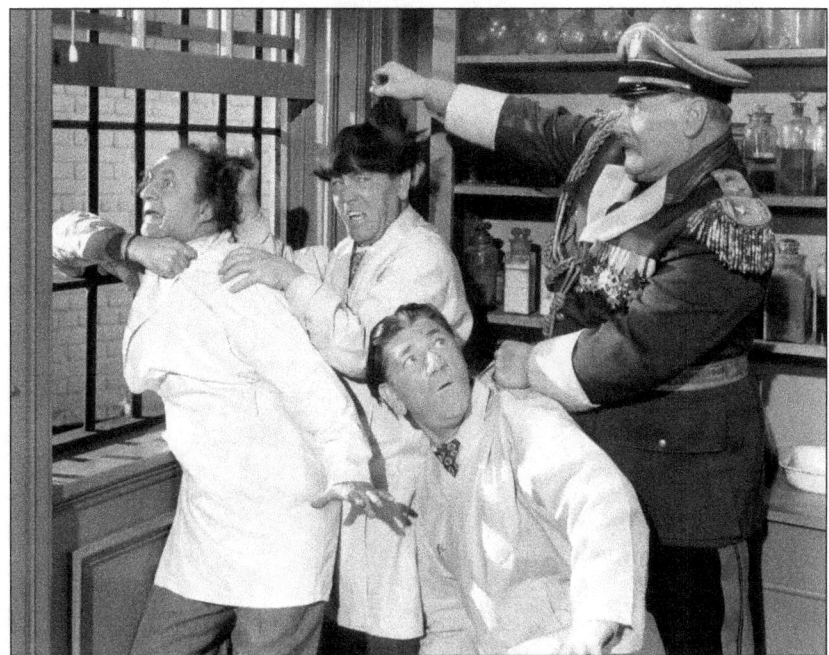

Fuelin' Around *(Columbia, 1949)* COURTESY OF RICH FINEGAN

Lt. Dungen, *Back From the Front*
Best Line: "Now I know you, you American swine!"
Highlight: Vernon's outrageous German accent.

Marshall Boring, *Higher than a Kite*
Best Line: Vernon: Ach, a lady — come here and sit on my lap.
    Larry: What lap?
Highlight: Vernon is a high-ranking Nazi officer who is delighted by the appearance of Carmen Miranda *(actually, Larry in drag)*.

Army Colonel, *Punchy Cowpunchers*
Best Line: "I need three good men… The Dillons are ruthless killers and these men that you select will probably never come back."
Highlight: Vernon looks at his empty hand after he extends it to shake Jacques O'Mahoney's.

General, *Fuelin' Around*
Best Line: "Unless you give us the formula at once, you, your daughter and your friends all will be shot!"
Highlight: Moe thinks the highly decorated general is a doorman.

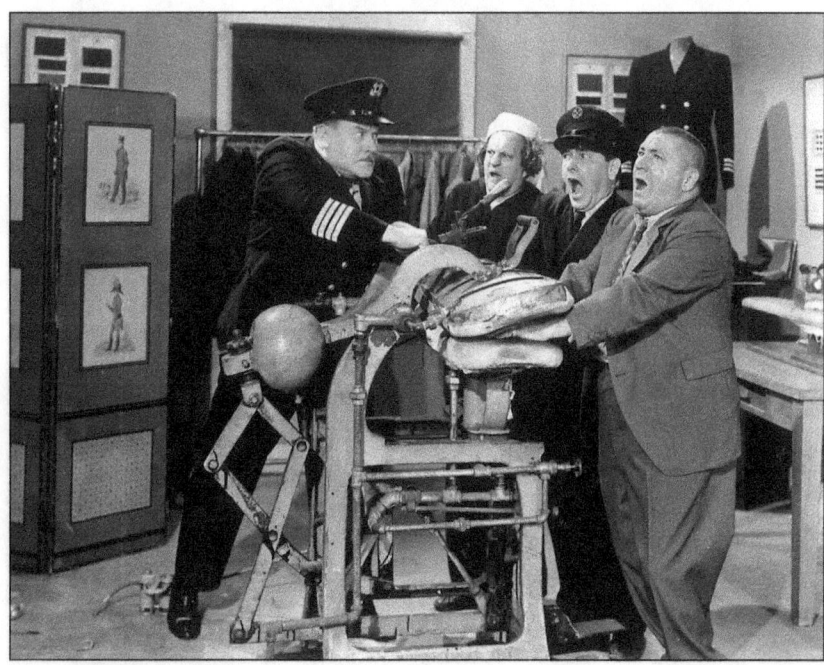

Booby Dupes *(Columbia, 1945)* COURTESY OF COMEDY III ENTERTAINMENT, INC.

Navy Captain, *Booby Dupes*
Best Line: "Here, press this uniform right away, my girl's waiting… make it snappy!"
Highlight: Vernon's head is soaked in ice cream after he jabs Curly with a beach umbrella.

Mr. Morgan, *Slippery Silks*
Best Line: "I'll tear you limb from limb!"
Highlight: Vernon gets poked in the eyes by Moe.

Moe's bridge partner, *No Census, No Feeling*
Best Line: "Yes, it's delicious." *(His face contradicts the sentiment).*
Highlight: Vernon mumbles, as does everyone at the party who drank alum-laced punch.

Poindexter Lawrence, *An Ache in Every Stake*
Best Line: "Now, I remember… *the ice men!*"
Highlight: It's Vernon's birthday and he gets cake in his face three different times.

Party Guest, *In the Sweet Pie and Pie*
Best Line: "Usually, I don't like parties, but I have a feeling I'll get a bang out of this one!"
Highlight: Vernon throws and receives pies with the other dinner guests.

Balbo the Magician, *Loco Boy Makes Good*
Best Line: "Wait 'til I get out there, brother — I'll wow 'em!"
Highlight: Vernon *(as a magician)* leaves his trick coat behind. Curly puts the magician's coat on by mistake. Mice, rabbits, birds, and a skunk all unexpectedly emerge from the pockets, creating laughs and havoc.

Man in Jail, *Three Smart Saps*
Best Line: "Now see here, you've been my tailor for years, and the day I need my clothes most, you have to disappoint me."
Highlight: Vernon is allegedly the crooked warden who "framed" the real warden.

Man in Car, *Even As I.O.U.*
Best Line: "Hey, just a second, these horses ran the day before yesterday. Give me my money back. POLICE!!! OFFICER!!!"
Highlight: Vernon calls for the cops and good old Bud Jamison responds.

Manager Editor of a newspaper (Fuller Bull), *Crash Goes the Hash*
Best Line: "I'll get a story or I'll tear the town apart. You're a great bunch of reporters…you're all fired…get out!!!"
Highlight: The Stooges inadvertently come through with a damning photo, drawing excited praise from boss Vernon. "*No Story?*" he says. "Why, this is the greatest scoop that ever hit this town!"

Wilson, the Magazine Editor, *Dutiful But Dumb*
Best Line: "Get out of here; you're fired!"
Highlight: Curly knocks over a standing display of framed photos and they fall like dominos onto Vernon.

Three Pests in a Mess *(Columbia, 1945)*. AUTHOR'S COLLECTION

Café Customer, *Busy Buddies*
Best Line: "Hey, these hotcakes must be made out of reclaimed rubber. Where's the chef? I can't eat these — let's see *you*."
Highlight: Vernon's fork and knife bend when he tries to cut into his hotcakes. Vernon then gives Moe "The Look."

Mr. Leander, *Idle Roomers*
Best Line: Vernon is married to Christine and have, as part of their "Big-Time" act, a werewolf in their luggage. "He's absolutely harmless, unless he hears music — then he goes insane."
Highlight: Vernon throws knives and darts at Curly.

Phillip Black, *Three Pests in a Mess*
Best Line: "Trouble at the cemetery? Oh, but I can't go, I'm at a masquerade party."
Highlight: Vernon dressed as a gravedigger, along with his associates *(a skeleton and a devil)*.

Insurance claims adjustor, *Hocus Pocus*
Best Line: "Thank you, boys!" *(He then rips up the settlement check).*
Highlight: Vernon exchanges slaps with Shemp, then stomps on Shemp's foot.

Mr. Bradley, *Three Arabian Nuts*
Best Line: "There's nothing magic about it [the lamp]; I bought it for fifty cents at a bazaar. You can have it if you want."
Highlight: Vernon is subjected to sitting on a hot plate, getting hit by a crowbar *(by Moe)*, getting hit by a mace *(by Larry)*, but the highlight is seeing the Stooges walk out with the results of the magic lamp; which includes girls and a wheelbarrow of money and jewels. The fadeout is on Vernon, repeatedly striking himself on the head with a hammer.

Nora's Father, *Scrambled Brains*
Best Line: "You stupid idiots, you've ruined my cake!"
Highlight: The Stooges and Vernon exchange punches and slaps while trapped in a telephone booth, but the capper is Vernon leaning over and biting Moe's nose.

Mr. Philander, *The Pest Man Wins*
Best Line: (Hostess to Vernon): "I just know you're going to like my pies." Before long, they are each on the receiving end of one.
Highlight: Vernon reacts to a mouse going into his pants by jumping and twitching. The Stooges join in with their own ridiculous dance.

Hotel Manager, *A Missed Fortune*
Best Line: "My vase! My beautiful vase! You've ruined my room!"
Highlight: Without trying, the Stooges break Vernon's $5,000 vase and everything else in their suite at Hotel Costa Plenty.

Uniformed Night Watchman with a gun, *Booty and the Beast*
Best Line: "What's going on here? Come along quietly — you'll get ten years for this."
Highlight: Moe tugs on a carpet and upends Vernon so the boys can escape.

Half-Shot Shooters *(Columbia, 1936).* COURTESY EDWARD WATZ

IRS Agent, *Income Tax Sappy*
Best Line: (As Vernon shakes his finger with contempt): "You men have ignored twenty summonses from the [Internal Revenue] Department."
Highlight: The Stooges try to escape by throwing the tablecloth over Vernon's head, only to stumble onto a wood-burning stove. Moe, Larry, and Shemp are captured and led off by IRS agents with the seats of their pants on fire.

The Boss, *Tassels in the Air*
Best Line: "Where are those guys...Larry? Curly? Moe? Don't explain — *you're fired!*"
Highlight: Vernon opens a misidentified door and we hear him fall down the elevator shaft.

Mr. Stutz, *Hotel Manager, Mutts to You*
Best Line: "I'm going to keep an eye on you guys."
Highlight: Vernon's does a double-take when he sees Larry's protruding belly.

Party Guest, *Three Little Sew and Sews*
Best Line: At the sight of a uniformed Naval officer *(Curly)* making out with a girl: "*Please*, sir!"
Highlight: Close-up of Vernon laughing at Curly's predicament. *(The Stooge has a sofa coil stuck to the seat of his pants.)*

Man in Office, *A-Ducking They Did Go*
Best Line: "I don't eat duck — I'm a vegetarian."
Highlight: In an attempt to hold a potential customer, the Stooges inadvertently tear off Vernon's clothes, including his pants, piece by piece *(this action occurs off camera)*.

Man in Restaurant, *Half-Shot Shooters*
Best Line: "Why, I oughta have you all arrested!"
Highlight: Vernon eating chicken in a restaurant when The Stooges send a dog in to steal it off the plate.

The Boss, *How High Is Up?*
Best Line: "Well it looks like good solid construction... Hey, who are those three new men?"
Highlight: Hot rivets are dropped down Vernon's shirt.

Mabel Langdon, Eunice and Vernon Dent, and Harry Langdon on the Dents' wedding day, in August 1938. COURTESY OF EDWARD WATZ

CHAPTER 14

EUNICE

Vernon's personal life changed forever in the spring of 1938 when he met a petite little spark of flame named Eunice. He was 43 years old, and like Ferdinand the Bull, Vernon's every sense was awakened to life's offerings.

When Eunice was interviewed by film historian and author Edward Watz in 1979, she explained that she and Vernon were introduced by a mutual friend at a party at Harry Langdon's house. Vernon was so smitten with this vivacious charmer that he proposed to her the very night they met.

Eunice said, "We met in April of 1938, and we were married that August. We saw no reason why we shouldn't be together." Vernon was on his third marriage; Eunice her second. Eunice had been employed as an escrow clerk at a local bank.

The Dents' extant marriage certificate lists Eunice's birth name as Hortense Eunice Boroughs. She was born in 1909, in New York. Her mother was the former Rose Zuckerman, originally from Minnesota. Eunice's father, Henry M. Boroughs, was born in Massachusetts; by 1920 the family lived in New York.

It is no wonder that the Harry Langdon family shared the joy of the Dents' new marriage. Vernon and Eunice not only met at their house, it appears that Harry and Vernon looked out for each other on a professional basis. And what greater honor is there than to be asked to be someone's Best Man and Matron of Honor?

"Mabel and Harry came out with us when we were married in Santa Barbara," Eunice recalled. "We had lunch at the El Facile Restaurant in Santa Barbara, which at that time was quite 'posh,' then we had dinner at Bob Murphy's Nightclub at La Cienega Boulevard. The four of us were there. And it was early, not 'nightclub time' at all. Virginia O'Brien, the girl singer was there, and she just started singing as we were having dinner. She sort of gave us a solo concert performance. We were very impressed with her — she was good! Of course, we had an awful lot of fun."

To mark the occasion of the latest Hollywood marriage, there were two small items in the newspapers. They are interesting to note because of different spellings and circumstances. This was from the *Los Angeles Times*:

Film Actor Marries in Santa Barbara

Aug. 27, 1938: Vernon Dent, motion picture actor, and Eunice Boroughs, daughter of Mr. and Mrs. Henry M. Boroughs of Boston, were married here today in a quiet ceremony performed by Rev. Robert N. McLean of the First Presbyterian Church.

Harry Langdon, film comedian and writer, was Best Man and Mrs. Langdon Matron of Honor. The Dents left for Washington State on a honeymoon trip.

And this was from the *Los Angeles Herald-Examiner:*

Langdon's Marital Success Spurs Film Couple to Nuptials

If marriage is a success for one film comedian it should be for another. That's the theory on which Miss Unice [*sic*] Burroughs [*sic*], secretary to a Hollywood banker, and Vernon Dent, film comic, will assume the bonds of matrimony tomorrow. Their wedding hinged on whether or not Harry Langdon, motion picture comedian, and his wife, stayed married five years.

The couple met five years ago at the Langdon home. When Dent proposed, Miss Burroughs shook her head and declared: "Hollywood marriages are jinxed. But, if the Langdons are still married five years from now, I might change my mind."

They did, and she did. And tomorrow the Langdons will be witnesses at the wedding of Dent and Miss Burroughs in Santa Barbara.

THE HONEYMOONERS

Eunice remembered that when she first met Vernon, "He used to trip just to amuse me, and in the beginning I really thought he was going to get hurt. But he knew instinctively how to do these things. He was part stuntman, I guess, but he learned this at a very early age. There was no training; he trained himself. He had no fear of falling."

The Dents eventually moved into their new house on Peach Street in Van Nuys. "There were only seven houses on this street," Eunice said. "I think we [had] the third house to be built here. This was an old walnut grove and [it] was very nice — this neighborhood turned out to be near all the major freeways."

"We used to entertain here, right after we bought the house," she continued. "It became the fashion to have outdoor barbeques, and Vern became very good at it.

"We were pretty young and Vern was actually the oldest [13 years older than I]. We used to have an awful lot of fun, because it was a difficult time [the years during World War II] to go anywhere."

"But Vernon as a person was a darling, sweet, gentle man with a wonderful sense of humor. He liked to do a lot of things, he was sensible — with his feet on the ground. So I was attracted to him, and he was to me. And that was what we did. He was under contract to Columbia Pictures when I married him."

Eunice fondly remembered that when they first married, Vernon was living in Culver City. It was December 10, 1938, and *Gone With the Wind* was being filmed on the nearby MGM lot. There were skeptics who didn't think a motion picture could capture the authenticity of Margaret Mitchell's celebrated novel. Characterization was one thing, but a literal burning of Atlanta seemed too vast of an undertaking. People in the business knew when production got to the point of the "burning" scene. It was reported to be the biggest use of extras and sets since the silent epics of D.W. Griffith and Cecil B. DeMille.

Vernon and Eunice sat on a hill overlooking the production and watched the mock "Burning of Atlanta." There was only one chance to get it right; the lighted embers glowed into the evening. It must have been a memorable night. Despite Eunice's enthusiasm for witnessing one of the most storied special effects captured on cinema, she admitted, "I'm not a movie buff, and this was one of Vernon's disappointments that I wasn't awed by all this stuff."

FAMOUS CO-STARS

In the course of his interviews, Edward Watz mentioned several of Vernon's legendary colleagues, hoping to trigger a fresh memory:

Andy Clyde?
"Yes, he was a good friend, but didn't have much to say. We had one of the first television sets on our street, back in the mid-1940s; he used to come over to visit."

Buster Keaton?

"Vernon worked with him, but just rather transitory, not very much. Vernon told me that he first worked a bit part with Buster in *The Cameraman*, a big MGM feature in the silent days. The next time they worked together was down in San Diego, in a cheap little short at the Navy base there [*Tars and Stripes*, in 1935]. Vernon later told me he was saddened by what had happened to Buster between the times they had last worked. After we were married, Vernon worked in Columbia shorts that starred Buster, and he was very happy when we learned that Buster found himself a very nice bride [Eleanor Norris]. With Vernon, it was an awestruck admiration for a comedian he felt was one of the very best. You'd think these comedians would all be more social with each other, but they weren't. It was a very serious business and, of course, they were beat at the end of the day; they had to get up very early again in the morning and work hard all day. Sometimes we had to go to the studio at five or six in the morning."

Vernon was thrilled to be working with Buster again. According to Eunice, Vernon considered Buster "the utmost of talent." Vernon was professionally fulfilled when they both worked together. Eunice conveyed how proud Vernon was when they got to work together at Columbia studios again in a series of two-reel shorts.

Arthur Ripley?

"He was very strange. I didn't know him very well; I met him at Mabel's house several times. I always found him difficult to talk with. I'm sure he simply dismissed me. He was dour, and he wasn't very pleasant. If we were in a gathering, I took myself away from him; I'd go help Mabel with the dishes or something. His wife was very charming. Often Arthur would devise a situation and then it was up to Harry and Vernon to work it out into a comedy routine. They would fill in and embellish the gags. Of course, the writers didn't care how dangerous it was. It was for Vernon and Harry to figure out the easiest way to do these routines."

Frank Capra?

"Oh, Frank Capra wouldn't make a movie without him. He always called Vernon for a part in several full-length pictures. Vernon was in *Mr. Smith Goes to Washington* and *Meet John Doe*." After Vernon retired, Capra called him for a part one last time. I believe the film was *Pocketful of Miracles* [1961]; unfortunately, Vernon was already blind."

The Three Stooges?
"They were weird — all four of them."
"But," Eunice added, "he liked them, and he understood them."
Eunice remembered some of the movie producers (including Jules White) and all the writers at Columbia. Eunice said, "Jack White, Harry Edwards, and Elwood Ullman would come by and watch baseball on TV with Vernon." Eunice also remembered, "At Columbia there was a girl casting director who used to give Vernon a call. I would talk to her for a few minutes. I practically never went to the studio. I went, maybe, when we were first married to see what was in it. It got so boring after a while that I never went again. The patience they had to have, it took a certain sort of temperament to do this."

Harry Langdon?
"Vernon dearly loved Harry. There was such a gentle camaraderie between them. They understood each other. It was really a touching association for both of them. I felt that as soon as I saw them together. Of course, Harry and Mabel's life was not much different from ours."
"Vernon and Harry were very close when working together, and he had a sympathetic audience in me, I simply let him talk knowing it was necessary," Eunice explained. "Harry and Vernon both manufactured their gags. They had gag writers, of course, but they were pretty resourceful themselves because they knew what they could do together."
Eunice retains fond memories of Harry on a personal level as well: "Harry and I had a ball, and we usually did. I was able to talk to Harry on any level. He knew that I didn't know anything about the picture business so he didn't even attempt to talk to me about this; he knew that I was not all that interested. He had plenty of people to talk about that. So we talked about lots of things, all different subjects, and I found him very intelligent, very warm. He was just a doll."

In 1983, Edward Watz transported a projector and several reels of film from his home in New Jersey to Van Nuys, California, to show Eunice some examples of her late husband's work. She was especially transfixed by his "Folly" comedies, co-starring Violet Joy/Duane Thompson. Like Violet, Eunice was tiny, shapely and beautiful. Without any prompting, Eunice made a spontaneous observation during the screening: "You know, I think now I know why Vernon fell in love with me; I reminded him of his little leading lady!"

CHAPTER 15

DON'T MENTION THE WAR

Once America declared war on Germany and Japan in late 1941, fear gripped the nation. The movies provided a pleasant distraction for the folks back home. Nevertheless, there were grim realities of combat from the newsreels. The features could be stark reality, some propaganda, and others light-hearted. A good example of the latter is *San Diego, I Love You*, released by Universal in 1944.

It was one of those cheerful "keep the morale up on the home front" features, and it had a terrific cast: Jon Hall, Edward Everett Horton, Irene Ryan, and Florence Lake. The highlight of the film comes when a bored bus driver (Buster Keaton, in a wonderful cameo) is persuaded to go off course and make an unscheduled trip to the beach. He is reluctant to do so at first, explaining that he could be fired if he ignored his familiar route. But with the enthusiastic encouragement of the passengers (including Vernon Dent), he slowly warms to the idea. At the end of this one-time lark, it is obvious that being a non-conformist agrees with the usually dour driver, for he flashes a dazzling smile (a rarity indeed for the Great Stoneface).

A few years earlier Vernon had appeared in a feature film, *Beast of Berlin* (1939). Instead of supplying the heavy German character, this time he played a German citizen being terrorized by Nazi soldiers. His scenes elicited much sympathy from American movie audiences.

In more familiar territory, he provided excellent support for Moe, Larry, and Curly in a handful of satirical Stooge shorts: *I'll Never Heil Again* (1941), *They Stooge to Conga* (1941), *Higher Than a Kite* (1943), and *Back From the Front* (1943). In *No Dough Boys* (1944), Vernon plays a Nazi spy, and the Stooges impersonate Japanese soldiers. The climactic scene has the Stooges rip Vernon's suit right off of him and expose his long-john underwear, which is decorated with little swastika patterns. Moe stands over Vernon with a globe of the world and says, "Here is to your new world order!" and smashes it over Vernon's head.

Moe, Larry, and Curly — all of the Jewish faith — were pleased to have the opportunity to poke some fun at the Axis powers, even though they may have been putting themselves at risk of retaliation. These were only two-reel comedies, but they were effective comedy-propaganda. In truth, no one knew what was safe, patriotic, or what was politically correct. The whole world seemed to be going crazy.

The same could be said of the events on the Home Front. Japanese-Americans were being placed in internment camps. Eunice recalls how this directly affected their household: "Vernon's Aunt Mabel had a lovely farm house with acreage — I think 50 acres — with prunes and apricots in Cupertino [California]. It was a charming house, an old Victorian home, which they fixed and modernized. They had imported Japanese to work on the fields and in the house, and when the war came in 1941 they were all…oh, that was heartbreaking because Vern had grown up with these Japanese — special Japanese families. The mother and father were in the house, as were two or three children. The aunty and uncle gave their children piano lessons and simply raised them like their own. And they were incarcerated during the war and we went to see them. We were heartbroken because, by this time, I knew who they were, and liked them. They were sent to Idaho or someplace. They came out of it alright, but it was quite a thing for Vernon and I."

A LIFE-ALTERING DIAGNOSIS

In 1943 a syndicated Hollywood columnist informed his readers that "Vernon Dent, onetime Keystone Cop [*sic*] and screen partner of Harry Langdon, is seriously ill at a Los Angeles hospital."

"Vernon thought he had hurt himself by accident, by mowing the lawn," Eunice recalled. "We had gotten one of the first electric lawn mowers, because he used to like to garden. He told me that since his families were ranchers, he knew all about gardening. I soon found out he didn't know a darn thing. I always let him, since he really enjoyed it. He was mowing the lawn, bumped his toe somehow; it got infected and didn't heal. That's how they discovered he was diabetic." Eunice also recalled that, while Vernon was in the hospital, their family dog was at home with a new litter of puppies. She managed to smuggle a cocker spaniel puppy into the hospital to cheer him up.

It has frequently been mentioned that Vernon's love of sweets contributed to the severity of his medical condition. Eunice remembers, "When Vernon and I were married he had the concession in Westlake Park, the boat concession. It was a very lucrative business…and it was so busy on Sundays that he used to get me to go down and hand out the food and candy, and I worked like a dog on Sundays. It was a very good business; he had the concession for years until they got a new park commissioner. We had it for about ten years. And he drank Coca-Cola; he loved sweets to an inordinate degree…I remember sending him to the market to do some shopping; all he would come home with was all of these sweets. I would be working and tell him I needed some scouring powder like Ajax, but he never would bring home any of this. He'd complain bitterly about spending money on anything as foolish as this."

Eunice and Mabel Langdon both remarked how Vernon always seemed to have a Coke in his hand — more than five or six a day. "And remember," Eunice pointed out, "this was pure sugar. He didn't buy the Cokes; we used to get the syrup from the boat house and mix it with the seltzer and make our own sodas, so you couldn't even count them. I knew that something was wrong. Diabetes is a malfunction of the pancreas. The sugar is not dissolved as in a normal body."

Although Vernon was a non-drinker, he always made sure that alcohol was available for his guests, even during the war years when spirits were expensive and in short supply. At one party, Eunice recalls, "Vernon and I got there and Harry immediately took me by the hand into a closet where Harry had stashed a bottle of bourbon. Every so often we'd make forays into this closet. Vernon didn't drink and he really didn't approve of my drinking."

A MISSED OPPORTUNITY

Mabel Langdon confided to Edward Watz, "I know that Harry had discussed with me in the 1930s that it would be great if Vernon and he were more like a team. But then with Laurel & Hardy being so prominent, it wouldn't have worked out at that particular time. I know that Vernon would've liked it. And I know that Harry would have, too."

The time for such a partnership would never come. After a brief illness, Harry Langdon died at St. Vincent's Hospital, on December 22, 1944. A small notice in the *Los Angeles Times* listed the survivors as his wife, Mabel, and his ten-year-old son, Harry, Jr. The article announced funeral arrangements, which were handled by Vernon.

When Harry, Jr. was a teenager, Mabel Langdon explained, "It was Uncle Vernon who gave him fatherly counseling and took him to baseball games. I'll never forget that."

SELECTED SHORT SUBJECTS

During the filming of the 97th Stooge short, *Half-Wits Holiday*, in May 1946, Curly Howard suffered a stroke. Vernon Dent was there, as part of the cast. Would Curly recover sufficiently to continue as the third Stooge? No one knew for sure. But the team was contractually obligated to continue with the series, and a replacement was needed. The most obvious choice was Moe and Curly's brother Shemp, who had been the first Stooge with Ted Healy.

With Shemp now in place as the third Stooge, Vernon continued his intermittent roles, some of which are considered classics. According to the first page of the original script of *Malice in the Palace* (by Felix Adler): "A pair of hands slowly parts the curtains as the camera trucks to a close-up, revealing the wicked face of Hassan Ben Sober [Vernon Dent], bearded and turbaned." A mysterious letter (delivered by a thrown knife) informs all: "Hassan Ben Sober, you are late, I got the diamond, you got the gate. (Signed) Omagosh, Emir of Shmow." Between anguished sobs, Hassan Ben Sober says, "This map is useless to me now. With that diamond, I could have quit my job at the Oasis Hotel!"

In addition to appearing with The Three Stooges at Columbia, Vernon turned up in support of Buster Keaton, Andy Clyde, Hugh Herbert, El Brendel, Monty Collins & Tom Kennedy, Schilling & Lane, Harry Von Zell, Wally Vernon & Eddie Quillan, Polly Moran, Smith & Dale, Billy Gilbert, Una Merkel, Slim Summerville, and Bert Wheeler.

The Heckler (1940) and *Mr. Noisy* (1946) featured Vernon playing more or less the same role: a spectator at a baseball game. In fact, the movies are virtually identical. "The Heckler" is Charley Chase and "Mr. Noisy" is Shemp Howard. Both portray obnoxious baseball fans (although each in his own unique way) who delight in yelling at the umpires and baiting the players. Of course, Vernon is the unlucky fan who is subjected to the late-arriving pest. With each rude and intolerable outburst by the star, Vernon burns in his seat with "The Look." *Mr. Noisy* is possibly the better of the two versions, with the interplay between Vernon and Shemp among the finest scenes for either comedian. Vernon's final rebuttal to the overbearing loudmouth — "Why don't you shut up?" — never fails to get a big laugh from audiences.

Another favorite role for Vernon was *Sappy Birthday* (1942), starring Andy Clyde. The opening shots capture the beginnings of a typical day. We hear roosters crowing, bottles of milk being delivered and newspapers being thrown. These sounds, pleasant as they seem, are only a distraction to Vernon. He's a police officer who works the night shift, and he needs his sleep. His next-door-neighbor, Andy Clyde, is oblivious to this and

Monty Collins, Charley Chase, and Vernon Dent in The Heckler *(Columbia, 1940).* COURTESY OF RICH FINEGAN

noisily goes about his morning routine, until Officer Dent imposes his displeasure. We know Andy is going to get it, but good.

Occasionally at Columbia Vernon was able to display his trained voice. In the Vera Vague short, *The Jury Goes Round 'N' Round* (1945), for example, Vernon gets on his fellow sequestered jurors' nerves by singing "There's No Place Like Home." This amusing two-reeler was nominated for an Academy Award as Best Short Subject.

Prior to February 1947 Vernon was earning $75 a day at Columbia. After that, he received $100 a day. Each two-reeler took approximately four days to film — sometimes three, but certainly never five. Averaging $300 per film may sound like an extremely modest wage by today's industry standards, but in 1947 the average working person's salary was in the neighborhood of $45 per week. So, while Vernon was hardly rich, he wasn't poor, either.*

---

* The information regarding Vernon's Columbia salary was obtained by Edward Watz, who had access to director Ed Bernds's call sheets.

Vernon Dent, Andy Clyde, Hank Mann, and James Finlayson at Mack Sennett's birthday party, circa 1950. COURTESY OF MARSHALL KORBY

CHAPTER 16

THE **FINAL CURTAIN**

The medium of television became mandatory home entertainment in America by the early 1950s. One of the reasons was *I Love Lucy*. This filmed series was three months into its run when, on Christmas Eve of 1951, CBS aired an episode entitled "Drafted." The climax of this episode has Lucy and Ricky Ricardo (Lucille Ball and Desi Arnaz) and their neighbors Fred and Ethel Mertz (William Frawley and Vivian Vance) each take turns tiptoeing into the scene, dressed as Santa Claus. They circle the festive tree singing "Jingle Bells" only to notice that there is one extra Santa Claus in the group — the *real* Santa Claus (Vernon). Everyone is agape with astonishment and wonder, but Santa finishes the song in a robust way.

This scene works even more when one learns how naturally gregarious Vernon was in real life. He must have loved playing Santa. According to Eunice, "Vernon was a very sentimental person. He had a very unhappy childhood."

Vernon was seen on television the following month, on New Year's Day of 1952, on *The Frank Sinatra Show*. This early variety program had a good mix of well-known celebrities (including Louis Armstrong, Yvonne DeCarlo, and Alan Young), skits, and singing. It's unfortunate that Vernon was not involved in some of the musical interludes of the show; he would have been more than able to hold his own. Instead, he was there to lend his usual support to fellow guest stars The Three Stooges.

On March 10, 1954, Vernon and a host of silent film veterans were on hand to salute their former boss, Mack Sennett, on an episode of Ralph Edwards's popular *This is Your Life* series. A running gag on the program had some "Keystone Cops" (played by Andy Clyde, Heinie Conklin, Hank Mann, Chester Conklin, and Vernon) chasing Del Lord, the director who had been responsible for some of Sennett's most memorable chase scenes. In fact, most of the original members of the

Keystone Cops had died by then. Vernon (who had never been a member of that legendary group) was filling in for the late Ford Sterling, even wearing his trademark Dutch chin whiskers. Fifty-nine-year-old Vernon performed well on the program, although his vision was rapidly failing. He had to wear specially constructed glasses so he could see his way around the lighted stage. At the end of the show, a clearly moved Mack Sennett thanked his former employees for the tribute. Vernon seemed moved as well. How fitting also that Vernon's last public appearance was with the man who 35 years earlier had introduced him to the movies: Hank Mann.

With his professional life now behind him, Vernon decided to take Eunice on a trip to Quebec, Canada. It was there, on June 2, 1953, that they watched Queen Elizabeth's coronation on television. The most gratifying moments, though, came from the people who recognized him as the man from the Columbia comedies.

"Vernon was always happy to talk with fans and sign autographs," Eunice recalled. The waiters, in particular, would give the Dents special attention.

FADE TO BLACK

There came a time when Vernon had to take daily insulin shots to control the symptoms of diabetes. The pain involved in taking these shots eventually wore him down. In a private moment with Larry Fine in the 1950s, Vernon confided to him, "I've had it with this crap," and stopped taking the shots. According to Larry, Vernon went blind a short time after that.

In November 1955 Shemp Howard died.* In *The Columbia Comedy Shorts*, Emil Sitka (who carried the torch as an eccentric comic co-star in the Stooge shorts) recalled a poignant vignette involving his colleague at Shemp's funeral.

> Vernon came into the parlor, wearing a yarmulke like everyone else since this was a Jewish ceremony. He was led in by his arm, and brought up to Shemp's casket. The man accompanying Vernon told him, "This is Shemp." Vernon was staring straight ahead at the wall — it was then that I realized he was blind. Vernon felt Shemp's

---

*Joe Besser, then Joe DeRita, took turns as the Third Stooge. Vernon has supported both comedians in their solo shorts at Columbia.

hand, then his face, very gently. Everyone else had been filing past the casket quickly, but Vernon took his time, giving a last goodbye to his friend. It was one of the most moving things I ever saw.

Despite his affliction, Vernon never lost his positive outlook on life. This was witnessed by journalist Alice Morse of the *Van Nuys News*

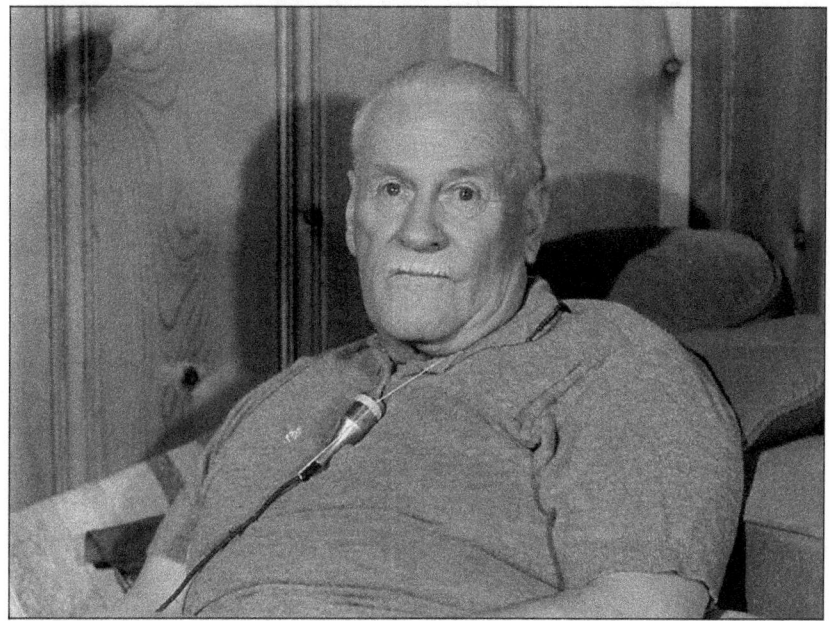

Vernon, circa 1957. COURTESY PAUL GIERUCKI.

when she visited the ailing actor at his home the year before his death. She wrote that Vernon and Eunice had surrounded themselves with animals, including a cat named Googie, and Cocker Spaniels named Ginger and Pigeon. They provided, she wrote, "warm and affectionate company for the blind 66-year-old actor, during the hours Eunice heads the escrow department at Security First National's Sun Valley branch. One of the dogs is of especial comfort to Vernon. Little Pigeon, too, lives in darkness."

Vernon suffered a coronary thrombosis on November 5, 1963. "He died very suddenly at home, and I was very grateful for that," Eunice recalled. "He hadn't been feeling well, and I told him I would be gone a few minutes to do some quick shopping. He said, 'I feel pretty good — let me go with you.' I was glad he was feeling better, and I went into the other room to get his jacket. From the other room, I heard Vernon very calmly say, 'Oh.' He had a heart attack, I know, because he died instantly. I called the paramedics, they came, and he was gone." He was 68 years old.

Vernon was laid to rest at Forest Lawn, Hollywood Hills, Hillside section, Lot #3796. His grave marker reads:

Vernon Bruce Dent
1895 — 1963
Gentle Presence

A gentle presence indeed. By all accounts, Vernon Dent was a kind man who gave freely of his time and talent. That talent, thankfully, is greatly in evidence even now. With the continuing popularity of The Three Stooges on television, at public film events and on DVD, Vernon Dent is better known today than he ever was during his lifetime. Devotees of early film comedy are drawn to his diverse contributions.

Until the end of his life, Vernon stayed true to his roots. He was nostalgic for his hometown. (It would have pleased him to know that San Jose now has a Dent Street, named in honor of his family's fruit-growing business.) Perhaps if his father had not been tragically murdered, Vernon might not have ventured beyond the peaceful environs of his youth. One can easily imagine him becoming a gentleman rancher. But if that had been the case, he would never have been a part of the burgeoning movie industry. He would never have worked with Mack Sennett. He would never have known and befriended Harry Langdon. And The Three Stooges would never have had such a memorable heavy.

That seems unthinkable now.

Dutiful but Dumb *(Columbia, 1941)*. AUTHOR'S COLLECTION

EPILOGUE

It was Thanksgiving weekend of 2009 — many years had passed since The Three Stooges' shorts served as an appetizer for the main bill at cinemas across the country. My wife and I were attending the annual Three Stooges Film Festival, held at the Alexandria Theatre, in Glendale, California. With the kids grown, it seemed the perfect time for us to travel out of town and take in this festival. We couldn't help but wonder, though, what would the crowd be like? Would there be imitation Stooges hitting and poking one another? Would Hell's Angels descend upon us? Or would we merely be deluged with a busload of well-behaved comedy film buffs?

When we finally arrived at the theater, we were surprised and delighted to see that the event was packed mostly with *families*. There were kids and folks of all ages, eager with anticipation. It was quite a sight. (I wonder how many of these attendees knew that this "Alex" theatre served as a main venue for screening Stooge shorts and gauging audience reactions prior to their original release.)

As we stood in line to obtain our tickets, we were behind a nice, elderly lady and a boy of about eight years old. The lady proudly explained to the box-office attendant that her late husband had "loved The Three Stooges," and she was bringing their grandson to see them on the big screen for the first time.

Inside the blackened cinema, everyone scrambled to find their seats. Cheers and applause erupted when the Stooges' images were projected onto the silver screen. Every bit of business, every remark, every sight gag resulted in a howling response from the audience. Even the supporting players received a round of applause when their characters were first introduced. The crowd went especially wild when Vernon did his stuff.

So now we have come full circle: The Three Stooges are once again considered wholesome family entertainment and are fully recognized as icons of American comedy. It looks like those boys have a bright future.

APPENDICES

PRAISE FOR VERNON DENT

"The most neglected heroes of silent comedy history have been those actors who forfeited their own stardom to become straight men in support of the lead comedians. Although this was seldom an altruistic gesture on their part, the very nature of screen comedy required comic foils and many talented men directed their careers towards that goal, knowing full well that while comedy leads come and go with the breeze, the good supporting character comic works forever. If honors were to be passed out in that category; the title of 'King of the Character Comics' would have to be given to Vernon Dent for his work in the twenties."

"Although surely not true, it seems that Dent appeared in every other comedy of the silent and early sound period. Despite the injustice of his obscurity, Dent's activities as a supporting comic embodied the duties of any top-quality straight man. His responsibility was to center as much attention as possible upon the lead comedian, working constantly to emphasize all of the comic action."

Kalton C. Lahue and Sam Gill,
as quoted in their 1970 book,
Clown Princes and Court Jesters

"[Vernon] Dent always allowed the audience to realize that he was doomed without ever appearing to know it himself. That is the mark of the consummate straight man. There was no character Dent couldn't play. He could be silly, gruff, boastful, or bashful. Even more impressive was his ability to transition seamlessly between personalities. The Stooges were lucky to work so closely with so gifted a talent."

Robert Kurson, as quoted in his 1998 book,
The Official Three Stooges Encyclopedia

"The portly Vernon Dent is best remembered as the exasperated foil in dozens of Three Stooges shorts. Custard pie comedy was nothing new to Dent. He played various comic roles in dozens of silent era comedies. More than the traditional menacing heavy, Dent played a wide variety of characters in silent films, from oily conmen to bumbling boyfriends, from eye-rolling brutes to big sissies."

Ron Smith, as quoted in his 1993 book,
Comic Support: Second Bananas in the Movies

"[Vernon Dent] was in the first six 2-reel comedies I directed. My producer, Hugh McCollum, recommended him for the first few, but after that I cast Vernon because I wanted him. He was the ideal actor — always performed; always ready to give a scene his best, even when there was danger of being hurt, as there often was in 2-reel comedies."

Edward Bernds, film editor and director,
(In a letter to historian James T. Mockoski)

"While doing research for the Columbia short comedies book, when we brought up the name of Vernon Dent it always elicited a reaction…Jack White cried when talking about Vernon. 'He was a very dear man,' he said."

Edward Watz, co-author,
The Columbia Comedy Shorts

The Columbia Comedy Shorts was dedicated as follows:
For Vernon Dent (1895-1963)
"May you always be kept in the foreground."
(From an inscribed photo presented to Vernon by Charley Chase.)

SONGWRITING CREDITS

"1915 Rag" (circa 1912)
(lyrics by Vernon Dent; music by Geo. Oscar Young.)

"Rhythmatic Drag" (circa 1912)
(lyrics by Vernon Dent; music by Geo. Oscar Young.)

"What Have I Done (To Make You Stop Loving Me)?" (1918)
(lyrics by Buddy DeSylva and Vernon Dent; music by Jimmie Blyler.)

"Girl of My Dreams" (1919)
(lyrics by Vernon Dent; music by Ben Light.)

SCREENWRITING CREDITS

Please 1933/12/15
Tied for Life 1933/7/2
Marriage Humor 1933/8/13
Hooks and Jabs 1933/8/25
On Ice 1933/10/6
Three Little Swigs 1933/10/11
Roaming Romeo 1933/12/29
Just an Echo 1934/1/19
Circus Hoodoo 1934/2/16
Petting Preferred 1934/4/27
No More Bridge 1934/16/03
His Marriage Mix-Up 1935/10/31
Hollywood Trouble 1935/1/1
The Mayor's Husband 1945/9/20

FILMED SINGING APPEARANCES

Ticklish Business (1929/8/25): "Don't Tickle Me" *(lyrics by Vernon Dent and Monty Collins; music by Stephen Roberts).*
Fainting Lover (1931/8/16): "The Waning Honeymoon" *(lyrics by Will M. Hough and Frank R. Adams; music by Joseph E. Howard).*
Marriage Humor (1933/8/18): "Good Little Black Sheep of Angels" *(music and lyrics by Harry Langdon).*
Hooks and Jabs (1933/8/25): "When You and I Were Young, Maggie" *(based on a poem by George Washington Johnson; set to music by James Butterfield).*
Please (1933/12/15): "Dear Old Girl" *(lyrics by Richard Henry Buck; music by Theodore Morse).*
Good Morning, Eve (1934/9/27): "Rhythm in the Bow" (Cliff Hess).
Mrs. Parkington (1944/10/12) Vernon is in a singing quartette with Billy Bletcher, Bud Jamison, and Harry Tyler *(Scenes deleted).*
The Jury Goes Round 'N' Round (1945/6/1): "There's No Place Like Home" *(lyrics by John Howard Payne; music by Sir Henry Bishop).*
Nob Hill (1945/11/15) Bud Jamison and Vernon are part of a singing quartet of waiters.
The Harvey Girls (1946/1/18): Vernon's voice is a dubbed in by a baritone.
I Love Lucy (1951/12/24): "Jingle Bells" *(James Lord Pierpont).*

Marriage Humor *(Paramount, 1933). Nancy Dover, Ethel Sykes, Harry Langdon, and Vernon Dent.* COURTESY OF COLE JOHNSON

SYNOPSES OF MISSING PARAMOUNT TWO-REEL COMEDIES

Marriage Humor (1933/8/13)
Story by Dean Ward and Vernon Dent

Harry [Langdon] and his wife work as butler and maid in the home of Mr. and Mrs. Vernon Dent. During a very heavy battle between Vernon and Ethyl [Sykes, the actress playing Vernon's wife], both Harry and Nancy Dover [the actress playing the maid] attempt to bring a tray full of food into the room. As the bottles and vases fly, both of them give up in despair. During the fracas, Mrs. Dent aims a vase at her husband and unintentionally hits Harry. She very sympathetically comforts him. Nancy, seeing this, immediately gets jealous. Mrs. Dent decides to leave her husband and Vernon suggests to Harry that they get rid of all the females in the house. So Mrs. Dent and Nancy leave together. Dent decides to celebrate so he digs into his supply of "giggle" water and he and Harry proceed to get very drunk. Both wives are having a fairly good time in their own way. The next morning, we see Vernon and Harry home in bed, feeling very bad. Vernon has D.T.'s and screams that he sees kangaroos and gorillas. Harry tells him that the kangaroo is merely a clothes rack. When a gorilla gets into bed with Harry, he thinks it is Vernon. A zebra prances into the room as do several other animals, and Harry suddenly comes to the realization that the animals are real. Meantime, an animal trainer breaks into the house demanding payment for the animals which he claims Harry and Vernon bought the night before. The wives, in the meanwhile, have decided to come back home and we see them sleeping very peacefully. To play a trick on the boys, the wives place models dressed like themselves in their places and hide in the closet. Harry, on seeing his wife, wants to make up. Vernon in a rage rushes over to the bed and chokes the supposed figure of Nancy. When he does this her head comes off. He picks up the figure of his wife and throws it out of the window. Just then, the girls poke their heads out of the closet and the two men dive through the window, screaming: "Ghosts!"

Roaming Romeo (1933/12/29)
Story by Dean Ward and Vernon Dent

Nell is awaiting the return of Harry [Langdon] to the swimming pool before she promises to marry Vernon. But Harry is in an orchard eating peaches when he is apprehended by the farmer and a sheriff with a gun. Harry runs home, escapes through [a] backdoor, hops into his flivver and starts off at break-neck speed only to find that he is pulling the house with him. He stops in front of Nell's home. She comes out with Vernon and greets Harry affectionately. This annoys Vernon. Nell admires the house on the back of Harry's car. He tells her he built it for her himself. Nell inspects the house and finds that she has only to press a button to bring down a folding bed, another button for a wash basin, and so-forth. Vernon decides to enter the house and have a look. He is so fat that as he steps on the porch the whole house tilts and Nell falls in Harry's lap. Vernon finds them thus when he enters. A fight ensues and the men decide to stake the girl on a golf match. After a lot of slapstick situation, Harry walks off the course with Nell.

Circus Hoodoo (1934/2/16)
Story by Dean Ward and Vernon Dent

The circus comes to town with its big tents, hula dancers, clowns, barkers. By the looks of the crowds, business is great. Yet the manager is worried for he is suspicious there is a hoodoo [one that brings bad luck] in the midst of his circus. He has recently lost an elephant and a tiger and his best bareback rider has broken his leg. He suspects the hoodoo is Harry Langdon and Vernon Dent, whose combined talents in the show make up the "Horse act." The reason for this suspicion is that Harry is constantly sneezing, so much so that each sneeze leaves him cross-eyed — and a cross-eyed person in a circus means bad luck. So the manager cancels the horse act. Harry and Vernon go into the umbrella business on the circus grounds — Harry furnishes the rain while Vernon sells the umbrellas. A couple of cops decide the rain act is not on the level and try to pull them in but the boys escape by a series of gags. Away from the circus grounds, the boys are mistaken by a couple of gangster's molls for the City Mayor and City Treasurer and are ensnared into going to [the girls'] apartment. The girls have their gangster boyfriends ready, to snap photographs of the "city mayor" and "city treasurer" and the gangsters, the boys win. Detectives arrive and present Harry with a check for a $1,000 reward for capturing the bandits. Harry feels a sneeze coming on and puts the check on the table. The sneeze over, Harry reaches for the reward only to see it go up in flames.

On Ice (1933/10/6)
Story by Dean Ward and Vernon Dent

Harry Langdon works on an ice wagon with Vernon Dent who owns the business. Vernon invites the charming blonde Marge (Diana Seaby), a waitress in a restaurant they serve with ice to go to the El Toro Café that evening. Marge says she'll go if Vernon gets a friend for Min, her girl friend. Vernon picks on Harry who is afraid to refuse his boss. Becoming nervous about the date, Harry gets mixed up in difficulties such as getting his ice tongs caught in a restaurant customer's coat and ruining the coat trying to extricate the tongs. As Harry and Vernon drive away in the ice truck, they hit an automobile and ruin it. It just so happens that it belongs to the same man whose coat was torn by Harry. That night, Harry has a terrific time trying to get out of the house. His wife (Ethyl Sykes) and her sister (Ruth Clifford) get suspicious. As it is pay night, Harry tries to hold out some of his salary but as usual, Ethyl manages to get it all, even by using very drastic measures. By a ruse, Harry manages to get out and meets Vernon and the girls in front of the El Toro. As they are seated, they discover that the waiter is the man whose coat and automobile they ruined that day. He presents them with a check to cover all damages to his car and coat. When Vernon sees they are not going to get out of the place until they make good, he tries to slip some money to Harry underneath the table but one of the girls grabs it and puts the money down her waist. Harry very cleverly gets the money back and everything is serene until Vernon spots Harry's wife and her sister looking for him. Harry ducks under the table. The waiter and Harry's wife get into an argument and a general disorder is started. As the two women arrive home, they discover that Harry is there ahead of them and he remonstrates with them for staying out late. He is just about getting away with it when Vernon and the girls arrive in a very "whoopee" mood. Harry's wife puts him out in the rain.

FILMOGRAPHY

Compiling an actor's filmography is quite a challenge; when that actor was as prolific as Vernon Dent, the task can seem impossible. Even *he* would have had no idea exactly how many films he had made.

The listing that follows represents many years of work on the author's part, and includes contributions from Richard Campos II, Marshall Korby, Lon Davis, Rich Finegan, Frank Flood, Cole Johnson, Sam Gill, Leonard Maltin, Steve Massa, Kit Parker, Richard M. Roberts, Steve Rydzewski, Warren M. Sherk, Brent Walker, Edward Watz, David Wyatt, and the late Richard E. Braff. Mr. Braff, in fact, was my first major contact. He was kind enough to send me his own filmography that he compiled on Vernon Dent. His comprehensive listing was posthumously published by McFarland & Co. as *The Braff Silent Short Film Working Papers*, in 2002.

I next had the good fortune to receive input from Dennis Campos II. For years, he had independently compiled his own listing of Vernon's films. He was generous enough to share a copy of his listings with me in 1998. There were many titles in common with Braff, but there were many inconsistencies as well. It needed further examination. Then it was promptly put in the back of the file cabinet for a number of years while I worked on my Edgar Kennedy project.

Trips to the Margaret Herrick Library to delve into the Mack Sennett files were more than fruitful. While compiling a filmography for Edgar Kennedy, it allowed me to also verify the Vernon Dent titles. After the publication of *Edgar Kennedy: Master of the Slow Burn*, in 2005, I was able to resume researching Vernon's career.

Taking into consideration that many of the silent comedies were made in comparative obscurity on low budgets and with limited distribution, it is no wonder that many of these films were not reviewed, nor have they survived the passage of time.

Many of the films were confirmed by reviews from the film trade journals of the day. Some series, including the Hank Mann series, had reviews that only mentioned the star, but none of the supporting players. The "stocky film-heavy" might very well be a reference to Vernon Dent, especially because we know he was the main support. Again, unless there is an existing photo, film or credit to verify a Dent appearance, we chose not to include the title in the filmography.

How many more Vernon Dent titles are there? No one knows for certain, but his familiar face pops up all the time unbilled in shorts and features throughout the 1920s, '30s and '40s. Some estimate that he could be in up to 100 additional titles. This filmography, therefore, should be considered a work in progress.

Key to Abbreviations:
D: Director
C: Cast
L: Length
P: Producer
DIST: Distributor
P/D: Producer *and* Distributor

A Gum Riot 1919/4/10 D: *Unknown* C: Hank Mann, Madge Kirby, Vernon Dent, Jess Weldon L: 2-Reels P: Morris Schlank Productions DIST: Arrow Film Corp. *(Hank Mann Comedies).*

An Auto Nut 1919 D: Robert Kerr [unconfirmed] C: James Parrott, Madge Kirby, Vernon Dent L: *Unknown* P: Alkire Photoplay Corporation DIST: Bulls-Eye *(Holly Comedies?).*

A Harem Hero 1919 D: *Unknown* C: Hank Mann, Madge Kirby, Vernon Dent L: 1-Reel P: Morris Schlank Productions DIST: Arrow Film Corporation *(Hank Mann Comedies).* [Note: Also listed as *A Harem Hen.*]

The Dentist 1919 D: *Unknown* C: Hank Mann, Madge Kirby, Vernon Dent, Dorothy Vernon L: 2-Reels P: Morris Schlank Productions DIST: Arrow Film Corp. *(Hank Mann Comedies).*

The Janitor 1919 D: *Unknown* C: Madge Kirby, Merta Sterling, Dorothy Vernon, Vernon Dent L: *Unknown* P: Morris Schlank Productions DIST: Arrow Film Corp. *(Hank Mann Comedies)*.

The Messenger 1919 D: *Unknown* C: Hank Mann, Vernon Dent L: 2-Reels P: Morris Schlank Productions DIST: Arrow Film Corp. *(Hank Mann Comedies)*.

In Hock 1919 D: *Unknown* C: Hank Mann, Vernon Dent L: 2-Reels P: Morris Schlank Productions DIST: Arrow Film Corp. *(Hank Mann Comedies)*.

The Bill Poster 1919 D: *Unknown* C: Hank Mann, Madge Kirby, Vernon Dent, Jess Weldon L: *Unknown* P: Morris Schlank Productions DIST: Arrow Film Corp. *(Hank Mann Comedies)*.

When Spirits Move 1920 D: Charles Parrott [Charley Chase] C: Hank Mann, Madge Kirby, Vernon Dent, James T. Kelley P: Morris Schlank Productions DIST: Arrow Film Corp. *(Hank Mann Comedies)*.

His Royal Slyness 1920/2/8 D: Hal Roach C: Harold Lloyd, Mildred Davis, Snub Pollard, Gus Leonard, Noah Young, Vernon Dent L: 2-Reels DIST: Pathé.

Broken Bubbles 1920/2/28 [other sources: 2/1/20] D: Hank Mann C: Hank Mann, Madge Kirby, Vernon Dent, James T. Kelly L: 2-Reels P: Morris Schlank Productions DIST: Arrow Film Corp. *(Hank Mann Comedies)*.

The Bell Hop 1920/3/22 D: *Unknown* C: Hank Mann, Jess C. Weldon, Madge Kirby, Vernon Dent L: 1-Reel P: Morris Schlank Productions DIST: Arrow Film Corp *(Hank Mann Comedies)*. [Note: Also known as *Hopping Bells* and *Hopping the Bells*.]

Don't Change Your Mrs. 1920/7/17 D: Charles Parrott C: Hank Mann, Vernon Dent, Madge Kirby L: *Unknown* P: Morris R. Schlank DIST: Arrow Film Corp. *(Hank Mann Comedies)*.

Roaming Romeo 1920 D: *Unknown* C: Hank Mann, Vernon Dent, Madge Kirby L: 2-Reels P: Morris Schlank Productions DIST: Arrow Film corp. *(Hank Mann Comedies).*

Mystic Mush 1920 D: Charles Parrott C: Hank Mann, Madge Kirby, Vernon Dent, James T. Kelly, Jess Weldon Charles Parrott L: 2-Reels P: Morris Schlank Productions DIST: Arrow Film Corp. *(Hank Mann Comedies).*

Way Out West 1920 D: Charley Chase C: Hank Mann, Vernon Dent, Madge Kirby, James T. Kelly L: *Unknown* P: Morris Schlank Productions DIST: Arrow Film Corp. *(Hank Mann Comedies).*

J-U-N-K 1920 D: *Unknown* C: Hank Mann, Vernon Dent, Madge Kirby, Jack Richardson, Dorothy Vernon L: 2-Reels P: Morris Schlank Productions DIST: Arrow Film Corp. *(Hank Mann Comedies).*

Naughty Nurses 1920 D: *Unknown* C: Hank Mann, Vernon Dent, Madge Kirby L: *Unknown* P: Morris Schlank Productions DIST: Arrow Film Corp. *(Hank Mann Comedies).*

The Paper Hanger 1920/2/15/ D: *Unknown* C: Hank Mann, Vernon Dent, Madge Kirby L: *Unknown* P: Morris Schlank Productions DIST: Arrow Film Co. *(Hank Mann Comedies).*

Up in the Air 1920/12/4 D: *Unknown* C: Hank Mann, Vernon Dent L: *Unknown* P: Morris Schlank Productions DIST: Arrow Film Corp. *(Hank Mann Comedies).*

Up and at 'Em 1921 D: *Unknown* C: Vernon Dent, Violet Joy L: 1-Reel P/D: Pacific Film Co. *(Folly Comedies)* [Note: Violet Joy later changed her name to Duane Thompson.]

Hail the Woman (feature) 1921/11/28 D: John Griffith Wray C: Florence Vidor, Lloyd Hughes, Theodore Roberts, Gertrude Claire, Madge Bellamy, Tully Marshall, Vernon Dent L: 8-Reels P: Ince/Assoc. First National.

Mummy's Nightmare 1922 D: *Unknown* C: George Ovey, Vernon Dent L: 1-Reel P/D: Pacific Film Co. *(Folly Comedies).*

Coming and Going 1922 D: *Unknown* C: Vernon Dent L: 1-Reel P/D: Pacific Film Co. *(Folly Comedies)*.

Fat and Sassy 1922 D: *Unknown* C: Vernon Dent, Violet Joy L: 1-Reel P/D: Pacific Film Co. *(Folly Comedies)*.

High and Mighty 1922 D: *Unknown* C: Vernon Dent L: 1-Reel P/D: Pacific Film Co. *(Folly Comedies)*.

Get the Hook 1922 D: *Unknown* C: Vernon Dent L: 1-Reel P/D: Pacific Film Co. *(Folly Comedies)*.

In at the Finish 1922 D: *Unknown* C: Vernon Dent L: 1-Reel P/D: Pacific Film Co. *(Folly Comedies)*.

Now or Never 1922 D: *Unknown* C: Vernon Dent, Violet Joy L: 1-Reel P/D: Pacific Film Co. *(Folly Comedies)*.

On the Jump 1922 D: *Unknown* C: Vernon Dent L: 1-Reels P/D: Pacific Film Co. *(Folly Comedies)*.

Sleeping Sickness 1922 D: *Unknown* C: Vernon Dent L: 1-Reel P/D: Pacific Film Co. *(Folly Comedies)*.

Slow But Sure 1922 D: *Unknown* C: Vernon Dent L: 1-Reel P/D: Pacific Film Co. *(Folly Comedies)*.

They're Off 1922 D: *Unknown* C: Vernon Dent L: 1-Reel P/D: Pacific Film Co. *(Folly Comedies)*.

Special Delivery 1922/4/30 D: Al St. John [Uncredited: Roscoe Arbuckle] C: Al St. John, Vernon Dent L: *Unknown* P/D: Fox *(Al St. John Comedies)*.

A Pair of Kings 1922/6/11 D: Larry Semon/Norman Taurog C: Larry Semon, Oliver Hardy, Vernon Dent, Lucille Carlisle, Al Thompson, Bill Hauber, Fred Lancaster L: 2-Reels P/D: Vitagraph *(Larry Semon Comedies)*.

Golf 1922/8/5 D: Tom Buckingham, Larry Semon C: Larry Semon, Oliver Hardy, Vernon Dent, William Hauber, Pete Gordon L: 2-Reels P/D: Vitagraph *(Larry Semon Comedies)*.

The Four-Flusher 3/18/23 D: Norman Taurog C: Joe Roberts, Leo Sulky, Vernon Dent L: 2-reels P/D: Fox *(Sunshine Comedies)*.

Soul of the Beast (feature) 1923/5/7 D: John Griffith Wray C: Madge Bellamy, Cullen Landis, Noah Berry Sr., Vernon Dent, Vola Vale, Harry Rattenburry, Carrie Clark Ward, Bert Sprotte, Lincoln Stedman, Larry Steers, Oscar the Elephant L: 5-Reels P: Thomas Ince DIST: Metro. [Note: Outside shots filmed with elephant in San Jose and Santa Cruz Mountains.]

Ain't Love Awful? 1923/5/26 D: Archie Mayo C: Bobby Dunn, Ena Gregory, Vernon Dent L: 2-Reels P: Century Film Corporation DIST: Universal [Working title: "The Imperfect Lover"] *(Century Comedies)*.

The Weekend 1923/8/30 D: Glen Lambert C: Bert Tracy, Vernon Dent, Miss Iolanthe L: 2-Reels P: Tracy Productions [Note: Filmed in Santa Cruz, California] *(Lightening Comedies)*.

The Extra Girl (feature) 1923/9/24 D: F. Richard Jones C: Mabel Normand, Vernon Dent, George Nichols, Ralph Graves, Charlotte Mineau, Carl Stockdale, Kewpie Morgan, Teddy the dog L: 6-Reels P: Sennett DIST: Assoc. Exhibitors.

Picking Peaches 1924/2/3 D: Erle C. Kenton C: Harry Langdon, Alberta Vaughn, Jack Cooper, Dot Farley, Vernon Dent L: 2-Reels P: Sennett DIST: Pathé.

The Half-Back of Notre Dame 1924/2/24 D: Del Lord C: Harry Gribbon, Jack Cooper, Madeline Hurlock, Louise Carver, Andy Clyde, Kewpie Morgan, Vernon Dent L: 2-Reels P: Sennett DIST: Pathé.

Shriek of Araby 1924/3/4 D: F. Richard Jones C: Ben Turpin, Kathryn McGuire, Luis Frondi, Dick Sutherland, Vernon Dent L: 5-Reels P: Sennett DIST: Allied Producers and Distributors Corp. [Note: Some historians dispute Vernon's appearance in this film. Thought lost for many years, the surviving print is thought to be incomplete. Vernon Dent can be identified by existing photos of the cast in production stills.]

The Hollywood Kid 1924/3/30 D: Roy Del Ruth C: Charlie Murray, Louise Carver, Jackie Lucas, Vernon Dent, Jack Cooper, Andy Clyde, Mack Sennett, Madeline Hurlock, Ben Turpin, Marie Prevost, Phyllis Haver, Billy Bevan, Ray Gray, Buddy Ross, Sunshine Hart, Teddy the dog, Sennett Bathing Girls [Beauties] L: 2-Reels P: Sennett DIST: Pathé.

Black Oxfords 1924/5/18 D: Del Lord C: Sid Smith, Vernon Dent, Jack Richardson, Anna Hernandez, Andy Clyde L: 2-Reels P: Sennett DIST: Pathé. [Working title: "A Tale of Two Nifties."]

The Lion and the Souse 1924/6/15 D: Harry Edwards C: Charlotte Mineau, Vernon Dent, Leo Sulky, Andy Clyde, Sid Smith, Numa (lion), Willie Hunter L: 2-Reels P: Sennett DIST: Pathé.

Romeo and Juliet 1924/8/3 D: Reggie Morris, Harry Sweet C: Ben Turpin, Natalie Kingston, Alice Day, Jack Curtis, Vernon Dent L: 2-Reels P: Sennett D: Pathé.

Wall Street Blues 1924/8/10 D: Del Lord C: Billy Bevan, Sid Smith, Andy Clyde, Natalie Kingston, Vernon Dent, Edgar Kennedy L: 2-Reels P: Sennett DIST: Pathé.

East of the Water Plug 1924/8/24 D: Frank Martin C: Ralph Graves, Alice Day, Vernon Dent, Andy Clyde, Billy Bevan, Sunshine Hart, Thelma Hill, Louise Carver L: 2-Reels P: Sennett DIST: Pathé.

Little Robinson Corkscrew 1924/9/21 D: Ralph Ceder C: Vernon Dent, Ralph Graves, Alice Day, Andy Clyde, Billy Bevan, Charlotte Mineau, Thelma Hill, Pat Kelly, Fanny Kelly L: 2-Reels P: Sennett DIST: Pathé.

Riders of the Purple Cows 1924/10/19 D: Ralph Ceder C: Ralph Graves, Alice Day, Andy Clyde, Vernon Dent, Tiny Ward, Larry McGrath, Barney Hellum L: 2-Reels P: Sennett DIST: Pathé.

All Night Long 1924/11/9 D: Harry Edwards C: Harry Langdon, Natalie Kingston, Fanny Kelly, Vernon Dent, Billy Gilbert L: 2-Reels P: Sennett DIST: Pathé.

Love's Sweet Piffle 1924/11/16 D: Edgar Kennedy C: Ralph Graves, Thelma Hill, Vernon Dent, Tiny Ward L: 2-Reels P: Sennett DIST: Pathé.

Feet of Mud 1924/12/7 D: Harry Edwards C: Harry Langdon, Florence D. Lee, Natalie Kingston, Vernon Dent L: 2-Reels P: Sennett DIST: Pathé.

Bull and Sand 1924/12/28 D: Del Lord C: Sid Smith, Vernon Dent, Madeline Hurlock, Andy Clyde, John J. Richardson, Tiny Ward L: 2-Reels P: Sennett DIST: Pathé *(Mack Sennett Comedies)*.

The Plumber 1925/1/11 D: Eddie Cline C: Ralph Graves, Alice Day, Marvin Loback, Elsie Tarron, Vernon Dent L: 2-Reels P: Sennett DIST: Pathé.

Boobs in the Wood 1925/2/1 D: Harry Edwards C: Harry Langdon, Marie Astaire, Vernon Dent L: 2-Reels P: Sennett DIST: Pathé.

The Beloved Bozo 1925/2/8 C: Ralph Graves, Alice Day, Marvin Loback, Vernon Dent, Eugenia Gilbert, Jack Richardson L: 2-Reels P: Sennett DIST: Pathé.

His Marriage Wow 1925/3/1 D: Harry Edwards C: Harry Langdon, Natalie Kingston, William McCall, Vernon Dent L: 2-Reels P: Sennett DIST: Pathé.

Plain Clothes 1925/03/29 D: Harry Edwards C: Harry Langdon, Claire Cushman, Vernon Dent, Harry Edwards L: 2-Reels P: Sennett DIST: Pathé.

Remember When? 1925/4/26 D: Harry Edwards C: Harry Langdon, Natalie Kingston, Vernon Dent L: 2-Reels P: Sennett DIST: Pathé.

Lucky Stars 1925/8/16) D: Harry Edwards C: Harry Langdon, Vernon Dent, Natalie Kingston, Ruth Taylor L: 2-Reels P: Sennett DIST: Pathé.

Hurry, Doctor! 1925/9/20 D: Lloyd Bacon C: Ralph Graves, Frank Whitson, Vernon Dent, Thelma Parr, Irving Bacon L: 2-Reels P: Sennett DIST: Pathé.

Love and Kisses 1925/9/27 D: Eddie Cline C: Alice Day, Raymond McKee, Sunshine Hart, Jack Cooper, Barbara Tennant, Vernon Dent L: 2-Reels P: Sennett DIST: Pathé.

Take Your Time 1925/11/15 D: Lloyd Bacon C: Ralph Graves, Vernon Dent, Thelma Parr, Marvin Loback, William McCall, Leo Sulky L: 2-Reels P: Sennett DIST: Pathé.

Isn't Love Cuckoo? 1925/11/22 D: Lloyd Bacon C: Raymond McKee, Ruth Hiatt, Eugenia Gilbert, Marvin Loback, Vernon Dent L: 2-Reels P: Sennett DIST: Pathé *(Mack Sennett Comedies)*.

There He Goes 1925/11/29 D: Harry Edwards C: Harry Langdon, Lloyd Bacon, Andy Clyde, Vernon Dent, Leo Sulky L: 3-Reels P: Sennett DIST: Pathé.

Saturday Afternoon 1926/1/31 D: Harry Edwards C: Harry Langdon, Vernon Dent, Ruth Hiatt, Peggy Montgomery L: 3-Reels P: Sennett DIST: Pathé.

The Funnymooners 1926/2/7 D: Lloyd Bacon C: Ralph Graves, Thelma Parr, Marvin Loback, Vernon Dent L: 2-Reels P: Sennett DIST: Pathé.

A Sea Dog's Tale 1926/7/11 D: Del Lord C: Andy Clyde, Vernon Dent, Madeline Hurlock, Billy Bevan L: 2-Reels P: Sennett DIST: Pathé.

Hubby's Quiet Little Game 1926/8/8 D: Del Lord C: Billy Bevan, Thelma Parr, Vernon Dent, David Morris, Irving Bacon L: 2-Reels P: Sennett DIST: Pathé.

Her Actor Friend 1926/8/22 D: Eddie Cline C: Alice Day, Eddie Quillan, Joe Young, Ruth Taylor, Vernon Dent L: 2-Reels P: Sennett DIST: Pathé.

Hoboken to Hollywood 1926/9/5 D: Del Lord C: Billy Bevan, Lenora Summers, Vernon Dent, Thelma Hill, Sunshine Hart L: 2-Reels P: Sennett DIST: Pathé.

Smith's Landlord 1926/9/19 D: Eddie Cline C: Raymond McKee, Ruth Hiatt, Mary Ann Jackson, Joe Young, Vernon Dent L: 2-Reels P: Sennett DIST: Pathé.

The Prodigal Bridegroom 1926/9/26 D: Lloyd Bacon C: Ben Turpin, Madeline Hurlock, Andy Clyde, Thelma Hill, Vernon Dent L: 2-Reels P: Sennett DIST: Pathé.

Masked Mamas 1926/10/31 D: Del Lord C: Billy Bevan, Vernon Dent, Thelma Parr, Barney Hellum, Irving Bacon L: 2-Reels P: Sennett DIST: Pathé.

The Divorce Dodger 1926/11/28 D: Del Lord C: Billy Bevan, Barbara Tennant, Barney Hellum, Thelma Hill, Vernon Dent, Bobbie Dunn L: 2-Reels P: Sennett DIST: Pathé.

Have Courage 1926/12/12 D: William H. Watson C: Billy Dooley, Natalie Joyce, Eddie Baker, Vernon Dent, Yola D'Avril L: 2-Reels P: Christie DIST: Educational *(Billy Dooley Comedies)*.

A Blonde's Revenge 1926/12/19 D: Del Lord C: Ben Turpin, Vernon Dent, Barbara Tennant, Thelma Parr L: 2-Reels P: Sennett DIST: Pathé.

Should Sleep Walkers Marry? 1926/12/23 D: Del Lord C: Billy Bevan, Thelma Parr, Barbara Tennant, Vernon Dent, Joe Young L: 2-Reels P: Sennett DIST: Pathé.

Flirty Four Flushers 1926/12/26 D: Eddie Cline C: Billy Bevan, Madeline Hurlock, Vernon Dent, Stanley Blystone, Thelma Hill L: 2-Reels P: Sennett DIST: Pathé.

A One-Mama Man 1927/3/6 D: James Parrott C: Charley Chase, Eugenia Gilbert, Gale Henry, Vernon Dent, Burr McIntosh L: 2-Reels P: Roach DIST: Pathé *(Charley Chase Comedies)*. [Note: Besides *His Royal Slyness* (1920), this was the only other Hal Roach entry for Vernon Dent.]

Cured in the Excitement 1927/4/17 D: Del Lord C: Billy Bevan, Madeline Hurlock, Vernon Dent, Thelma Hill L: 2-Reels P: Sennett DIST: Pathé.

His First Flame (feature) 1927/5/8 D: Harry Edwards C: Harry Langdon, Natalie Kingston, Ruth Hiatt, Vernon Dent, Bud Jamison, Dot Farley L: 5-Reels P: Sennett DIST: Pathé.

The Pride of Pikeville 1927/6/5 D: Alf Goulding C: Ben Turpin, Thelma Hill, Andy Clyde, Ruth Taylor, Stanley Blystone, Vernon Dent L: 2-Reels P: Sennett DIST: Pathé.

The Golf Nut 1927/9/4 D: Harry Edwards C: Billy Bevan, Vernon Dent, Eddie Quillan, Mary Mayberry L: 2-Reels P: Sennett DIST: Pathé.

Gold Digger of Weepah 1927/10/2 D: Harry Edwards C: Billy Bevan, Sunshine Hart, Matty Kemp, Vernon Dent L: 2-Reels P: Sennett DIST: Pathé.

Smith's Cook 1927/10/16 D: Mary Ann Jackson, Raymond McKee, Ruth Hiatt, Molly Moran, Johnny Burke, C: Vernon Dent L: 2-Reels P: Sennett DIST: Pathé.

For Sale, A Bungalow 1927/10/30 D: Earle Rodney C: Madeline Hurlock, Eddie Quillan, Andy Clyde, Irving Bacon, Vernon Dent L: 2-Reels P: Sennett DIST: Pathé.

Fiddlesticks 1927/11/27 D: Harry Edwards C: Harry Langdon, Vernon Dent L: 2-Reels P: Sennett DIST: Pathé.

The Bullfighter 1927/11/27 D: Eddie Cline C: Billy Bevan, Madeline Hurlock, Eddie Quillan, Andy Clyde, Vernon Dent L: 2-Reels P: Sennett DIST: Pathé.

The Girl From Everywhere 1927/12/4 D: Eddie Cline C: Daphne Pollard, Dot Farley, Mack Swain, Carole Lombard, Madeline Hurlock, Andy Clyde, Mary Ann Jackson, Ruth Hiatt, Louise Carver, Vernon Dent L: 4-reels *(originally)* P: Sennett DIST: Pathé.

Smith's Modiste Shop 1927/12/11 D: Alf Goulding C: Mary Ann Jackson, Raymond McKee, Ruth Hiatt, Vernon Dent, Irving Bacon, Andy Clyde L: 2-Reels P: Sennett DIST: Pathé.

The Beach Club 1928/1/22 D: Harry Edwards C: Billy Bevan, Vernon Dent, Johnny Burke, Andy Clyde L: 2-Reels P: Sennett DIST: Pathé *(Mack Sennett Comedies).*

Smith's Army Life 1928/2/5 D: Alf Goulding C: Raymond McKee, Ruth Hiatt, Mary Ann Jackson, Vernon Dent, Glen Cavender L: 2-Reels P: Sennett DIST: Pathé *(Smith Family Series).*

Who's Lyin' 1928/6/10 D: Stephen Roberts C: Monty Collins, George Davis, Vernon Dent, Betty Boyd, Robert Graves, Eva Thatcher L: 2-Reels P: Jack White DIST: Educational *(Mermaid Comedies).*

The Best Man 1928/2/19 D: Harry Edwards C: Billy Bevan, Vernon Dent, Alma Bennett, Andy Clyde, Irving Bacon, Sunshine Hart L: 2-Reels P: Sennett DIST: Pathé.

The Bicycle Flirt 1928/3/18 D: Harry Edwards C: Billy Bevan, Vernon Dent, Dot Farley, Carole Lombard, Leota Winters, Irving Bacon, Andy Clyde L: 2-Reels P: Sennett DIST: Pathé *(Mack Sennett Comedies).*

Golf Widows (feature) 1928/5/1 D: Erle C. Kenton C: Vera Reynolds, Harrison Ford, John Patrick, Sally Rand, Will Stanton, Vernon Dent, Kathleen Key L: 56 minutes P/D: Columbia.

His Favorite Wife 1928/7/22 D: Orville O. Dull C: Tyler Brooke, Cortland Van Bibber, Vernon Dent L: 2-Reels P/D: Fox *(Van Bibber Comedies).*

Smith's Restaurant 1928/8/19 D: Phil Whitman C: Raymond McKee, Ruth Hiatt, Mary Ann Jackson, Daphne Pollard, Vernon Dent L: 2-Reels P: Sennett DIST: Pathé.

Her Mother's Back 1928/8/19 D: Jasper Blystone C: Billy Bletcher, Vernon Dent L: 2-Reels P/D: Fox *(Imperial Comedies)*.

His Unlucky Night 1928/8/12 D: Harry Edwards C: Billy Bevan, Vernon Dent, Dot Farley, Carole Lombard, Sunshine Hart, Bud Jamison, Andy Clyde, Otto Fries L: 2-Reels P: Sennett DIST: Pathé.

A Dumb Waiter 1928/9/16 D: Harry Edwards C: Johnny Burke, Ethel Gray, Vernon Dent L: 2-Reels P: Sennett DIST: Pathé.

The Cameraman (feature) 1928/9/22 D: Edward Sedgwick C: Buster Keaton, Marceline Day, Harold Goodwin, Sidney Bracey, Harry Gribbon, Vernon Dent, Charles Lindbergh *(archive footage)* L: 8-Reels P/D: MGM.

The Campus Carmen, 1928/9/23 D: Alf Goulding C: Daphne Pollard, Johnny Burke, Carole Lombard, Madeline Fields, Vernon Dent L: 2-Reels P: Sennett DIST: Pathé.

Soldier Man 1928/9/30 D: Harry Edwards C: Harry Langdon, Frank Whitson, Natalie Kingston, Vernon Dent L: 2-Reels P: Sennett DIST: Pathé.

A Jim Jam Janitor 1928/11/11 D: Harry Edwards C: Johnny Burke, Carmelita Geraghty, Vernon Dent, Glen Cavender L: 2-Reels P: Sennett DIST: Pathé.

Campus Vamp 1928/11/25 D: Harry Edwards C: Carole Lombard, Sally Eilers, Vernon Dent, Carmelita Geraghty, Johnny Burke, Matty Kemp L: 2-Reels P: Sennett DIST: Pathé.

Murder Will Out 1928/12/01 D: Jules White C: Vernon Dent, Georgia O'Dell, Al Thompson, Ford West, Jackie Levine L: 1-Reel P: Jack White DIST: Educational *(Cameo Comedies)*.

Hubby's Weekend Trip 1928/12/2 D: Harry Edwards C: Vernon Dent L: 2-Reels P: Sennett DIST: Pathé.

The Lion's Roar 1928/12/9 D: Mack Sennett C: Johnny Burke, Daphne Pollard, Billy Bevan, Vernon Dent L: 2-Reels P: Sennett DIST: Educational. [Note: First Sennett talkie.]

Social Prestige 1928/12/23 D: Stephen Roberts C: Monty Collins, Vernon Dent, Betty Boyd, Robert Graves L: 1-Reel P: Jack White DIST: Educational *(Mermaid Comedies)*.

In the Morning 1928/12/30 D: Francis J. Martin C: Vernon Dent L: 1-Reel P: Jack White DIST: Educational *(Cameo Comedies)*.

What a Trip 1929/1/2 D: Francis J Martin C: Vernon Dent, Amber Norman, Jack Richardson L: 1-Reel P: Jack White DIST: Educational *(Cameo Comedies)*.

Clunked On the Corner 1929/1/6 D: Harry Edwards C: Johnny Burke, Carmelita Geraghty, Vernon Dent L: 2-Reels P: Sennett DIST: Pathé.

The Bride's Relations 1929/1/13 D: Mack Sennett C: Johnny Burke, Thelma Hill, Andy Clyde, Louise Carver, Harry Gribbon, Vernon Dent L: 2-reels P: Mack Sennett DIST: Educational.

Calling Hubby's Bluff 1929/2/3/ D: Harry Edwards C: Billy Bevan, Carmelita Geraghty, Vernon Dent L: 2-Reels P: Sennett DIST: Pathé *(Mack Sennett Comedies)*.

The Old Barn 1929/2/3 D: Mack Sennett C: Johnny Burke, Thelma Hill, Daphne Pollard, Andy Clyde, Irving Bacon, Vernon Dent L: 2-Reels P: Sennett DIST: Educational *(Mack Sennett Comedies)*.

Whoopee Boys 1929/2/10 D: Stephen Roberts C: Monty Collins, Vernon Dent, Estelle Bradley, Eva Thatcher, Robert Graves, Al Thompson L: 2-Reels P: Jack White DIST: Educational *(Mermaid Comedies)*. [Note: The film debut of comedy team Collins & Dent.]

Button My Back 1929/2/11 D: Phil Whitman C: Billy Bevan, Carmelita Geraghty, Irving Bacon, Alice Ward, Vernon Dent L: 2-Reels P: Sennett DIST: Pathé.

Ladies Must Eat 1929/3/3 D: Harry Edwards C: Johnny Burke, Daphne Pollard, Vernon Dent, Natalie Joyce, Andy Clyde L: 2-Reels P: Sennett DIST: Pathé.

Foolish Husbands 1929/3/17 D: Phil Whitman C: Billy Bevan, Dot Farley, Vernon Dent, Carmelita Geraghty, Irving Bacon, Sunshine Hart, Otto Fries L: 2-Reels P: Sennett DIST: Pathé *(Mack Sennett Comedies)*.

Parlor Pests 1929/3/24 D: Stephen Roberts C: Vernon Dent, Monty Collins, Eva Thatcher Estelle Bradley, Al Thompson, Robert Graves L: 1-Reel P: Jack White DIST: Educational Film Exchanges *(Mermaid Comedies)*.

Those Two Boys 1929/3/30 D: Stephen Roberts C: Vernon Dent, Monty Collins, Robert Graves, Al Thompson L: 2-Reels P: Jack White DIST: Educational *(Mermaid Comedies)*.

Wise Wimmen 1929/3/31 C: Glen Cavender, Vernon Dent, Jerry Drew (Clem Beauchamp), Lucille Hutton L: 1-Reel P: Jack White DIST: Educational *(Ideal Comedies)*.

Pink Pajamas 1929/4/21 D: Phil Whitman C: Billy Bevan, Natalie Joyce, Alice Ward, Vernon Dent L: 2-Reels P: Sennett DIST: Pathé.

Howling Hollywood 1929/4/21 D: James Jones C: George Davis, Vernon Dent, Arthur Housman, Al Thompson, Ella McKenzie, Fred Spencer L: 2-reels P: Jack White DIST: Educational *(Mermaid Comedies)*.

The Bee's Buzz 1929/4/27 D: Mack Sennett C: Harry Gribbon, Andy Clyde, Barbara Leonard, Vernon Dent L: 2-Reels P: Sennett DIST: Educational.

The Big Palooka 1929/5/12 D: Mack Sennett C: Harry Gribbon, Andy Clyde, Thelma Hill, Vernon Dent L: 2-Reels P: Sennett DIST: Educational.

Household Blues 1929/5/14 D: Jules White C: Vernon Dent, Monty Collins, Eva Thatcher, Robert Burns L: 1-Reel P: Jack White DIST: Educational *(Cameo Comedies)*.

Don't Get Jealous 1929/5/19 D: Eddie Cline C: Billy Bevan, Carmelita Geraghty, Vernon Dent, Andy Clyde, Carole Lombard L: 2-Reels P: Sennett DIST: Pathé.

Girl Crazy 1929/6/9 D: Alf Goulding C: Andy Clyde, Vernon Dent, Alma Bennett, Irving Bacon L: 2-Reels P: Sennett DIST: Educational.

What a Day 1929/6/16 D: Stephen Roberts C: Monty Collins, Vernon Dent L: 2-Reels P: Jack White DIST: Educational *(Mermaid Comedies)*.

Motoring Mamas 1929/6/16 D: Phil Whitman C: Billy Bevan, Alice Ward, Vernon Dent, Natalie Joyce, Glen Cavender L: 2-Reels P: Sennett DIST: Pathé.

A Close Shave 1929/6/23 D: Harry Edwards C: Johnny Burke, Vernon Dent, Carmelita Geraghty L: 2-Reels P: Sennett DIST: Pathé.

Jazz Mamas 1929/6/29 D: Mack Sennett C: Virginia Lee Corbin, Vernon Dent, Jack Cooper, Jack Richardson, Bathing Girls L: 2-Reels P: Sennett DIST: Educational Film Exchanges. [Note: "In Multi-Color."]

The Barber's Daughter 1929/7/21 D: Mack Sennett C: Andy Clyde, Thelma Hill, Vernon Dent, Addie McPhail, Milton Holmes, Ben Hall L: 2-Reels P: Sennett DIST: Educational.

Ticklish Business 1929/8/24 D: Stephen Roberts C: Vernon Dent, Monty Collins, Addie McPhail, Phyllis Crane, William Irving, Jerry Drew L: 2-Reels P: Jack White DIST: Educational *(Mermaid Comedies)*.

Hot Sports 1929/9/11 D: Jules White C: Vernon Dent, Monty Collins, Betty Boyd, Eva Thatcher, Robert Graves L: 1-Reel P: Jack White DIST: Educational Film Exchanges *(Cameo Comedies)*.

Watch Your Friends 1929/10/9 D: Richard Smith C: Lou Archer, Vernon Dent L: 2-Reels P/D: Universal *(All-Star Comedies)*.

The Talkies 1929/10/27 D: Stephen Roberts C: Vernon Dent, Monty Collins, Lloyd Ingraham, Francis Ford, Mary Jane Temple L: 2-Reels P: Jack White DIST: Educational *(Mermaid Comedies)*.

Sunday Morning 1929/12/4 D: Harry Edwards C: Vernon Dent, Lou Archer L: 1-Reel P/D: Universal *(All-Star Comedies)*.

Up and Down Stairs 1930/1/25 D: Harry Edwards C: Vernon Dent, Lou Archer, Dorothy Coburn, Charlotte Merriam L: 2-Reels P/D: Universal *(All-Star Comedies)*.

Vernon's Aunt 1930/2/19 D: Harry Edwards C: Vernon Dent, Lou Archer, Blanche Gilmore L: 2-Reels P/D: Universal *(All-Star Comedies)*.

Honeymoon Zeppelin 1930/4/13 D: Mack Sennett C: Marjorie Beebe, Daphne Pollard, Nick Stuart, Lew Kelly, Vernon Dent L: 2-Reels P: Sennett DIST: Educational.

Good-Bye Legs 1930/7/27 D: Mack Sennett C: Andy Clyde, Daphne Pollard, Ann Christy, Nick Stuart, Vernon Dent, Ann Christy, Will Hays, Tom Dempsey L: 2-Reels P: Sennett DIST: Educational.

Johnny's Weekend Trip 1930/9/14 D: William Watson C: Johnny Hines, Adrienne Dore, Vernon Dent, Estelle Bradley, Helen Bolton, Frank Rice. L: 2-Reels P: Christie DIST: Educational *(Gayety Comedies)*.

Midnight Daddies (feature) 1930/10/3 D: Mack Sennett C: Harry Gribbon, Andy Clyde, Vernon Dent, Jack Cooper, Irving Bacon, Alma Bennett, Addie McPhail, Natalie Joyce, Katherine Ward L: 60 minutes P: Sennett DIST: Sono Art-World Wide.

Take Your Medicine 1930/10/26 D: Eddie Cline C: Andy Clyde, Patsy O'Leary, Frank Eastman, Blanche Payson, Vernon Dent L: 1-Reel P: Sennett DIST: Educational. [Note: In color.]

Crazy House 1930/11/1 D: Jack Cummings C: Benny Rubin, Polly Moran, Karl Dane, Vernon Dent, Cliff Edwards, Gus Shy L: 2-Reels P/D: MGM. [MGM Colortone Revue.]

Too Hot to Handle 1930/11/15 D: Lewis R. Foster C: Louise Fazenda, Fern Emmett, Harry Bernard, Lyle Tayo, Vernon Dent L: 2-Reels P: Larry Darmour Productions DIST: RKO Radio Pictures *(Louise Fazenda Comedies)*.

Dance Hall Marge 1931/1/18 D: Mack Sennett/Del Lord C: Harry Gribbon, Marjorie Beebe, Frank Eastman, Vernon Dent L: 2-Reels P: Sennett DIST: Educational.

Girls Will Be Boys 1931/1/25 D: William Watson C: Charlotte Greenwood, Vernon Dent, Eddie Baker, Snub Pollard L: 2-Reels P: Christie DIST: Educational *(Vanity Comedies)*.

Talking Turkey 1931/1/25 D: Mark Sandrich C: Benny Rubin, Theodore Lorch, Vernon Dent L: 2-Reels P/D: RKO Radio *(Broadway Headliners Series)*.

The Bride's Mistake 1931/3/1 D: Earle Rodney C: Marjorie Beebe, Kenneth Thomson, Vernon Dent L: 2-Reels P: Sennett DIST: Educational.

Gents of Leisure 1931/5/9 D: Del Lord C: Chester Conklin, Vernon Dent, Bud Jamison, Ethel Sykes, Stanley Blystone, Bobby Dunn L: 2-reels P: Phil Ryan Productions, Ltd. DIST: Paramount *(Chester Conklin Comedies, released as part of Paramount Two-Reel Comedies series)*.

Don't Divorce Him 1931/5/31 D: William Watson C: Clyde Cook, Edgar Kennedy, Vernon Dent, John T. Murray, Jessie Le Seur, Betty Lorraine L: 2-Reels P: Christie DIST: Educational *(Tuxedo Comedies)*.

A College Racket 1931/6/14 D: Harold Beaudine C: Glenn Tryon, Vernon Dent, Eddie Baker, Betty Lorraine, Donald Keith, Tom Dempsey, Glen Cavender L: 2-Reels P: Christie DIST: Educational *(Vanity Comedies)*.

The 13th Alarm 1931/7/4 D: Del Lord C: Chester Conklin, Vernon Dent, Broderick O'Farrell, Stella Adams L: 2-Reels P: Phil Ryan Productions, Ltd. DIST: Paramount *(Chester Conklin Comedies, released as part of Paramount Two-Reel Comedies series)*.

Fainting Lover 1931/8/16 D: Mack Sennett C: Andy Clyde, Addie McPhail, Wade Boteler, Anna Dodge, Vernon Dent L: 2-Reels P: Sennett DIST: Educational.

Murder at Midnight 1931/9/1 *(feature)* D: Frank R. Strayer C: Aileen Pringle, Alice White, Hale Hamilton, Robert Elliott, Clara Blandick, Brandon Hurst, Vernon Dent L: 69 minutes P: Tiffany Productions.

The Cannonball 1931/9/6 D: Del Lord C: Andy Clyde, Irene Thompson, Lew Sargent, Vernon Dent, George Gray L: 2-Reels P: Sennett DIST: Educational.

The Freshman's Finish 1931/9/20 D: William Watson C: Carlyle Moore, Helen Mann, Vernon Dent L: 2-Reels P: Christie DIST: Educational *(Vanity Comedies)*.

Beach Pajamas 1931/9/21 D: William Goodrich (Roscoe Arbuckle) C: Louis John Bartels, Ena Gregory, Vernon Dent, James Finlayson L: 2-Reels P/D: RKO Pathé Pictures *(Traveling Man Comedies)*.

Up Pops the Landlord 1931 [Note: Unreleased two-reel comedy, produced by Joe Quillan and starring his son Eddie and the Quillan Family. According to Eddie (in a 1988 interview with Edward Watz), Vernon played the role of the landlord.]

The Girl Rush 1931/10/25 D: William Watson C: Vernon Dent, Helen Mann, Eddie Tamblyn, Vera Steadman, Ronnie Rondell, Jack Duffy L: 2-Reels P: Christie DIST: Educational *(Vanity Comedies)*.

All-American Kickback 1931/11/29 D: Del Lord C: Harry Gribbon, Vernon Dent, Dorothy Granger: L: 2-Reels P: Sennett DIST: Educational.

Dragnet Patrol (feature) 1931/12/15 D: Frank R. Strayer C: Glenn Tryon, Vera Reynolds, Walter Long, George "Gabby" Hayes, Marjorie Beebe, Vernon Dent L: 59 minutes P: Mayfair DIST: Action Pictures.

Hollywood Halfbacks 1931/12/23 D: Charles Lamont C: Johnny Mack Brown, Betty Compson, Arthur Lake, Vernon Dent L: 2-Reels P: Foy Productions, Ltd. DIST: Universal *(Thalians Comedies)*.

Dream House 1932/1/17 D: Del Lord C: Bing Crosby, Ann Christy, Katherine Ward, Eddie Phillips, Vernon Dent L: 2-Reels P: Sennett DIST: Educational.

Texas Cyclone (feature) 1932/2/24 D: D. Ross Lederman C: Tim McCoy, John Wayne, Vernon Dent, Shirley Grey, Wheeler Oakman, Walter Brennan L: 63 minutes P/D: Columbia.

Business and Pleasure (feature) 1932/3/6 D: David Butler C: Will Rogers, Jetta Goudal, Joel McCrea, Dorothy Peterson, Boris Karloff, Oscar Apfel, Jed Prouty, Vernon Dent L: 77 minutes P/D: Fox.

The Riding Tornado (feature) 1932/5/4 D: D. Ross Lederman C: Tim McCoy, Shirley Grey, Montagu Love, Wheeler Oakman, Wallace MacDonald, Russell Simpson, Vernon Dent L: 64 minutes P/D: Columbia.

Million Dollar Legs (feature) 1932/7/8 D: Edward F. Cline C: W.C. Fields, Jack Oakie, Susan Fleming, Lyda Roberti, Andy Clyde, Ben Turpin, Dickie Moore, Billy Gilbert, Hugh Herbert, Vernon Dent L: 64 minutes P/D: Paramount.

For the Love of Ludwig 1932/7/24 D: Emil Herberger C: Andy Clyde, Vernon Dent, Wade Boteler, Addie McPhail L: 2-Reels P: Sennett DIST: Educational *(Mack Sennett Comedies)*.

Daring Danger (feature) 1932/7/27 D: D. Ross Lederman C: Tim McCoy, Alberta Vaughn, Wallace MacDonald, Robert Ellis, Richard Alexander, Murdock MacQuarie, Vernon Dent, Edward LeSaint L: 57 minutes P/D: Columbia.

A Hollywood Handicap 1932/8/10 D: Charles Lamont C: Marion Byron, Anita Stewart, John Wayne, Vernon Dent, Dickie Moore L: 2-Reels P: Foy Productions, Ltd. DIST: Universal *(Thalians Comedies)*.

The Iceman's Ball 1932/8/13 D: Mark Sandrich C: Bobby Clark, Paul McCullough, James Finlayson, Fred Kelsey, Walter Brennan, Vernon Dent L: 2-Reels P/D: RKO Radio Pictures *(Clark & McCullough Comedies)*.

Just a Pain in a Parlor 1932/8/26 D: George Marshall C: Harry Sweet, Monty Collins, Vernon Dent L: 2-Reels P/D: RKO Radio Pictures *(Harry Sweet Comedies).*

The Singing Plumber 1932/9/23 D: Leslie Pearce C: Donald Novis, J. Farrell MacDonald, Aggie Herring, Babe Kane, Matt McHugh, Vernon Dent L: 2-Reels P: Sennett DIST: Educational *(Mack Sennett Star Comedies).*

Sun Kissed Sweeties 1932/10/30 D: Harry Edwards C: Andy Clyde, Vernon Dent, Faye Pierre, Monty Collins, Thelma Hill, Stanley Blystone L: 2-Reels P/D: Educational *(Andy Clyde Comedies).*

The Big Flash 1932/11/6 D: Arvid E. Gillstrom C: Harry Langdon, Vernon Dent, Ruth Hiatt, Bobby Dunn L: 2-Reels P/D: Educational *(Mermaid Comedies).*

A Fool About Women 1932/11/27 D: Harry Edwards C: Andy Clyde, Vernon Dent, Faye Pierre, Fern Emmett, Tom Dempsey, Melbourne McDowell L: 2-Reels P/D: Educational *(Andy Clyde Comedies).*

Tired Feet 1933/1/1 D: Arvid E. Gillstrom C: Harry Langdon, Vernon Dent, Eddie Baker L: 2-Reels P/D: Educational *(Mermaid Comedies).*

Artists Muddles 1933/1/29 D: Harry Edwards C: Andy Clyde, Vernon Dent L: 2-Reels P: Educational DIST: Fox *(Andy Clyde Comedies).*

The Hitchhiker 1933/2/12 D: Arvid E. Gillstrom C: Harry Langdon, Vernon Dent, Ruth Clifford, William Irving, Chris Marie Meeker L: 2-Reels P: Educational DIST: Fox *(Mermaid Comedies).*

Knight Duty 1933/5/7 D: Arvid E. Gillstrom C: Harry Langdon, Vernon Dent L: 2-Reels P: Educational DIST: Fox *(Mermaid Comedies).*

Tied for Life 1933/7/2 D: Arvid E. Gillstrom C: Harry Langdon, Vernon Dent, Eddie Baker, Nell O'Day, Mabel Forrest, Elaine Whipple L: 2-Reels P: Educational DIST: Fox *(Mermaid Comedies).* [Note: Story by Dean Ward and Vernon Dent.]

Marriage Humor 1933/8/13 D: Harry Edwards C: Harry Langdon, Vernon Dent, Judith Barrett, Ethyl Sykes, Nancy Dover L: 2-Reels P: Arvid E. Gillstrom DIST: Paramount *(Harry Langdon Comedies)*.

Hooks and Jabs 1933/8/25 D: Arvid E. Gillstrom C: Harry Langdon, Vernon Dent L: 2-Reels P: Educational DIST: Fox *(Mermaid Comedies)*. [Note: Vernon Dent has writing credit.]

On Ice 1933/10/6 D: Arvid E. Gillstrom C: Harry Langdon, Vernon Dent, Diana Seaby L: 2-Reels P: Arvid E. Gillstrom DIST: Paramount *(Harry Langdon Comedies)*.

Three Little Swigs 1933/10/11 D: Arvid E. Gillstrom C: Leon Errol, Vernon Dent L: 2-Reels P: Arvid E. Gillstrom DIST: Paramount *(Leon Errol Comedies)*.

Please 1933/12/15 D: Arvid E. Gillstrom C: Bing Crosby, Vernon Dent, Mary Kornman, Dickie Kibbie L: 2-Reels P: Arvid E. Gillstrom DIST: Paramount *(Bing Crosby Comedies)*.

Roaming Romeo, 1933/12/29 D: Arvid E. Gillstrom C: Harry Langdon, Vernon Dent, Nell O'Day, Jack Henderson, Les Goodwin L: 2-Reels P: Arvid E. Gillstrom DIST: Paramount *(Harry Langdon Comedies)*.

Just an Echo 1934/1/19 D: Arvid E. Gillstrom C: Bing Crosby, Vernon Dent, Mary Kornman L: 2-Reels P: Arvid E. Gillstrom DIST: Paramount *(Bing Crosby Comedies)*.

Circus Hoodoo 1934/2/16 D: Arvid E. Gillstrom C: Harry Langdon, Vernon Dent, Eleanor Hunt, Matthew Betz, Diana Seaby, James C. Morton, Tom Kennedy L: 2-Reels P: Arvid E. Gillstrom DIST: Paramount *(Harry Langdon Comedies)*.

You're Telling Me! (feature) 1934/4/5 D: Erle C. Kenton C: W.C. Fields, Joan Marsh, Larry "Buster" Crabbe, Vernon Dent L: 64 minutes P/D: Paramount.

Petting Preferred 1934/4/27 D: Arvid E. Gillstrom C: Harry Langdon, Vernon Dent L: 2-Reels P: Arvid E. Gillstrom DIST: Paramount *(Harry Langdon Comedies)*.

Manhattan Melodrama (feature) 1934/5/4 D: W. S. Van Dyke C: Clark Gable, William Powell, Myrna Loy, Mickey Rooney, Leo Carrillo, Isabel Jewell, Vernon Dent L: 93 minutes P/D: MGM.

Good Morning, Eve 1934/9/22 D: Roy Mack C: Leon Errol, Vernon Dent, June MacCloy, Maxine Doyle, Harry Seymour, L: 2-Reels P: Vitaphone Corp. DIST: Warner Bros. *(Broadway Brevities)*. [Note: This novelty short was filmed in Technicolor.]

Hollywood Trouble 1935/1/1 D: Jack Townley C: John Harron, Grady Sutton, Vernon Dent, Gertrude Short, Franklin Pangborn L: 2-Reels P: Jack Townley Productions DIST: Universal *(Thalians Comedies)*. [Note: Vernon has writing credit.]

Tars and Stripes 1935/5/3 D: Buster Keaton *(uncredited)*, Charles Lamont C: Buster Keaton, Vernon Dent, Dorothea Kent L: 2-Reels P: Educational DIST: Fox *(Star Personality Comedies)*.

His Marriage Mix-Up 1935/10/31 D: Preston Black C: Harry Langdon, Dorothy Granger, Vernon Dent, Robert "Bobby" Burns L: 2-Reels P/D: Columbia *(Broadway Comedies)*. [Note: Vernon has writing credit.]

Tuned Out 1935/11/15 D: Alfred J. Goulding C: Ruth Etting, Herbert Rawlinson, Vernon Dent, Irving Bacon L: 2-Reels P/D: RKO Radio (Headliner Series).

Unrelated Relations 1935/12/5 D: Del Lord C: Monty Collins, Ruth Skinner, Mary Foy, Louise Carver, Vernon Dent, Jack Kenney, Tommy Bond L: 2-Reels P/D: Columbia *(Broadway Comedies)*.

I Don't Remember 1935/12/26 D: Preston Black (Jack White) C: Harry Langdon, Geneva Mitchell, Mary Carr, Vernon Dent, Robert "Bobby" Burns, Charles "Heinie" Conklin, Lynton Brent, Harry Semels, Al Thompson, Bobby Barber L: 2-Reels P/D: Columbia *(Broadway Comedies)*.

Share the Wealth 1936/3/16 D: Del Lord C: Andy Clyde, Mary Gordon, Vernon Dent, James C. Morton, Al Thompson L: 2-Reels P/D: Columbia *(Broadway Comedies)*.

Half-Shot Shooters 1936/4/30 D: Preston Black (Jack White) C: Moe Howard, Larry Fine, Curly Howard, Stanley Blystone, Vernon Dent, Harry Semels, Charles "Heinie" Conklin, Bert Young L: 2-Reels P/D: Columbia *(Three Stooges Series)*.

Dog Blight 1936/6/12 D: Jean W. Yarbrough C: Jack Norton, Maxine Jennings, Vernon Dent L: 2-Reels P/D: RKO Radio *(Radio Flash Comedies)*.

San Francisco (feature) 1936/6/26 D: W. S. Van Dyke C: Clark Gable, Spencer Tracy, Jeanette MacDonald, Ted Healy, Edgar Kennedy, Vernon Dent L: 115 minutes P/D: MGM.

Oh, Duchess! 1936/10/9 D: Charles Lamont C: Polly Moran, Vernon Dent, Mary Blake, Al Thompson, Jack "Tiny" Lipson, Symona Boniface, Bob McKenzie, Eva McKenzie L: 2-Reels P/D: Columbia *(Broadway Comedies)*.

The Fugitive Sheriff (feature) 1936/10/20 D: Spencer Gordon Bennet C: Ken Maynard, Beth Marion, Virginia True Boardman, Edmund Cobb, Walter Miller, Hal Price, John Elliot, Vernon Dent L: 58 minutes P/D: Columbia [Note: Vernon appears uncredited as a bunkhouse singer.]

Slippery Silks 1936/12/27 D: Preston Black (Jack White) C: Moe Howard, Larry Fine, Curly Howard, Vernon Dent, Symona Boniface, Eddie Laughton, William Irving, Jack "Tiny" Lipson, Gertrude Messinger, Beatrice Curtis L: 2-Reels P/D: Columbia *(Three Stooges Series)*.

Dizzy Doctors 1937/3/19 D: Del Lord C: Moe Howard, Larry Fine, Curly Howard, Vernon Dent, Bud Jamison, June Gittelson, Eva Murray, Ione Leslie, Louise Carver, Ella McKenzie, Wilfred Lucas, Al Thompson, James C. Morton L: 2-Reels P/D: Columbia *(Three Stooges Series)*.

Back to the Woods 1937/5/14 D: Preston Black (Jack White) C: Moe Howard, Larry Fine, Curly Howard, Vernon Dent, Bud Jamison, Harlene Wood, Ethelreda Leopold, Cy Schindell, Bert Young, Beatrice Curtis L: 2-Reels P/D: Columbia *(Three Stooges Series)*.

Easy Living (feature) 1937/7/7 D: Mitchell Leisen C: Jean Arthur, Edward Arnold, Ray Milland, Vernon Dent L: 88 minutes P/D: Paramount.

Calling All Doctors 1937/7/22 D: Charles Lamont C: Charley Chase, Lucille Lund, John T. Murray, Bobby Watson, James C. Morton, Vernon Dent L: 2-Reels P/D: Columbia *(Broadway Comedies)*.

Calling All Curtains 1937/10/1 D: Del Lord C: Tom Kennedy, Monty Collins, Bud Jamison, Vernon Dent, William Irving, Marjorie Cameron L: 2-Reels P/D: Columbia *(Broadway Comedies)*.

The Awful Truth (feature) 1937/10/21 D: Leo McCarey C: Irene Dunn, Cary Grant, Ralph Bellamy, Cecil Cunningham, Mary Forbes, Joyce Compton, Molly Lamont, Vernon Dent L: 91 minutes P/D: Columbia.

Gracie at the Bat 1937/10/29 D: Del Lord C: Andy Clyde, Louise Stanley, Ann Doran, Leora Thatcher, Bud Jamison, Vernon Dent, Bess Flowers L: 2-Reels P/D: Columbia *(Broadway Comedies)*.

Murder in Greenwich Village (feature) 1937/11/3 D: Albert S. Rogell C: Richard Arlen, Fay Wray, Raymond Walburn, Vernon Dent L: 68 minutes P/D: Columbia.

Paid to Dance (feature) 1937/11/4 D: C.C. Coleman, Jr. C: Don Terry, Jacqueline Wells, Rita Hayworth, Arthur Loft, Paul Stanton, Paul Fix, Louise Stanley, Ralph Byrd, Beatrice Curtis, Bess Flowers, Beatrice Blinn, Jane Hamilton, Dick Curtis, Al Herman, Vernon Dent, Bud Jamison L: 55 minutes P/D: Columbia.

Outlaws of the Prairie (feature) 1937/12/1 D: Sam Nelson C: Charles Starrett, Donald Grayson, Iris Meredith, Norman Willis, Dick Curtis, Vernon Dent, Sons of the Pioneers L: 59 minutes P/D: Columbia.

All-American Sweetheart (feature) 1937/12/20 D: Lambert Hillyer C: Patricia Farr, Scott Colton, Gene Morgan, Jimmy Eagles, Arthur Loft, Bud Jamison, Vernon Dent L: 62 minutes P/D: Columbia.

The Shadow (feature) 1937/12/22 D: Charles C. Coleman C: Rita Hayworth, Charles Quigley, Marc Lawrence, Arthur Loft, Dick Curtis, Marjorie Main, Bess Flowers, Vernon Dent L: 59 minutes P/D: Columbia.

Fiddling Around 1938/1/21 D: Charles Lamont C: Monty Collins, Tom Kennedy, Gino Corrado, William Irving, Vernon Dent, Bud Jamison L: 2-Reels P/D: Columbia *(Broadway Comedies)*.

Little Miss Roughneck (feature) 1938/1/23 D: Aubrey Scotto C: Edith Fellows, Leo Carrillo, Scott Kolk, Julie Bishop, Vernon Dent, Bud Jamison L: 64 minutes P/D: Columbia.

Who Killed Gail Preston? (feature) 1938/2/24 D: Leon Barsha C: Don Terry, Rita Hayworth, Robert Paige, Wyn Cahoon, Gene Morgan, Marc Lawrence, Vernon Dent L: 60 minutes P/D: Columbia.

Wee Wee Monsieur 1938/2/28 D: Del Lord C: Moe Howard, Larry Fine, Curly Howard, Vernon Dent, Bud Jamison, William Irving, Harry Semels, John Lester Johnson, Ethelreda Leopold L: 2-Reels P/D: Columbia *(Three Stooges Series)*.

Start Cheering (feature) 1938/3/3 D: Albert S. Rogell C: Jimmy Durante, Walter Connolly, Joan Perry, Charles Starrett, Gertrude Niesen, Hal LeRoy, Broderick Crawford, The Three Stooges (Moe Howard, Larry Fine, and Curly Howard), Vernon Dent L: 78 minutes P/D: Columbia.

The Old Raid Mule 1938/3/4 D: Charley Chase C: Andy Clyde, Olin Howland, Ann Doran, Vernon Dent, Bud Jamison L: 2-Reels P/D: Columbia *(Broadway Comedies)*.

When G-Men Step In (feature) 1938/3/17 D: Charles C. Coleman C: Don Terry, Julie Bishop, Robert Paige, Vernon Dent L: 60 minutes P/D: Columbia.

Time Out for Trouble 1938/3/18 D: Del Lord C: Charley Chase, Louis Stanley, Ann Doran, Dick Curtis, Vernon Dent, Bud Jamison L: 2-Reels P/D: Columbia *(Broadway Comedies)*.

Tassels in the Air 1938/4/1 D: Charley Chase C: Moe Howard, Larry Fine, Curly Howard, Vernon Dent, Bess Flowers, Bud Jamison L: 2-Reels P/D: Columbia *(Three Stooges Series)*.

The Mind Needer 1938/4/29 D: Del Lord C: Charley Chase, Ann Doran, Vernon Dent, John T. Murray, Bess Flowers L: 2-Reels P/D: Columbia *(Broadway Comedies)*.

Vivacious Lady (feature) 1938/5/10 D: George Stevens C: James Stewart, Ginger Rogers, James Ellison, Beulah Bondi, Charles Coburn, Frances Mercer, Grady Sutton, Jack Carson, Franklin Pangborn, Hattie McDaniel, Vernon Dent L: 90 minutes P/D: RKO.

Ankles Away 1938/5/13 D: Charley Chase C: Andy Clyde, Ann Doran, Gene Morgan, Gino Corrado, Bess Flowers, Vernon Dent L: 2-Reels P/D: Columbia *(Broadway Comedies)*.

The Lone Wolf in Paris (feature) 1938/5/25 D: Albert S. Rogell C: Francis Lederer, Frances Drake, Walter Kingsford, Leona Maricle, Vernon Dent L: 66 minutes P/D: Columbia.

Reformatory (feature) 1938/6/20 D: Lewis D. Collins C: Jack Holt, Bobby Jordan, Tommy Bupp, Ward Bond, Vernon Dent L: 61 minutes P/D: Columbia.

Many Sappy Returns 1938/8/19 D: Del Lord C: Charley Chase, Vernon Dent, Ann Doran, John T. Murray, Fred Kelsey L: 2-Reels P/D: Columbia *(Broadway Comedies)*.

Juvenile Court (feature) 1938/9/15 D: D. Ross Lederman C: Paul Kelly, Rita Hayworth, Frankie Darro, Hal E. Chester, Don Lattore, David Gorcey, Richard Selzer, Allan Ramsay, Charles Hart, Howard C. Hickman, Harry Bernard, Vernon Dent L: 60 minutes P/D: Columbia.

Mutts to You 1938/10/14 D: Charley Chase C: Moe Howard, Larry Fine, Curly Howard, Vernon Dent, Bess Flowers, Lane Chandler, Bud Jamison L: 2-Reels P/D: Columbia *(Three Stooges Series)*.

Thanks for the Memory (feature) 1938/11/11 D: George Archainbaud C: Bob Hope, Shirley Ross, Charles Butterworth, Otto Kruger, Roscoe Karns, Hedda Hopper, Eddie Anderson, Vernon Dent L: 77 minutes P/D: Paramount.

A Doggone Mix-up 1938/12/4 D: Charles Lamont C: Harry Langdon, Ann Doran, Vernon Dent, Bud Jamison L: 2-Reels P/D: Columbia *(Broadway Comedies)*.

Home on the Rage 1938/12/9 D: Del Lord C: Andy Clyde, Shemp Howard, Lela Bliss, Vernon Dent L: 2-Reels P/D: Columbia *(Broadway Comedies)*.

You Can't Take it With You (feature) 1938/12/26 D: Frank Capra C: Jean Arthur, Lionel Barrymore, James Stewart, Edward Arnold, Mischa Auer, Ann Miller, Spring Byington, Eddie "Rochester" Anderson, Donald Meek, Vernon Dent L: 127 minutes P/D: Columbia.

Three Little Sew and Sews 1939/1/6 D: Del Lord C: Moe Howard, Larry Fine, Curly Howard, Vernon Dent, Phyllis Barry, Harry Semels, James C. Morton, Bud Jamison L: 2-Reels P/D: Columbia *(Three Stooges Series)*.

Mutiny on the Body 1939/2/10 D: Charley Chase C: Joe Smith, Charlie Dale, Chester Conklin, Guy Usher, Cy Schindell, Marjorie Deanne, Joe Ploski, Vernon Dent L: 2-Reels P/D: Columbia *(Broadway Comedies)*.

Stanley and Livingstone (feature) 1939/3/1 D: Henry King C: Spencer Tracy, Nancy Kelly, Richard Greene, Walter Brennan, Charles Coburn, Cedric Hardwicke, Henry Hull, Henry Travers, Miles Mander, Vernon Dent L: 101 minutes P/D: 20th Century-Fox.

A-Ducking They Did Go 1939/4/7 D: Del Lord C: Moe Howard, Larry Fine, Curly Howard, Vernon Dent, Lynton Brent, Bud Jamison, Cy Schindell L: 2-Reels P/D: Columbia *(Three Stooges Series)*.

A Star is Shorn 1939/4/21 D: Del Lord C: Danny Webb, Mary Treen, Ethelreda Leopold, Eugene Anderson, Jr., Victor Travers, Dudley Dickerson, Cy Schindell, Gene Stone, Raymond Brown, Al Thompson, Beatrice Blinn, Vernon Dent, John Tyrrell L: 2-Reels P/D: Columbia *(Broadway Comedies)*.

Yes, We Have No Bonanza 1939/5/19 D: Del Lord C: Moe Howard, Larry Fine, Curly Howard, Vernon Dent, Dick Curtis, Lynton Brent, Suzanne Kaaren, Jean Carmen, Lola Jensen L: 2-Reels P/D: Columbia *(Three Stooges Series)*.

The Lone Wolf Spy Hunt (feature) 1939/5/30 D: Peter Godfrey C: Warren William, Ida Lupino, Ralph Morgan, Thurston Hall, Vernon Dent L: 67 minutes P/D: Columbia.

Only Angels Have Wings (feature) 1939/5/15 D: Howard Hawks, C: Cary Grant, Jean Arthur, Richard Barthelmess, Vernon Dent L: 121 minutes P/D: Columbia.

Now It Can Be Sold 1939/6/2 D: Del Lord C: Andy Clyde, Tommy Bond, Anita Garvin, Vernon Dent L: 2-Reels P/D: Columbia *(Broadway Comedies)*.

Saved By the Belle 1939/6/30 D: Charley Chase C: Moe Howard, Larry Fine, Curly Howard, Vernon Dent L: 2-Reels P/D: Columbia *(Three Stooges Series)*.

Sue My Lawyer 1939/9/16 D: Jules White C: Harry Langdon, Ann Doran, Monty Collins, Bud Jamison, Vernon Dent L: 2-Reels P/D: Columbia *(Broadway Comedies)*.

Hitler, Beast of Berlin (feature) 1939/10/8 D: Sam Newfield C: Alan Ladd, Roland Drew, Steffi Duna, Greta Granstedt, Lucian Prival, Vernon Dent L: 87 minutes P: Sigmund Neufeld Productions DIST: Producers Distributing Corporation.

Mr. Smith Goes to Washington (feature) 1939/10/19 D: Frank Capra C: James Stewart, Jean Arthur, Claude Rains, Edward Arnold, Guy Kibbee, Thomas Mitchell, Eugene Pallette, Beulah Bondi, Harry Carey, Charles Lane, Jack Carson, Vernon Dent L: 129 minutes P/D: Columbia.

Teacher's Pest 1939/11/3 D: Del Lord C: Charley Chase, Ruth Skinner, Chester Conklin, Richard Fiske, Bud Jamison, Hank Bell, Vernon Dent L: 2-Reels P/D: Columbia *(Broadway Comedies)*.

Mendelssohn's Wedding March 1939/11/4 D: James Fitzpatrick C: Mary Anderson, E. Alyn Warren, Vernon Dent L: 1-Reel P/D: MGM. [Note: Filmed in Technicolor.]

The Lone Wolf Strikes (feature) 1940/1/26 D: Sidney Salkow C: Alan Baxter, Astrid Allwyn, Montagu Love, Robert Wilcox, Don Beddoe, Fred A. Kelsey, Vernon Dent L: 57 minutes P/D: Columbia.

Mr. Clyde Goes to Broadway 1940/2/2 D: Del Lord C: Andy Clyde, Vivian Oakland, John T. Murray, Vernon Dent L: 2-Reels P/D: Columbia *(Broadway Comedies)*.

The Doctor Takes a Wife (feature) 1940/2/14 D: Alexander Hall C: Ray Milland, Loretta Young, Reginald Gardiner, Gail Patrick, Edmund Gwenn, Frank Sully, Gordon Jones, Vernon Dent L: 89 minutes P/D: Columbia.

The Heckler 1940/2/16 D: Del Lord C: Charley Chase, Vernon Dent, Monty Collins, Bruce Bennett, Richard Fiske, Bud Jamison, Bess Flowers, Charles "Heinie" Conklin L: 2-Reels P/D: Columbia *(Broadway Comedies)*.

Pardon My Berth Marks 1940/3/22 D: Jules White C: Buster Keaton, Dorothy Appleby, Richard Fiske, Vernon Dent L: 2-Reels P/D: Columbia *(Broadway Comedies)*.

Money Squawks 1940/4/5 D: Jules White C: Andy Clyde, Shemp Howard, Vernon Dent L: 2-Reels P/D: Columbia *(Broadway Comedies)*.

Nutty but Nice 1940/6/14 D: Jules White C: Moe Howard, Larry Fine, Curly Howard, Vernon Dent, John Tyrrell, Cy Schindell, Ned Glass, Lynton Brent, Eddie Garcia, Bert Young, Ethelreda Leopold, Lew Davis, Charles Dorety, Johnny Kascier L: 2-Reels P/D: Columbia *(Three Stooges Series)*.

His Bridal Fright 1940/7/12 D: Del Lord C: Charley Chase, Iris Meredith, Bud Jamison, Richard Fiske, Dudley Dickerson, Bruce Bennett, Vernon Dent L: 2-Reels P/D: Columbia *(Broadway Comedies)*.

How High is Up? 1940/7/26 D: Del Lord C: Moe Howard, Larry Fine, Curly Howard, Vernon Dent, Bruce Bennett, Edmund Cobb, Bert Young, Cy Schindell L: 2-Reels P/D: Columbia *(Three Stooges Series)*.

The Lady in Question (feature) 1940/8/7 D: Charles Vidor C: Brian Aherne, Rita Hayworth, Glenn Ford, Irene Rich, Evelyn Keyes, Edward Norris, Vernon Dent, William Castle, Jack Rice L: 80 minutes P/D: Columbia.

From Nurse to Worse 1940/8/23 D: Jules White C: Moe Howard, Larry Fine, Curly Howard, Vernon Dent, Lynton Brent, John Tyrrell, Dorothy Appleby, Cy Schindell, Marjorie "Babe" Kane, Joe Palma, Dudley Dickerson, Al Thompson, Blanche Payson L: 2-Reels P/D: Columbia *(Three Stooges Series)*.

He Stayed for Breakfast (feature) 1940/8/31 D: Alexander Hall C: Loretta Young, Melvyn Douglas, Alan Marshal, Eugene Pallette, Una O'Connor, Curt Bois, Grady Sutton, Frank Sully, Vernon Dent L: 89 minutes P/D: Columbia. [Note: Vernon Dent has an uncredited role as a chef.]

No Census, No Feeling 1940/10/4 D: Del Lord C: Moe Howard, Larry Fine, Curly Howard, Vernon Dent, Symona Boniface, Marjorie "Babe" Kane, Max Davidson, Bruce Bennett, Bert Young L: 2-Reels P/D: Columbia *(Three Stooges Series)*.

The Villain Still Pursued Her (feature) 1940/10/11 D: Edward Cline C: Billy Gilbert, Anita Louise, Margaret Hamilton, Alan Mowbray, Richard Cromwell, Joyce Compton, Buster Keaton, Diane Fisher, Hugh Herbert, Franklin Pangborn, Charles Judels L: 66 minutes P: Franklin-Blank Productions DIST: RKO.

Cold Turkey 1940/10/18 D: Del Lord C: Harry Langdon, Ann Doran, Monty Collins, Bud Jamison, Vernon Dent L: 2-Reels P/D: Columbia *(All-Star Comedies)*.

A Bundle of Bliss 1940/11/1 D: Jules White C: Andy Clyde, Esther Howard, Dorothy Appleby, Fred Kelsey, Vernon Dent, Blanche Payson L: 2-Reels P/D: Columbia *(All-Star Comedies)*.

Blondes and Blunders 1940/11/29 D: Del Lord C: Walter Catlett, Billy Gilbert, Vernon Dent, Ann Doran, Marion Martin, Bud Jamison L: 2-Reels P/D: Columbia *(All-Star Comedies)*.

Fresh as a Freshman 1941/1/29 D: Jules White C: David Durand, Paul Hurst, Wally Vernon, Dorothy Vaughn, Adele Pearce, Rita Rio, Vernon Dent L: 2-Reels P/D: Columbia *(Glove Slingers Series)*.

So Long, Mr. Chumps 1941/2/7 D: Jules White C: Moe Howard, Larry Fine, Curly Howard, Vernon Dent, Eddie Laughton, Dorothy Appleby, John Tyrrell, Bruce Bennett, Bert Young L: 2-Reels P/D: Columbia *(Three Stooges Series)*.

You're the One (feature) 1941/2/19 D: Ralph Murphy C: Bonnie Baker, Orrin Tucker, Albert Dekker, Edward Everett Horton, Jerry Colonna, Walter Catlett, Charles Lane, Vernon Dent L: 83 minutes P/D: Paramount.

So You Won't Squawk 1941/2/21 D: Del Lord C: Buster Keaton, Eddie Fetherstone, Bud Jamison, Matt McHugh, Vernon Dent, Hank Mann L: 2-Reels P/D: Columbia *(All-Star Comedies)*.

Yumpin' Yimminy! 1941/3/7 D: Jules White C: El Brendel, Fred Kelsey, Don Brody, Vernon Dent, Dorothy Appleby L: 2-Reels P/D: Columbia *(All-Star Comedies)*.

Dutiful but Dumb 1941/3/21 D: Del Lord C: Moe Howard, Larry Fine, Curly Howard, Vernon Dent, Bud Jamison, Fred Kelsey, Chester Conklin L: 2-Reels P/D: Columbia *(Three Stooges Series)*.

Glove Affair 1941/4/4 D: Jules White C: David Durand, Dorothy Vaughn, Paul Hurst, Roscoe Ates, Vernon Dent L: 2-Reels P/D: Columbia *(Glove Slingers Series)*.

The Ring and the Belle 1941/5/2 D: Del Lord C: Andy Clyde, Vivian Oakland, Dudley Dickerson, Vernon Dent L: 2-Reels P/D: Columbia *(Broadway Comedies)*.

Meet John Doe (feature) 1941/5/3 D: Frank Capra C: Gary Cooper, Barbara Stanwyck, Edward Arnold, Walter Brennan, Spring Byington, James Gleason, Gene Lockhart, Vernon Dent L: 132 minutes P/D: Warner Bros.

Adventure in Washington (feature) 1941/5/29 D: Alfred E. Green C: Herbert Marshall, Virginia Bruce, Gene Reynolds, Samuel Hinds, Ralph Morgan, Charles Smith, Dickie Jones, Tommy Bonds, Bess Flowers, Vernon Dent *(uncredited man in gymnasium)* L: 84 minutes P/D: Columbia

Yankee Doodle Andy 1941/6/13 D: Jules White C: Andy Clyde, Dorothy Appleby, Tom Kennedy, Vernon Dent, Bud Jamison L: 2-Reels P/D: Columbia *(All-Star Comedies)*.

San Antonio Rose (feature) 1941/6/20 D: Charles Lamont C: Robert Paige, Jane Frazee, Eve Arden, Lon Chaney, Jr., Shemp Howard, The Merry Macs, Richard Lane, Luis Alberni, Luis DaPron, Vernon Dent L: 63 minutes P/D: Universal.

I'll Never Heil Again 1941/7/11 D: Jules White C: Moe Howard, Larry Fine, Curly Howard, Vernon Dent L: 2-Reels P/D: Columbia *(Three Stooges Series)*.

Host to a Ghost 1941/8/8 D: Del Lord C: Andy Clyde, Dudley Dickerson, Monty Collins, Lew Kelly, Vernon Dent L: 2-Reels P/D: Columbia *(All-Star Comedies)*.

An Ache in Every Stake 1941/8/24 D: Del Lord C: Moe Howard, Larry Fine, Curly Howard, Vernon Dent, Bess Flowers, Symona Boniface, Bud Jamison, Gino Corrado, Blanche Payson L: 2-Reels P/D: Columbia *(Three Stooges Series)*.

Half Shot at Sunrise 1941/9/4 D: Del Lord C: Roscoe Karns, Ann Doran, Marion Martin, Bobby Larson, Vernon Dent, Bess Flowers, Bud Jamison, Monty Collins L: 2-Reels P/D: Columbia *(All-Star Comedies)*.

In the Sweet Pie and Pie 1941/10/16 D: Jules White C: Moe Howard, Larry Fine, Curly Howard, Vernon Dent, Dorothy Appleby, Mary Ainslee, Ethelreda Leopold, Richard Fiske, Symona Boniface L: 2-Reels P/D: Columbia *(Three Stooges Series)*.

Lovable Trouble 1941/10/23 D: Del Lord C: Andy Clyde, Ann Doran, Esther Howard, Luana Walters, Vernon Dent L: 2-Reels P/D: Columbia *(All-Star Comedies)*.

Sweet Spirits of the Nighter 1941/12/25 D: Del Lord C: El Brendel, Tom Kennedy, Lew Kelly, Frank Lackteen, Duke York, Vernon Dent, Bud Jamison, Hank Mann L: 2-Reels P/D: Columbia *(El Brendel Series)*.

Bedtime Story (feature) 1941/12/25 D: Alexander Hall C: Frederic March, Loretta Young, Robert Benchley, Allyn Joslyn, Eve Arden, Helen Westley, Joyce Compton, Tim Ryan, Clarence Kolb, Vernon Dent L: 85 minutes P/D: Columbia.

Loco Boy Makes Good 1942/1/8 D: Jules White C: Moe Howard, Larry Fine, Curly Howard, Vernon Dent, Dorothy Appleby, John Tyrrell, Eddie Laughton, Bud Jamison L: 2-Reels P/D: Columbia *(Three Stooges Series)*.

Sappy Birthday 1942/2/5 D: Harry Edwards C: Andy Clyde, Matt McHugh, Esther Howard, Vernon Dent L: 2-Reels P/D: Columbia *(All-Star Comedies)*.

Cactus Makes Perfect 1942/2/26 D: Del Lord C: Moe Howard, Larry Fine, Curly Howard, Vernon Dent, Monty Collins, Ernie Adams L: 2-Reels P/D: Columbia *(Three Stooges Series)*.

My Favorite Blonde (feature) 1943/3/8 D: Sidney Lanfield C: Bob Hope, Madeleine Carroll, Gale Sondergaard, George Succor, Victor Varconi, Vernon Dent L: 78 minutes P/D: Paramount.

House of Errors (feature) 1942/4/10 D: Bernard B. Ray C: Harry Langdon, Charley Rogers, Marian Marsh, Ray Walker, John Holland, Betty Blythe, Richard Kipling, Vernon Dent L: 65 minutes P: Producers Releasing Corporation (PRC).

Matri-Phony 1942/7/2 D: Edward Bernds C: Moe Howard, Larry Fine, Curly Howard, Vernon Dent, Marjorie Deanne, Monty Collins, Cy Schindell, Al Thompson L: 2-Reels P/D: Columbia *(Three Stooges Series)*.

All Work and No Pay 1942/7/16 D: Del Lord C: Andy Clyde, Frank Lackteen, Duke York, Eddie Laughton, Vernon Dent, Blanche Payson, Bud Jamison L: 2-Reels P/D: Columbia *(All-Star Comedies)*.

Three Smart Saps 1942/7/30 D: Jules White C: Moe Howard, Larry Fine, Curly Howard, Vernon Dent, Barbara Slater, Ruth Skinner, Julie Gibson, Julie Duncan, Bud Jamison, John Tyrrell, Sally Cairns, Frank Terry L: 2-Reels P/D: Columbia *(Three Stooges Series)*.

Even As I. O. U. 1942/9/18 D: Del Lord C: Moe Howard, Larry Fine, Curly Howard, Vernon Dent, Ruth Skinner, Stanley Blystone, Wheaton Chambers, Bud Jamison, Charles "Heinie" Conklin, Jack Gardner, Billy Bletcher L: 2-Reels P/D: Columbia *(Three Stooges Series)*.

Sappy Pappy 1942/10/30 D: Harry Edwards C: Andy Clyde, Vivian Oakland, Vernon Dent L: 2-Reels P/D: Columbia *(All-Star Comedies)*.

The Glass Key (feature) 1942/10/23 D: Stuart Heisler C: Brian Donlevy, Alan Ladd, Veronica Lake, William Bendix, Bonita Granville, Richard Denning, Joseph Calleia, Vernon Dent L: 85 minutes P/D: Paramount.

They Stooge to Conga 1943/1/1 D: Del Lord C: Moe Howard, Larry Fine, Curly Howard, Vernon Dent, John Tyrrell, Dudley Dickerson, Lloyd Bridges, Stanley Brown L: 2-Reels P/D: Columbia *(Three Stooges Series)*.

His Wedding Scare 1943/1/15 D: Del Lord C: El Brendel, Louise Currie, Monty Collins, Vernon Dent, Dudley Dickerson, Lloyd Bridges, Stanley Blystone L: 2-Reels P/D: Columbia *(El Brendel Series)*.

A Blitz on the Fritz 1943/1/22 D: Jules White C: Harry Langdon, Louise Currie, Douglas Leavitt, Bud Jamison, Vernon Dent, Jack Lipson, Blanche Payson, Joe Palma, Stanley Blystone, Bud Fine L: 2-Reels P/D: Columbia *(All-Star Comedies)*.

Wolf in Thief's Clothing 1943/2/12 D: Jules White C: Andy Clyde, Emmett Lynn, Esther Howard, Stanley Brown, Spec O'Donnell, Bud Jamison, Esther Howard, Stanley Brown, Bud Jamison, Vernon Dent L: 2-Reels P/D: Columbia *(All-Star Comedies)*.

A Maid Made Mad 1943/3/19 D: Del Lord C: Andy Clyde, Barbara Pepper, Gwen Kenyon, Vernon Dent, Blanche Payson L: 2-Reels P/D: Columbia *(All-Star Comedies)*.

I Spied for You 1943/4/30 D: Jules White C: El Brendel, Vernon Dent, Kathryn Keys, Bud Jamison, Stanley Blystone, Barbara Slater L: 2-Reels P/D: Columbia *(El Brendel Series)*.

Back From the Front 1943/5/28 D: Jules White C: Moe Howard, Larry Fine, Curly Howard, Vernon Dent, Bud Jamison, Adele Mara, Stanley Blystone, Heinie Conklin L: 2-Reels P/D: Columbia *(Three Stooges Series)*.

Here Comes Mr. Zerk 1943/7/23 D: Jules White C: Harry Langdon, Shirley Patterson, John T. Murray, Fred Kelsey, Bob McKenzie, Dudley Dickerson, Hank Mann, Vernon Dent, Charles "Heinie" Conklin, Eva McKenzie, Blanche Payson, Joyce Gardner L: 2-Reels P/D: Columbia *(All-Star Comedies)*.

Higher Than a Kite 1943/7/30 D: Del Lord C: Moe Howard, Larry Fine, Curly Howard, Vernon Dent, Dick Curtis, Duke York, Johnny Kascier L: 2-Reels P/D Columbia *(Three Stooges Series)*.

Farmer for a Day 1943/8/20 D: Jules White C: Andy Clyde, Betty Blythe, Douglas Leavitt, Adele Mara, Vernon Dent L: 2-Reels P/D: Columbia *(All-Star Comedies)*.

Quack Service 1943/9/3 D: Harry Edwards C: Una Merkel, Gwen Kenyon, Monty Collins, Dudley Dickerson, Blanche Payson, Vernon Dent, Bud Jamison, Snub Pollard, Stanley Brown L: 2-Reels P/D: Columbia *(All-Star Comedies)*.

Garden of Eatin' 1943/10/22 D: Harry Edwards C: Slim Summerville, Bobby Larson, Chester Conklin, Marjorie Kane, Christine McIntyre, Snub Pollard, Vernon Dent L: 2-Reels P/D: Columbia *(All-Star Comedies)*.

Who's Hugh? 1943/12/17 D: Harry Edwards C: Hugh Herbert, Christine McIntyre, Constance Worth, Eddie Gribbon, George Lewis, Charlie Hall, Vernon Dent, Fred Kelsey, Joe Palma, Fred Toones L: 2-Reels P/D: Columbia *(All-Star Comedies)*.

Cowboy in the Clouds (feature) 1943/12/23 D: Benjamin H. Kline C: Charles Starrett, Dick Curtis, Dub Taylor, Julie Duncan, Jimmy Wakely, Charles King, Vernon Dent, Davison Clark L: 54 minutes P/D: Columbia.

True to Life (feature) 1943/12/24 D: George Marshall C: Mary Martin, Franchot Tone, Dick Powell, Victor Moore, Mabel Paige, William Demarest, Ernest Truex, Vernon Dent L: 94 minutes P/D: Paramount.

To Heir is Human 1944/1/14 D: Harold Godsoe C: Una Merkel, Harry Langdon, Christine McIntyre, Vernon Dent L: 2-Reels P/D: Columbia *(All-Star Comedies)*.

Chip Off the Old Block (feature) 1944/2/1 D: Charles Lamont C: Donald O'Connor, Peggy Ryan, Ann Blyth, Helen Vinson, Helen Broderick, Arthur Treacher, Vernon Dent L: 71 minutes P/D: Universal.

Crash Goes the Hash 1944/2/5 D: Jules White C: Moe Howard, Larry Fine, Curly Howard, Vernon Dent, Dick Curtis, Symona Boniface, John Tyrrell, Johnny Kascier, Wally Rose, Judy Malcolm, Victor Travers, Beatrice Blinn, Ida Mae Johnson, Elise Grover L: 2-Reels P/D: Columbia *(Three Stooges Series)*.

Bachelor Daze 1944/2/17 D: Jules White C: Slim Summerville, Emmett Lynn, Minerva Urecal, Vernon Dent, Victor Travers, Al Thompson, Frank Sully L: 2-Reels P/D: Columbia *(All-Star Comedies)*.

His Tale is Told 1944/3/4 D: Harry Edwards C: Andy Clyde, Vernon Dent, Christine McIntyre, Ann Doran, Mabel Forrest, Bud Jamison, Charles "Heinie" Conklin, Jack Norton, Snub Pollard L: 2-Reels P/D: Columbia *(All-Star Comedies)*.

Busy Buddies 1944/3/18 D: Del Lord C: Moe Howard, Larry Fine, Curly Howard, Vernon Dent, Fred Kelsey, Eddie Gribbon, John Tyrrell, Eddie Laughton, Victor Travers, Johnny Kascier L: 2-Reels P/D: Columbia *(Three Stooges Series)*.

Her Primitive Man (feature) 1944/3/30 D: Charles Lamont C: Louise Albritton, Robert Paige, Robert Benchley, Edward Everett Horton, Helen Broderick, Stephanie Bachelor, Walter Catlett, Irving Bacon, Vernon Dent L: 79 Minutes P/D: Universal.

Defective Detectives 1944/4/3 D: Harry Edwards C: Harry Langdon, Vernon Dent, Christine McIntyre, John Tyrrell, Eddie Laughton, Snub Pollard, Dick Botiller L: 2-Reels P/D: Columbia *(All-Star Comedies)*.

Jam Session (feature) 1944/4/13 D: Charles Barton C: Ann Miller, Jess Barker, Charles Brown, Eddie Kane, Louis Armstrong, Duke Ellington, Glen Gray, Teddy Powell, Charlie Barnet, Nan Wynn, Pied Pipers, Vernon Dent L: 77 minutes P/D: Columbia.

Address Unknown (feature) 1944/6/1 D: William Cameron Menzies C: Paul Lukas, Carl Esmond, Peter van Eyck, Mady Christians, Morris Carnovsky, Frank Faylen, Vernon Dent L: 75 minutes P/D: Columbia.

Once Upon a Time (feature) 1944/6/29 D: Alexander Hall C: Cary Grant, Janet Blair, James Gleason, Ted Donaldson, Art Baker, Vernon Dent L: 89 minutes P/D: Columbia.

Idle Roomers 1944/7/16 D: Del Lord C: Moe Howard, Larry Fine, Curly Howard, Vernon Dent, Christine McIntyre, Duke York, Eddie Laughton, Joanne Frank, Esther Howard L: 2-Reels P/D: Columbia *(Three Stooges Series)*.

Secret Command (feature) 1944/7/30 D: A. Edward Sutherland C: Pat O'Brien, Carole Landis, Chester Morris, Ruth Warrick, Barton MacLane, Tom Tully, Wallace Ford, Frank Sully, Vernon Dent L: 82 minutes P/D: Columbia.

Wedded Bliss 1944/8/18 D: Harry Edwards C: Billy Gilbert, Christine McIntyre, Vernon Dent L: 2-Reels P/D: Columbia *(All-Star Comedies)*.

Kansas City Kitty (feature) 1944/8/24 D: Del Lord C: Joan Davis, Bob Crosby, Jane Frazee, Erik Rolf, Tim Ryan, Christine McIntyre, Vernon Dent, Bud Jamison, Doodles Weaver, Andy Williams L: 71 minutes P/D: Columbia. [Note: Vernon and Bud Jamison are repo men from A-1 Piano Company.]

San Diego, I Love You (feature) 1944/9/29 D: Reginald Le Borg C: Jon Hall, Louise Allbritton, Edward Everett Horton, Eric Blore, Buster Keaton, Irene Ryan, Florence Lake, Rudy Wissler, Peter Miles, Vernon Dent L: 83 minutes P/D: Universal.

Bonnie Lassie 1944/10/6 D: William Shea C: David Brooks, Gloria Saunders, Joan Woodbury, Mary Gordon, Alec Craig, David Clyde, John Miller, Johnny Coy, Vernon Dent L: 2-Reels P/D: Paramount.

Strife of the Party 1944/10/13 D: Harry Edwards C: Vera Vague, Lorin Raker, Joe Forte, Gwen Donovan, Vernon Dent, Symona Boniface, Joe Palma, Charles "Heinie" Conklin L: 2-Reels P/D: Columbia *(All-Star Comedies)*.

No Dough Boys 1944/11/24 D: Jules White C: Moe Howard, Larry Fine, Curly Howard, Vernon Dent, Christine McIntyre, Kelly Flint, Judy Malcolm L: 2-Reels P/D: Columbia *(Three Stooges Series)*.

Heather and Yon 1944/12/8 D: Harry Edwards C: Andy Clyde, Isabel Withers, Jack Norton, Vernon Dent, Snub Pollard, Charles "Heinie" Conklin L: 2-Reels P/D: Columbia *(All-Star Comedies)*.

She Snoops to Conquer 1944/12/29 D: Jules White C: Vera Vague, Weldon Heyburn Vernon Dent L: 2-Reels P/D: Columbia *(All-Star Comedies)*.

Let's Go Steady (feature) 1945/1/4 D: Del Lord C: Pat Parrish, Jackie Moran, June Preisser, Jimmy Lloyd, Arnold Stang, Mel Torme, Vernon Dent L: 60 minutes P/D: Columbia.

She Gets Her Man (feature) 1945/1/12 D: Erle C. Kenton C: Joan Davis, William Gargan, Leon Errol, Vivian Austin, Milburn Stone, Russell Hicks, Donald MacBride, Paul Stanton, Vernon Dent L: 65 minutes P/D: Universal.

Three Pests in a Mess 1945/1/19 D: Del Lord C: Moe Howard, Larry Fine, Curly Howard, Vernon Dent, Christine McIntyre, Brian O'Hara, Snub Pollard, Robert Williams, Charles "Heinie" Conklin L: 2-Reels P/D: Columbia *(Three Stooges Series)*.

Sagebrush Heroes (feature) 1945/2/1 D: Benjamin H. Kline C: Charles Starrett, Dub Taylor, Constance Worth, Paul Conrad, Eddie Laughton, Vernon Dent L: 54 minutes P/D: Columbia.

Snooper Service 1945/2/2 D: Harry Edwards C: Harry Langdon, El Brendel, Vernon Dent, Dick Curtis, Fred Kelsey L: 2-Reels P/D: Columbia *(All-Star Comedies)*.

Sing Me a Song of Texas (feature) 1945/2/8 D: Vernon Keays C: Rosemary Lane, Hal McIntyre, Tom Tyler, Slim Summerville, Noah Beery, Pinky Tomlin, Vernon Dent L: 66 minutes P/D: Columbia.

See My Lawyer 1945/3/9 *(feature)* D: Edward F. Cline C: Ole Olsen, Chic Johnson, Alan Curtis, Grace McDonald, Noah Beery Jr., Franklin Pangborn, Gus Schilling, Vernon Dent L: 67 minutes P/D: Universal.

Booby Dupes 1945/3/17 D: Del Lord C: Moe Howard, Larry Fine, Curly Howard, Vernon Dent, Rebel Randall, John Tyrrell, Dorothy Vernon Dent, Snub Pollard L: 2-Reels P/D: Columbia *(Three Stooges Series)*.

Having Wonderful Crime (feature) 1945/4/12 D: A. Edward Sutherland C: Pat O'Brien, George Murphy, Carole Landis, Lenore Aubert, George Zucco, Vernon Dent L: 70 minutes P/D: RKO

Rockin' in the Rockies (feature) 1945/4/17 D: Vernon Keays C: Moe Howard, Larry Fine, Curly Howard, Mary Beth Hughes, Jay Kirby, Gladys Blake, Tim Ryan, Jack Clifford, Forrest Taylor, Vernon Dent, The Hoosier Hotshots, The Cappy Barra Boys, and Spade Cooley L: 63 minutes P/D: Columbia.

The Jury Goes Round 'N' Round 1945/6/1 D: Jules White C: Vera Vague, Barton Yarborough, Judy Malcolm, Joe Palma, Vernon Dent, June Bryde (Gittelson) L: 2-Reels P/D: Columbia *(All-Star Comedies)*. [Note: Vernon sings in this short.]

Idiots Deluxe 1945/7/20 D: Jules White C: Moe Howard, Larry Fine, Curly Howard, Vernon Dent, Paul Kruger, Eddie Laughton L: 2-Reels P/D: Columbia *(Three Stooges Series).*

I Love a Bandleader (feature) 1945/9/13 D: Del Lord C: Phil Harris, Eddie "Rochester" Anderson, Leslie Brooks, Walter Catlett, Frank Sully, Vernon Dent L: 70 minutes P/D: Columbia.

Song of the Prairie (feature) 1945/9/27 D: Ray Nazarro C: Ken Curtis, June Storey, Andy Clyde, Guinn "Big Boy" Williams, Jeff Donnell, Grady Sutton, Thurston Hall, Vernon Dent L: 62 minutes P/D: Columbia.

The Mayor's Husband 1945/9/20 D: Harry Edwards C: Hugh Herbert, Christine McIntyre, Vernon Dent, Robert Williams, Dick Curtis L: 2-Reels P/D: Columbia *(All-Star Comedies).* [Note: Vernon receives writing credit.]

Nob Hill 1945/11/15 *(feature)* D: Henry Hathaway C: George Raft, Joan Bennett, Vivian Blaine, Peggy Ann Garner, Alan Reed, Vernon Dent L: 95 Minutes P/D: 20th Century Fox.

Snafu (feature) 1945/11/2 D: Jack Moss C: Robert Benchley, Barbara Jo Allen, Conrad Janis, Nanette Parks, Janis Wilson, Jimmy Lloyd, Vernon Dent L: 85 Minutes P/D: Columbia.

Calling All Fibbers 1945/11/29 D: Jules White C: Vera Vague, Etta McDaniel, Frank Sully, Vernon Dent, John Tyrrell L: 2-Reels P/D: Columbia *(All-Star Comedies).*

High Blood Pleasure 1945/12/6 D: Jules White C: Gus Schilling, Richard Lane, Vernon Dent, Lynton Brent, Harry Semels, Symona Boniface, Johnny Kascier, Victor Travers L: 2-Reels P/D: Columbia *(All-Star Comedies).*

Beer Barrel Polecats 1946/1/10 D: Jules White C: Moe Howard, Larry Fine, Curly Howard, Vernon Dent, Eddie Laughton, Robert Williams, Bruce Bennett, Joe Palma, Al Thompson, Blackie Whiteford L: 2-Reels P/D: Columbia *(Three Stooges Series).*

The Harvey Girls (feature) 1946/1/18 D: George Sidney C: Judy Garland, John Hodiak, Ray Bolger, Angela Lansbury, Preston Foster, Virginia O'Brien, Marjorie Main, Chill Wills, Selena Royle, Cyd Charisse, Vernon Dent L: 102 minutes P/D: MGM. [Note: Vernon's singing part was dubbed by another actor.]

The Blonde Stayed On 1946/1/24 D: Harry Edwards C: Andy Clyde, Christine McIntyre, Gladys Blake, Vernon Dent L: 2-Reels P/D: Columbia *(All-Star Comedies).*

When the Wife's Away 1946/2/1 D: Edward Bernds C: Hugh Herbert, Vernon Dent, Christine McIntyre, Frank "Billy" Mitchell L: 2-Reels P/D: Columbia *(All-Star Comedies).*

A Bird in the Head 1946/2/28 D: Edward Bernds C: Moe Howard, Larry Fine, Curly Howard, Vernon Dent, Robert Williams, Frank Lackteen, Art Miles L: 2-Reels P/D: Columbia *(Three Stooges Series).*

Mr. Noisy 1946/3/22 D: Edward Bernds C: Shemp Howard, Vernon Dent, Matt Willis, Brian O'Hara, Walter Soderling, Daniel Kerry, Wally Rose, John Ince, Claire James, Marilyn Johnson, Don Gordon, Bess Flowers L: 2-Reels P/D: Columbia *(All-Star Comedies).*

Night Editor (feature) 1946/3/29 D: Henry Levin C: William Gargan, Janis Carter, Jeff Donnell, Coulter Irwin, Charles D. Brown, Paul E. Burns, Harry Shannon, Frank Wilcox, Anthony Caruso, Vernon Dent L: 68 Minutes P/D: Columbia.

That Texas Jamboree (feature) 1946/5/16 D: Ray Nazarro C: Ken Curtis, Jeff Donnell, Andy Clyde, Carolina Cotton, Vernon Dent L: 59 Minutes P/D: Columbia.

Renegades (feature) 1946/6/13 D: George Sherman C: Larry Parks, Edgar Buchanan, Forrest Tucker, Frank Sully, Evelyn Keyes, Willard Parker, Jim Bannon, Vernon Dent, John Hamilton, Syd Saylor, Will Stanton L: 87 Minutes P/D: Columbia.

Dangerous Business (feature) 1946/6/20 D: D. Ross Lederman C: Forrest Tucker, Lynn Merrick, Gerald Mohr, Gus Schilling, Shemp Howard, Frank Sully, Cora Witherspoon, Thurston Hall, Vernon Dent, Eddie Dunn L: 60 minutes P/D: Columbia.

You Can't Fool a Fool 1946/7/11 D: Jules White C: Andy Clyde, Fred Kelsey, Esther Howard, Charles "Heinie" Conklin, Vernon Dent, Ted Lorch L: 2-Reels P/D: Columbia *(All-Star Comedies)*.

Cowboy Blues 1946/7/18 *(feature)* D: Ray Nazarro C: Ken Curtis, Jeff Donnell, Guy Kibbee, Guinn Williams, Isabel Randolph, Mark Roberts, Vernon Dent L: 62 minutes P/D: Columbia.

Hot Water 1946/7/25 D: Edward Bernds C: Gus Schilling, Richard Lane, Christine McIntyre, Dick Curtis, Rebel Randall, Helga Storme, Judy Malcolm, Vernon Dent L: 2-Reels P/D: Columbia *(All-Star Comedies)*.

Headin' For a Weddin' 1946/8/15 D: Jules White C: Vera Vague, Claire Carleton, William Hall, Jack Rice, Vernon Dent, Joe Palma, Al Thompson, Charles "Heinie" Conklin L: 2-Reels P/D: Columbia *(All-Star Comedies)*.

Pardon My Terror 1946/9/12 D: Edward Bernds, C: Gus Schilling, Richard Lane, Christine McIntyre, Lynne Lyons, Kenneth MacDonald, Dick Wessel, Phil Van Zandt, Vernon Dent, Emil Sitka, Dudley Dickerson L: 2-Reels P/D: Columbia *(All-Star Comedies)*.

It's Great to Be Young (feature) 1946/9/12 D: Del Lord C: Leslie Brooks, Jimmy Lloyd, Jeff Donnell, Bob Haymes, Jack Williams, Jack Fina, Frank Orth, Ann Codee, Pat Yankee, Frank Sully, Vernon Dent, Grady Sutton L: 69 minutes P/D: Columbia.

Society Mugs 1946/9/19 D: Edward Bernds C: Shemp Howard, Vernon Dent, Tom Kennedy, Christine McIntyre, Rebel Randall, Charles Williams, Etta McDaniel, Bess Flowers, Gene Roth, Snub Pollard, Helen Benda L: 2-Reels P/D: Columbia *(All-Star Comedies)*.

Three Little Pirates 1946/12/5 D: Edward Bernds C: Moe Howard, Larry Fine, Curly Howard, Vernon Dent, Christine McIntyre, Robert Stevens, Dorothy DeHaven, Ethan Laidlaw, Joe Palma, Jack Parker, Larry McGrath, Al Thompson L: 2-Reels P/D: Columbia *(Three Stooges Series)*.

Lone Star Moonlight (feature) 1946/12/12 D: Ray Nazzarro C: Ken Curtis, Joan Barton, Guy Kibbee, Robert Kellard, Claudia Drake, Arthur Loft, Vernon Dent L: 67 minutes P/D: Columbia.

Half-Wits Holiday 1947/1/9 D: Jules White C: Moe Howard, Larry Fine, Curly Howard, Vernon Dent, Barbara Slater, Ted Lorch, Emil Sitka, Symona Boniface, Al Thompson, Johnny Kascier L: 2-Reels P/D: Columbia *(Three Stooges Series)*.

Meet Mr. Mischief 1947/1/23 D: Edward Bernds C: Harry Von Zell, Ralf Harolde, Christine McIntyre, Charles Wilson, Dudley Dickerson, Emil Sitka, Phil Arnold, Fred Kelsey, Vernon Dent L: 2-Reels P/D: Columbia *(All-Star Comedies)*.

Nervous Shakedown 1947/3/13 D: Del Lord C: Hugh Herbert, Dudley Dickerson, Kenneth, MacDonald, Dick Wessel, Frank Lackteen, Vernon Dent L: 2-Reels P/D: Columbia *(All-Star Comedies)*.

The Good Bad Egg 1947/3/20 D: Jules White C: Joe DeRita, Symona Boniface, Bobby Burns, Lew Davis, Vernon Dent L: 2-Reels P/D: Columbia: *(All-Star Comedies)*.

Bride and Gloom 1947/3/27 D: Edward Bernds C: Shemp Howard, Christine McIntyre, Jean Donahue, Dick Curtis, Vernon Dent, Emil Sitka, Vernon Dent L: 2-Reels P/D: Columbia *(All-Star Comedies)*.

Two Jills and a Jack 1947/4/14 D: Jules White C: Andy Clyde, Christine McIntyre, Vernon Dent L: 2-Reels P/D: Columbia *(All-Star Comedies)*.

Out West 1947/4/24 D: Edward Bernds C: Moe Howard, Larry Fine, Shemp Howard, Vernon Dent, Christine McIntyre, Jacques O'Mahoney, Jack Norman, Stanley Blystone, George Chesebro, Frank Ellis, Charles "Heinie" Conklin, Blackie Whiteford L: 2-Reels P/D: Columbia *(Three Stooges Series)*.

The Sea of Grass (feature) 1947/4/25 D: Elia Kazan C: Spencer Tracy, Katharine Hepburn, Melvyn Douglas, Phyllis Thaxter, Edgar Buchanan, Harry Carey, Robert Armstrong, Vernon Dent L: 123 minutes P/D: MGM.

Wedding Belle 1947/8/9 D: Edward Bernds C: Gus Schilling, Richard Lane, Christine McIntyre, Lynne Lyons, Sammy Stein, Billy Curtis, Symona Boniface, Judy Malcolm, Vernon Dent L: 2-Reels P/D: Columbia *(All-Star Comedies)*.

The Secret Life of Walter Mitty (feature) 1947/9/1 D: Norman Z. McLeod C: Danny Kaye, Virginia Mayo, Boris Karloff, Vernon Dent L: 110 minutes P/D: Goldwyn/RKO.

Wild Harvest (feature) 1947/9/26 D: Tay Garnett C: Alan Ladd, Dorothy Lamour, Robert Preston, Lloyd Nolan, Richard Erdman, Allen Jenkins, Will Wright, Griff Barnett, Anthony Caruso, Vernon Dent L: 92 minutes P/D: Paramount.

Merton of the Movies (feature) 1947/10/11 D: Robert Alton C: Red Skelton, Virginia O'Brien, Gloria Grahame, Leon Ames L: 82 minutes P/D: MGM. [Note: Vernon Dent, Chester Conklin and Heinie Conklin have cameos as Keystone Cops.]

It Had to be You (feature) 1947/10/22 D: Don Hartman C: Ginger Rogers, Cornel Wilde, Percy Waram, Spring Byington, Ron Randell, Vernon Dent L: 98 minutes P/D: Columbia.

Sing a Song of Six Pants 1947/10/30 D: Jules White C: Moe Howard, Larry Fine, Shemp Howard, Vernon Dent, Virginia Hunter, Harold Brauer, Phil Arnold, Cy Schindell L: 2-Reels P/D: Columbia *(Three Stooges Series)*.

Should Husbands Marry? 1947/11/13 D: Del Lord C: Hugh Herbert, Christine McIntyre, Matt McHugh, Marion Martin, Dudley Dickerson, Dorothy Granger, Vernon Dent L: 2-Reels P/D: Columbia *(All-Star Comedies)*.

Shivering Sherlocks 1948/1/8 D: Del Lord C: Moe Howard, Larry Fine, Shemp Howard, Vernon Dent, Christine McIntyre, Kenneth MacDonald, Frank Lackteen, Duke York, Stanley Blystone, Joe Palma L: 2-Reels P/D: Columbia *(Three Stooges Series)*.

Two Nuts in a Rut 1948/2/19 D: Edward Bernds C: Gus Schilling, Richard Lane, Christine McIntyre, Dick Wessel, Claire Carleton, Lynne Lyons, Symona Boniface, Vernon Dent, Emil Sitka, Ted Stanhope, Johnny Kascier L: 2-Reels P/D: Columbia *(All-Star Comedies)*.

Squareheads of the Round Table 1948/3/4 D: Edward Bernds C: Moe Howard, Larry Fine, Shemp Howard, Vernon Dent, Christine McIntyre, Jacques O'Mahoney, Phil Van Zandt, Harold Brauer, Joe Palma, Douglas Coppin, Joe Garcia L: 2-Reels P/D: Columbia *(Three Stooges Series)*.

Eight-Ball Andy 1948/3/11 D: Edward Bernds C: Andy Clyde, Vernon Dent, Dick Wessel, Christine McIntyre, Lucille Browne, Vera Lewis, Murray Alper, Emil Sitka, Charles "Heinie" Conklin L: 2-Reels P/D: Columbia *(All-Star Comedies)*.

Fiddlers Three 1948/5/6 D: Jules White C: Moe Howard, Larry Fine, Shemp Howard, Vernon Dent, Phil Van Zandt, Virginia Hunter, Joe Palma, Sherry O'Neil, Cy Schindell, Al Thompson L: 2-Reels P/D: Columbia *(Three Stooges Series)*.

The Sheepish Wolf 1948/5/27 D: Edward Bernds C: Harry Von Zell, Christine McIntyre, George Lewis, Lynne Lyons, Lennie Bremen, Harry O. Tyler, Vernon Dent, Emil Sitka, Symona Boniface, Fred Sears, Red Breen Victor Travers L: 2-Reels P/D: Columbia *(All-Star Comedies)*.

Heavenly Daze 1948/9/2 D: Jules White C: Moe Howard, Larry Fine, Shemp Howard, Vernon Dent, Sam McDaniel, Symona Boniface, Victor Travers, Marti Shelton, Judy Malcolm L: 2-Reels P/D: Columbia *(Three Stooges Series)*.

Mummy's Dummies 1948/11/4 D: Edward Bernds C: Moe Howard, Larry Fine, Shemp Howard, Vernon Dent, Ralph Dunn, Phil Van Zandt, Dee Green, Jean Spangler, Virginia Ellsworth, Suzanne Ridgeway, Cy Malis, Vivian Mason L: 2-Reels P/D: Columbia *(Three Stooges Series)*.

A Pinch in Time 1948/11/11 D: Del Lord C: Hugh Herbert, Christine McIntyre, Matt McHugh, Kenneth MacDonald, Symona Boniface, Vernon Dent, Lynne Lyons, Emil Sitka, Charles "Heinie" Conklin, Robert Williams, Chester Conklin L: 2-Reels P/D: Columbia *(All-Star Comedies)*.

Parlor, Bedroom and Wrath 1948/12/16 D: Jules White C: Wally Vernon, Eddie Quillan, Christine McIntyre, Billy Gray, Laura Lee Michel, Lonnie Thomas, Vernon Dent L: 2-Reels P/D: Columbia *(All-Star Comedies)*.

He's in Again 1949/1/13 D: Edward Bernds C: Gus Schilling, Richard Lane, Christine McIntyre, Vernon Dent, Robert Williams, Jack Overman L: 2-Reels P/D: Columbia *(All-Star Comedies)*.

Make Believe Ballroom (feature) 1949/4/1 D: Joseph Stanley C: Jerome Courtland, Ruth Warrick, Virginia Welles, Al Jarvis, Frankie Laine, Nat "King" Cole, Jimmy Dorsey, Toni Harper, Kay Starr, Vernon Dent L: 79 minutes P/D: Columbia.

Trapped by a Blonde 1949/4/7 D: Del Lord C: Hugh Herbert, Christie McIntyre, Matt McHugh, Robert Williams, Vernon Dent, Jack Overman L: 2-Reels P/D: Columbia. *(All-Star Comedies)*.

A Connecticut Yankee in King Arthur's Court (feature) 1949/4/22 D: Tay Garnett C: Bing Crosby, Rhonda Fleming, Cedric Hardwicke, William Bendix, Murvyn Vye, Vernon Dent, Babe London L: 106 minutes P/D: Paramount.

Hokus Pokus 1949/5/5 D: Jules White C: Moe Howard, Larry Fine, Shemp Howard, Vernon Dent, Mary Ainslee, David Bond, Jimmy Lloyd, Ned Glass L: 2-Reels P/D: Columbia *(Three Stooges Series)*.

The Doolins of Oklahoma (feature) 1949/5/27 D: Gordon Douglas
C: Randolph Scott, George Macready, Louise Albritton, John Ireland,
Virginia Huston, Charles Kemper, Noah Beery Jr., Lee Patrick, Jock
Mahoney, Vernon Dent, Eddie Dunn L: 90 minutes DIST: Columbia.

Fuelin' Around 1949/7/7 D: Edward Bernds C: Moe Howard, Larry
Fine, Shemp Howard, Vernon Dent, Christine McIntyre, Emil Sitka,
Phil Van Zandt, Jacques O'Mahoney, Harold Brauer, Andre Pola
L: 2-Reels P/D: Columbia *(Three Stooges Series)*.

Clunked in the Clink 1949/7/13 D: Jules White C: Vera Vague,
Christine McIntyre, Douglas Fowley, Vernon Dent L: 2-Reels
P/D: Columbia *(All-Star Comedies)*.

The Girl from Jones Beach (feature) 1949/7/16 D: Peter Godfrey
C: Ronald Reagan, Virginia Mayo, Eddie Bracken, Dona Drake, Henry
Travers, Paul Harvey, Vernon Dent L: 78 Minutes P/D: Warner Bros.

Malice in the Palace 1949/9/1 D: Jules White C: Moe Howard, Larry
Fine, Shemp Howard, Vernon Dent, George Lewis, Frank Lackteen,
Johnny Kascier L: 2-Reels P/D: Columbia *(Three Stooges Series)*.

Waiting in the Lurch 1949/9/8 D: Edward Bernds C: Joe Besser,
Vernon Dent, Christine McIntyre, Rodney Bell, Andre Pola, James
Logan, Charles Hamilton, Joe Palma L: 2-Reels P/D: Columbia *(All-Star Comedies)*.

Super-Wolf 1949/10/13 D: Del Lord C: Hugh Herbert, Christine
McIntyre, Jack Rice, Henry Kulky, Vernon Dent L: 2-Reels
P/D: Columbia *(All-Star Comedies)*.

Let Down Your Aerial 1949/11/17 D: Edward Bernds C: Wally
Vernon, Eddie Quillan, Jean Willes, Matt McHugh, Vernon Dent,
Stanley Blystone L: 2-Reels P/D: Columbia *(All-Star Comedies)*.

And Baby Makes Three (feature) 1949/12/2 D: Henry Levin C: Robert
Young, Barbara Hale, Robert Hutton, James Carter, Billie Burke, Lloyd
Corrigan, Vernon Dent, Emil Sitka L: 84 minutes P/D: Columbia.

Punchy Cowpunchers 1950/1/5 D: Edward Bernds C: Moe Howard, Larry Fine, Shemp Howard, Vernon Dent, Jacques O'Mahoney, Christine McIntyre, Kenneth MacDonald, Emil Sitka, Dick Wessel, Bob Cason L: 2-Reels P/D: Columbia *(Three Stooges Series)*.

Good Humor Man (feature) 1950/6/1 D: Lloyd Bacon C: Jack Carson, Lola Albright, Jean Wallace, George Reeves, Vernon Dent, Emil Sitka, Richard Egan L: 80 minutes P/D: Columbia.

One Shivery Night 1950/7/13 D: Del Lord C: Hugh Herbert, Dudley Dickerson, Phil Van Zandt, Robert Williams, Vernon Dent L: 2-Reels P/D: Columbia *(All-Star Comedies)*.

Innocently Guilty 1950/8/21 D: Jules White C: Bert Wheeler, Christine McIntyre, Nanette Bordeaux, Margie Liszt, Joe Palma, Vernon Dent L: 2-Reels P/D: Columbia *(All-Star Comedies)*.

Studio Stoops 1950/10/5 D: Edward Bernds C: Moe Howard, Larry Fine, Shemp Howard, Vernon Dent, Kenneth MacDonald, Christine McIntyre, Charles Jordan, Joe Palma, Stanley Price L: 2-Reels P/D: Columbia *(Three Stooges Series)*.

Three Arabian Nuts 1951/1/4 D: Edward Bernds C: Moe Howard, Larry Fine, Shemp Howard, Vernon Dent, Phil Van Zandt, Dick Curtis, Wesley Bly L: 2-Reels P/D: Columbia *(Three Stooges Series)*.

The Awful Sleuth 1951/4/19 D: Richard Quine C: Bert Wheeler, Jean Willes, Minerva Urecal, Ben Welden, Tom Kennedy, Vernon Dent L: 2-Reels P/D: Columbia *(All-Star Comedies)*.

Scrambled Brains 1951/7/7 D: Jules White C: Moe Howard, Larry Fine, Shemp Howard, Vernon Dent, Babe London, Emil Sitka, Royce Milne, Johnny Kascier L: 2-Reels P/D: Columbia *(Three Stooges Series)*.

Bonanza Town (feature) 1951/7/26 D: Fred F. Sears C: Charles Starrett, Fred F. Sears, Luther Crockett, Myron Healey, Charles Horvath, Slim Duncan, Smiley Burnette, Vernon Dent L: 56 minutes P/D: Columbia.

Sunny Side of the Street 1951/9/? *(feature)* D: Richard Quine C: Frankie Laine, Billy Daniels, Terry Moore, Jerome Courtland, Toni Arden, Audrey Long, Dick Wesson, Lynn Bari, William Tracy, Willard Waterman, Jonathan Hale, Vernon Dent L: 71 minutes P/D: Columbia.

The Tooth Will Out 1951/10/4 D: Edward Bernds C: Moe Howard, Larry Fine, Shemp Howard, Vernon Dent, Margie Liszt, Dick Curtis, Emil Sitka, Slim Gaut L: 2-Reels P/D: Columbia *(Three Stooges Series)*.

Trouble in Laws 1951/10/11 D: Hugh McCollum C: Hugh Herbert, Charles Williams, Kitty McHugh, Jean Bates, Vernon Dent, Dick Wessel, Mike Mahoney L: 2-Reels P/D: Columbia *(All-Star Comedies)*.

Pest Man Wins 1951/12/6 D: Jules White C: Moe Howard, Larry Fine, Shemp Howard, Vernon Dent, Margie Liszt, Emil Sitka, Nanette Bordeaux, Helen Dickson, Symona Boniface, Eddie Laughton, Charles "Heinie" Conklin, Al Thompson, Victor Travers L: 2-Reels P/D: Columbia *(Three Stooges Series)*.

A Missed Fortune 1952/1/3 D: Jules White C: Moe Howard, Larry Fine, Shemp Howard, Vernon Dent, Nanette Bordeaux, Suzanne Ridgeway, Vivian Mason, Stanley Blystone L: 2-Reels P/D: Columbia *(Three Stooges Series)*.

Listen, Judge 1952/3/6 D: Edward Bernds C: Moe Howard, Larry Fine, Shemp Howard, Vernon Dent, Kitty McHugh, Mary Emory, John Hamilton, Emil Sitka, Gil Perkins, Chick Collins L: 2-Reels P/D: Columbia *(Three Stooges Series)*.

Booty and the Beast 1953/3/5 D: Jules White C: Moe Howard, Larry Fine, Shemp Howard, Vernon Dent, Kenneth MacDonald, Charles "Heinie" Conklin, Dudley Dickerson, Blackie Whiteford L: 2-Reels P/D: Columbia *(Three Stooges Series)*.

Doggie in the Bedroom 1954/1/7 D: Jules White C: Wally Vernon, Eddie Quillan, Vernon Dent, Christine McIntyre, Billy Gray, Laura Lee Michel, Lonnie Thomas, Joe Palma L: 2-Reels P/D: Columbia *(All-Star Comedies)*.

Income Tax Sappy 1954/2/4 D: Jules White C: Moe Howard, Larry Fine, Shemp Howard, Vernon Dent, Benny Rubin, Marjorie Liszt, Nanette Bordeaux, Joe Palma L: 2-Reels P/D: Columbia *(Three Stooges Series)*.

Musty Musketeers 1954/5/3 D: Jules White C: Moe Howard, Larry Fine, Shemp Howard, Vernon Dent, Phil Van Zandt, Virginia Hunter, Sherry O'Neil, Charles "Heinie" Conklin, Wanda Perry, Diana Darin, Norma Randall, Joe Palma L: 2-Reels P/D: Columbia *(Three Stooges Series)*.

Knutzy Knights 1954/9/2 D: Jules White C: Moe Howard, Larry Fine, Shemp Howard, Vernon Dent, Christine McIntyre, Jacques O'Mahoney, Phil Van Zandt, Harold Brauer, Joe Palma, Ruth Godfrey, Joe Garcia, Douglas Coppin L: 2-Reels P/D: Columbia *(Three Stooges Series)*.

Vernon appears in the following Columbia titles via stock footage:

Oh, Say Can You Sue 1953/9/10 D: Jules White C: Andy Clyde, Vernon Dent, Christine McIntyre L: 2-Reels P/D: Columbia *(All-Star Comedies)*. [Note: Also contains new footage featuring Vernon Dent.]

The Fire Chaser 1954/9/30 D: Jules White C: Joe Besser, Vernon Dent, Christine McIntyre, Rodney Bell, James Logan, Andre Pola, Charles Hamilton, Joe Palma L: 2-Reels P/D: Columbia *(All-Star Comedies)*.

Rip, Sew and Stitch 1953/9/3 D: Jules White C: Moe Howard, Larry Fine, Shemp Howard, Vernon Dent, Harold Brauer, Cy Schindell, Phil Arnold L: 2-Reels P/D: Columbia *(Three Stooges Series)*.

Pals and Gals 1954/6/3 D: Jules White C: Moe Howard Larry Fine, Shemp Howard, Vernon Dent, Christine McIntyre, George Chesebro, Norman Willes, Charles "Heinie" Conklin, Fran Ellis, Stanley Blystone, Joe Palma L: 2-Reels P/D: Columbia *(Three Stooges Series)*. [Note: Also contains new footage with Vernon Dent.]

His Pest Friend 1955/1/20 D: Jules White C: Wally Vernon, Eddie Quillan, Vernon Dent, Jean Willes, Matt McHugh L: 2-Reels P/D: Columbia *(All-Star Comedies)*.

Of Cash and Hash 1955/2/3 D: Jules White C: Moe Howard, Larry Fine, Shemp Howard, Christine McIntyre, Kenneth MacDonald, Frank Lackteen, Vernon Dent, Duke York, Cy Schindell L: 2-Reels P/D: Columbia *(Three Stooges Series)*.

Bedlam in Paradise 1955/4/14 D: Jules White C: Moe Howard, Larry Fine, Shemp Howard, Sylvia Lewis, Phil Van Zandt, Vernon Dent, Symona Boniface, Victor Travers, Marti Shelton, Judy Malcolm, L: 2-Reels P/D: Columbia *(Three Stooges Series)*.

Flagpole Jitters 1956/4/5 D: Jules White C: Moe Howard, Larry Fine, Shemp Howard, David Bond, Mary Ainslee, Vernon Dent, Frank Sully, Don Harvey, Ned Glass, Barbara Bartay, Beverly Thomas L: 2-Reels P/D: Columbia *(Three Stooges Series)*.

Rumpus in the Harem 1956/6/21 D: Jules White C: Moe Howard, Larry Fine, Shemp Howard, Vernon Dent, George Lewis, Harriett Tarler, Diana Darrin, Ruth Godfrey White, Joe Palma L: 2-Reels P/D: Columbia *(Three Stooges Series)*.

Hot Stuff 1956/9/6 D: Jules White C: Moe Howard, Larry Fine, Shemp Howard, Christine McIntyre, Emil Sitka, Phil Van Zandt, Vernon Dent, Gene Roth, Connie Cezan, Evelyn Lovequist, Jacques O'Mahoney, Andre Pola, Joe Palma L: 2-Reels P/D: Columbia *(Three Stooges Series)*.

Guns A-Poppin' 1957/6/13 D: Jules White C: Moe Howard, Larry Fine, Joe Besser, Vernon Dent, Frank Sully, Joe Palma L: 2-Reels P/D: Columbia *(Three Stooges Series)*.

TELEVISION APPEARANCES

I Love Lucy "Drafted" 1951/12/24 CBS [Note: Vernon appears briefly as Santa Claus at the episode's close; this footage was also used in the "I Love Lucy Christmas Show," broadcast on 1956/12/24.]

The Frank Sinatra Show 1952/1/1 CBS [Note: Vernon appears in a New Year's Eve party sketch with Frank Sinatra and The Three Stooges (Moe, Larry, and Shemp). Other guests appearing on this live broadcast: musician Louis Armstrong, actress Yvonne DeCarlo, actor Alan Young, impressionist George DeWitt, and orchestra leader Axel Stordahl.]

This Is Your Life 1954/3/10; repeated 1956/7/11 NBC [Note: Vernon appears briefly as a Keystone Cop — along with Andy Clyde, Chester Conklin, Charles "Heinie" Conklin, and Hank Mann — in host Ralph Edwards's tribute to Mack Sennett at the El Capitan Theater in Hollywood. Other surprise guests: author Cameron Shipp, Sennett's former girlfriend Rose Guilfoil, opera singer Fritzi Scheff, director Del Lord, and actors Dell Henderson, Phyllis Haver, Franklin Pangborn, Minta Durfee, Alberta Vaughn, Jack Mulhall, Sally Eilers, Louise Fazenda, and Harold Lloyd.]

THEATRICAL COMPILATIONS

The Road to Hollywood 1947/7/4 D: Bud Pollard (also editor and host) P: Robert M. Savini DIST: Astor L: 55 minutes [Note: Vernon appears in a scene from the 1932 Bing Crosby short, *Dream House*.]

Down Memory Lane 1949/8/2 D: Phil Karlson C: Steve Allen, Mack Sennett, Franklin Pangborn L: 70 Minutes P: Mack Sennett (Original source) Aubrey Schenck Productions. DIST: Eagle-Lion Films. [Note: Vernon appears in clips from Sennett comedies, including *The Hollywood Kid* (1924).]

The Golden Age of Comedy, 1957/12/26 D: Robert Youngson C: Stan Laurel & Oliver Hardy, Billy Bevan, Charley Chase, Andy Clyde, Harry Gribbon, Jean Harlow, Harry Langdon, Carole Lombard, Will Rogers, Ben Turpin, Vernon Dent, Kewpie Morgan, Jack Richardson, Mack Sennett L: 79 minutes P/D: Distributors Corporation of America (DCA). [Note: Another helping of Vernon in *The Hollywood Kid* (1924).]

When Comedy Was King 1960/3/29 D: Robert Youngson C: Roscoe "Fatty" Arbuckle, Wallace Berry, Charles Chaplin, Charley Chase, Buster Keaton, Edgar Kennedy, Harry Langdon, Laurel & Hardy, Mabel Normand, Gloria Swanson, Ben Turpin, Billy Bevan, Andy Clyde, Chester Conklin, Vernon Dent, Stuart Erwin, James Finlayson, Madeline Hurlock, Charles Murray, Daphne Pollard, Mack Swain, Al St. John, Bobby Vernon L: 81 minutes P/D: 20th Century-Fox. [Note: Vernon appears in a clip from the 1924 Billy Bevan short, *Wall Street Blues*.]

Stop! Look! and Laugh! 1960/7/1 D: Don Appell/Louis Brandt C: Moe Howard, Larry Fine, Curly Howard, Vernon Dent, Bud Jamison, Paul Winchell, the Marquis Chimps L: 68 minutes P/D: Columbia Studios (Harry Romm Productions). [Note: Vernon appears in clips from the Three Stooges comedies *How High is Up?* (1940) and *Higher Than a Kite* (1943).]

30 Years of Fun 1963/2/10 D: Robert Youngson C: Billy Bevan, Eric Campbell, Charles Chaplin, Sydney Chaplin, Charley Chase, Andy Clyde, Douglas Fairbanks, Greta Garbo, Stan Laurel, Oliver Hardy, Buster Keaton, Mabel Normand, Mary Pickford, Snub Pollard, King Vidor L: 85 minutes P/D: 20th Century-Fox. [Note: Vernon appears in a clip from the 1928 Billy Bevan short, *The Best Man*.]

The Sound of Laughter 1963/12/17 D: John O'Shaughnessy C: Ed Wynn (master of ceremonies); archival footage of Buster Keaton, Danny Kaye, Bing Crosby, Bob Hope, Harry Langdon, Milton Berle, the Ritz Brothers, Vernon Dent. L: 72 minutes P/D: Independently produced and distributed. All clips from Educational shorts [Note: Vernon appears in clips from the 1933 Langdon short *The Hitchhiker* and the 1931 Al Christie comedy *The Freshman's Finish*.]

The Three Stooges Follies 1974/11/1 D: Spencer Gordon Bennett C: Moe Howard, Larry Fine, Curly Howard, Barbara Jo Allen, Buster Keaton, Lewis Wilson, Douglas Croft, Kate Smith, Dorothy Appleby, Phil Arnold, Vernon Dent L: 106 min. P/D: Columbia. [Note: Vernon appears as a sheriff in the 1939 Three Stooges comedy *Yes, We Have No Bonanza*.]

SOURCES

BOOKS

Alioto, Laura L. *Images of America-Seal Beach*. Charleston, SC, Chicago IL, Portsmouth NH, San Francisco, CA: Arcadia Publishing, 2005.

Beilharz, Edwin A., and Donald O. DeMers. *San Jose — California's First City*. Tulsa, OK: Continental Heritage Pres, Inc., 1980.

Boston, Linda Larson. *San Jose's Vaudeville House: Theatre Jose* (self-published), 2000.

Braff, Richard E. *Braff Silent Short Film Working Papers*. Jefferson, NC: McFarland & Co., 1998.

Bruskin, David N. *Behind the Three Stooges: The White Brothers: Jack, Jules and Sam White*. Los Angeles, CA: A Directors Guild of America Publication, 1993.

Capra, Frank. *The Name Above the Title*. New York: Macmillan, 1971.

Davis, Lon. *Silent Lives: 100 Biographies of the Silent Film Era*. Albany, GA: BearManor Media, 2008.

Davis, Lon and Debra. *Stooges Among Us*. Albany, GA: BearManor Media, 2008.

Dowlding, William J. *Beatlesongs*. New York: Simon & Schuster, 1989.

Douglas, Jack. *Historical Footnotes of Santa Clara Valley*. San Jose, CA: The Rosicrucian Press, 1993.

Foote, H. S. *Pen Pictures of the Garden of the World* (or *Santa Clara County, California*). Chicago: The Lewis Publishing Co., 1888.

Fernett, Gene. *American Film Studios*. Jefferson, NC: McFarland & Co., 1988.

Fowler, Gene. *Father Goose: The Story of Mack Sennett*. New York: Covici-Friede, 1934.

Gilbert, Lauren Miranda, and Bob Johnson. *Images of America-San Jose's Historic Downtown*. Charleston, SC, Chicago, IL, Portsmouth, NH, San Francisco, CA: Arcadia Publishing, 2004.

Touring Historic Willow Glen, Ten Walking Loops. San Jose, CA: Historic Committee of the Willow Glen Neighborhood Association, in conjunction with the Preservation Action Council of San Jose, 2007.

Kurson, Robert. *The Official Three Stooges Encyclopedia: The Ultimate Knucklehead's Guide to Stoogedom, from Amalgamated Morons to Ziller, Zeller, and Zoller.* Chicago, IL: Contemporary Books, Comedy III, 1998.

Lahue, Kalton C. *World of Laughter: The Motion Picture Comedy Short 1910–1930.* Norman, OK: University of Oklahoma Press. 1972.

———. *Mack Sennett's Keystone: The Man, the Myth and the Comedies.* South Brunswick & New York: A.S. Barnes & Co., 1971.

Lahue, Kalton C., and Sam Gill. *Clown Princes and Court Jesters: Some Great Comics of the Silent Screen.* New York: A.S. Barnes & Co., 1970.

Lenburg, Jeff, with Joan Howard Maurer and Greg Lenburg. *The Three Stooges Scrapbook.* New York: The Citadel Press, 1982.

Liebman, Roy. *The Wampas Baby Stars: A Biographical Dictionary, 1922–1934.* Jefferson, NC: McFarland & Co., 2000.

Lipsky, Dr. William *Images of America: San Francisco's Panama-Pacific International Exposition.* Charleston, SC, Chicago IL, Portsmouth NH, San Francisco CA: Arcadia Publishing, 2005.

Maltin, Leonard. *The Great Movie Comedians: From Charlie Chaplin to Woody Allen.* New York: Crown Publishers, 1978.

———. *The Great Movie Shorts.* New York: Bonanza Books, 1972.

———. *Movie Comedy Teams.* New York: Signet Books, 1970.

Manly, William Lewis. *Death Valley in '49: An Autobiography of a Pioneer.* Torrington, WY: The Narrative Press, 2001.

Mitchell, Glenn. *A-Z of Silent Film Comedy: An Illustrated Companion.* London: BT Batsford Ltd., 1998.

Miller, Blair. *American Silent Film Comedies: An Illustrated Encyclopedia of Persons, Studios and Terminology.* Jefferson, NC: McFarland & Co., 2008.

O'Hare, Sheila, and Irene Berry. *Images of America: Santa Cruz, California.* Charleston, SC, Chicago, IL, Portsmouth, NH, San Francisco, CA: Arcadia Publishing, 2002.

Okuda, Ted, with Edward Watz. *The Columbia Comedy Shorts: Two-Reel Hollywood Film Comedies, 1933–1958.* Jefferson, NC: McFarland & Co., 1986.

Rambo, Ralph. *Adventure Valley.* San Jose, CA: The Rosicrucian Press, Ltd., 1970.

Rambo, Ralph. *Pen and Inklings Nostalgic Views of Santa Clara Valley.* San Jose, CA: The Rosicrucian Press, 1984.

Schelly, William. *Harry Langdon: His Life and Films.* Jefferson, NC: McFarland & Co., Inc., 2008.

Sennett, Mack, with Cameron Shipp. *King of Comedy.* New York: Doubleday & Co., 1954.

Sherk, Warren M. (editor). *The Films of Mack Sennett: Credit Documentation for the Mack Sennett Collection at the Margaret Herrick Library.* Lanham, MD: Scarecrow Press, 1998.

Smith, Ron. *Comic Support: Second Bananas in the Movies.* New York: Citadel Press, 1993.

Spehr, Paul C., with Gunnar Lundquist. *American Film Personnel and Company Credits, 1908–1920.* Jefferson, NC: McFarland & Co., Inc., 1996.

Sunshine, Fruit and Flowers, and Its Resources. San Jose, CA: San Jose Mercury Publishing and Printing Company, 1885; San Jose Historical Museum Association (reprint), 1986.

Tillmany, Jack, with Jennifer Dowling. *Images of America: Theatres of Oakland.* Charleston, SC, Chicago, IL, Portsmouth, NH, San Francisco, CA: Arcadia Publishing, 2006.

Walker, Brent E. *Mack Sennett's Fun Factory: A History and Filmography of His Studio and His Keystone and Mack Sennett Comedies, with Biographies of Players and Personnel.* Jefferson, NC: McFarland & Co., Inc., 2010.

Watson, Coy, Jr. *The Keystone Kid: Tales of Early Hollywood.* Santa Monica, CA: Santa Monica Press, 2001.

Watz, Edward. *Wheeler & Woolsey: The Vaudeville Comic Duo and their Films, 1929–1937.* Jefferson, NC: McFarland & Co., 2001.

NEWSPAPERS

San Jose Evening News
June 6, 1894
September 18, 1899
Nov. 7, 1900
June 4, 1904
April, 19, 1906
April 27, 1908
June 25, 1909
June 26, 1909
Dec. 3, 1909
January 13, 1910
January 13, 1922
May 3, 1922

San Jose Mercury and Herald
April 3, 1899
March 17, 1907
January 6, 1907
June 26, 1909
June 27, 1909
June 29, 1909
April 6, 1915
June 6, 1915
October 6, 1917
January 22, 1922
January 7, 1922
April 26, 1922
May 3, 1922

Oakland Tribune
June 19, 1912
February 9, 1913
February 27, 1913
March 22, 1913
September 10, 1913
September 19, 1913
Nov. 17, 1914.
July 1, 1915

Los Angeles Times
December 17, 1919
February 20, 1921
January 25, 1922
July 23, 1922
February 4, 1923
May 6, 1923
April 4, 1924
August 15, 1924
June 30, 1926
November 27, 1927
August 28, 1938

Los Angeles Herald Examiner
August 26, 1938

Salt Lake Telegram
August 7, 1921

San Francisco Chronicle
May 21, 1922

Santa Cruz Evening News
March 26, 1922
March 29, 1922
April 8, 1922
April 12, 1922
April 20, 1922
April 21, 1922
April 24, 1922
April 28, 1922
August 14, 1923
August 25, 1923

The Oregonian
September 25, 1921

Edwardsville (IL) Intelligencer
April 6, 1943

Van Nuys (CA) News
January 11, 1962

Davenport (IA) Democrat and Leader
November 25, 1923

MAGAZINES

Moving Picture World
May 5, 1923

Motion Picture News
March 30, 1929
August 24, 1929
February 1, 1930

Motion Picture Herald
January 24, 1931

Classic Film Collector
(The forerunner of *Classic Images*)
Fall 1976

The Three Stooges Journal
#114, Summer 2005

STUDIO PRESS RELEASES

Christie Film Company
Plumb Crazy, June 3, 1923
Don't Divorce Him, May 5, 1931
The Girl Rush, October 25, 1931

Educational Pictures
The Lion's Roar, December 9, 1928
A College Racket, June 14, 1931
Fainting Lover, August 16, 1931
Dream House, January 17, 1932
Sunkissed Sweeties, October 30, 1932

Cameo Comedies
Murder Will Out, December 1928
In the Morning, December 30, 1928

Jack White Mermaid Comedies
The Whoopie Boys, February 10, 1929
Parlor Pests, March 24, 1929
Those Two Boys, March 5, 1929
Ticklish Business, August 25, 1929
The Talkies, October 1929

UNPUBLISHED INTERVIEWS

James T. Mockoski, with Eunice (Dent) Friend (November 20, 1997)

Edward Watz, with Eunice (Dent) Friend (July 9, 1979)

Lon Davis, with Larry Fine (August 18, 1974)

SOURCES 247

OTHER SOURCES

Coroner's Jury Report (June 24, 1909)

Death Certificate (#1490, February 19, 1938)

Script for *Malice in the Palace* by Felix Adler (April 19, 1949)

Letter from Edward Bernds to James T. Mockoski (February 24, 1997)

Langdon and Dent in His Marriage Wow *(Sennett, 1925).* COURTESY OF EDWARD WATZ

ABOUT THE AUTHOR

Bill Cassara lives with his wife, Michelle, in Salinas, California. In 1975, after attending schools in San Jose, he became a volunteer docent for the San Jose Historical Museum. Upon graduating from San Jose State University, he dedicated himself to a career in law enforcement. He was hired as a deputy sheriff with the Santa Clara County Sheriff's Office in 1978. For 27 years he served the Monterey County Sheriff's Office, retiring as a sergeant for the Internal Investigations Unit.

Bill has been a lifetime movie buff and in 1984, founded the "Midnight Patrol" tent in the Sons of the Desert organization (An international Laurel & Hardy society). He has chaired many events for the Monterey County Film Commission, including salutes to Doris Day and Clint Eastwood.

In addition to writing numerous articles and film-related essays, Bill authored an acclaimed book, *Edgar Kennedy — Master of the Slow Burn* (BearManor Media, 2005).

INDEX

Adler, Felix 164
A-Ducking They Did Go 153
Agee, James 13
Agnews 28
Alexandria Theatre 175
All Night Long 95, 98
Alviso, CA 22
Alum Rock Park 22
American Thomas Flyer 33
An Auto Nut 65
Anderson, G.M. (Broncho Billy) 80-81
Anna May the Elephant 78, 82-84, 100
Arbuckle, Clyde 9
Arbuckle, Roscoe "Fatty," 9-10, 32-33, 54-55, 60, 66, 91
Archer, Lou (Louis Archambeau) 121
Arch Rock 90
Armory Hall 47
Armstrong, Louis 169
Arnaz, Desi 169
Arrow Film Corporation 65, 109

Back From the Front 145, 147, 161
Back to the Woods 143
Ball, Lucille 169
Battleship Dent 60-61
Beast of Berlin 161
Beatty, James 54
Beer Barrel Polecats 144
Beery, Noah 78-79
Beery, Wallace 91
Bell, Fred 55-56, 60
Bell Hop, The 65
Bellamy, Madge 78-79, 82, 84-85
Benedict, Brooks 127

Ben Lomond, CA 180
Bercovich's Cigar Store 28
Berkeley, CA 45
Bernds, Edward 178
Bevan, Billy 91, 96, 98, 109-110, 112
Big Flash, The 127
Bill Poster, The 65
Bird in the Head, A 139
Black Oxfords 95
Blystone, Stanley 136
Bob Murphy's Nightclub 155
Boobs in the Wood 98
Booby Dupes 148
Booty and the Beast 151
Bordeaux, Joseph 54
Boroughs, Henry M. 155-156
Boroughs, Hortense Eunice 155-156
Boulder Creek, CA 80-83
Bowen, Bobbie 48
Bowen, Charles 48
Braff, Richard E. 187
Bramhall Park 24
Brendel, El 164
B.F. Brissac 80
Broken Bubbles 65
Brookdale, CA 81
Broncho Billy (See Anderson, G.M.)
Brotherhood of Railroad Trainmen 34
Brown, Randy 84
Bruckman, Clyde 100
Bryan, William Jennings 27
Bull and Sand 96
Bunny, John 91
Burbank, Frances 23
Burke, Johnny 109

Burt, Frank 53
Busch, Mae 91
Busy Buddies 150
Butterfield, James Austin 128

California Motion Picture Corporation 61
Call, Minnie, (See Dent, Minnie)
Call, Maggie 55
Call, William 55
Capra, Frank 97, 99, 102, 106, 158
Cameraman, The 130, 158
Campos, Dennis II 187
Carmel, CA 77
Carver, Louise 91
Casa Del Rey Hotel 90
Cassara, Bill 14, 249
Cassara, Diana 24
Cassara, John 9
Cassidy, Frank A. 79
Cavender, Glen 54
Chandler, Laura 24
Chaplin, Charlie 91-93, 97, 100
Chaplin, Syd 91
Chase, Charley (Charles Parrott) 18, 65, 85, 109, 111, 164-165, 178
Cherry Avenue 23
Christie, Al (Christie Comedies) 72, 111, 122-123, 138
Circus Hoodoo 128
Clark & McCullough 116
Clover Leaf Dramatic Society 47
Clyde, Andy 109, 123, 132, 157, 164-165, 168
Coconut Grove, The 124
Collins, Monty 113-118, 121, 131, 136, 164-165
Columbia Pictures 170, 174
Conklin, Chester 136, 169
Connecticut Yankee in King Arthur's Court, A 104
Coogan, Jackie 92
Cook, Clyde 122
Coming and Going 67
Corbett, James J. 61
Coyote River 22
Crash Goes the Hash 149
Creeps 121
Cress, G. A. 82-83
Crosby, Bing (Harry Lillis Crosby) 124-125, 128-129

Culver City, CA 66-67, 78, 80, 83, 96, 157
Cupertino, CA 9, 22, 56, 71, 77, 162
Currier, Clara M. 109
Curtner Avenue 23-24, 51

Daniels, Bebe 60
Davis, Lon 187
Dashaway Livery Shop 9
Dash Saloon 25, 28
Day, Alice 97, 109
DeCarlo, Yvonne 239
DeMille, Cecil B.
Dent, Enoch 23
Dent, Eunice 10, 14, 155-159, 162-163, 170-171, 246 (See also Boroughs, Hortense Eunice)
Dent, Fanny (Fay) (See Fanny Mossman)
Dent, Gale 34
Dent, Grace 137
Dent, John Captain 60
Dent, Julia 23
Dent Melville E. 25, 45
Dent, Minnie (Call) 55-56, 66
Dent, Rawley E. 23-25, 51
Dent, Vernon 9-10, 12-14, 16-19, 21, 23, 25-26, 31-32, 46-48, 50, 52-53, 55-56, 60-62, 65, 67, 69-71, 77-78, 85, 90, 93-98, 100, 102-106, 109-110, 112-118, 120-122, 124, 126-129, 131-132, 136-138, 141, 146, 154-156, 161-162, 164-165, 168, 172, 177-178
Dent, William E. 21, 23, 25-27-28, 31, 34-36, 39-41
Dentist, The 65
Derby, The 59
Detroit, Michigan 121
Dickerson, Dudley 18
Dizzy Doctors 139
Don't Change Your Mrs. 65
Don't Divorce Him 122
Dover, Nancy 182-183
Dream House 124-125, 246
Durfee, Minta (Arbuckle) 136, 239
Dutiful But Dumb 149, 174

Eagles Hall 27, 34
East of the Water Plug 96
Educational Pictures 108
Edwards, Harry 121, 159

INDEX

Edwards, Ralph 169
El Camino Real 22
Electric Light Tower 22
El Facile Restaurant 155
Elks Club 35
Errol, Leon 130
Essanay Studios 80-81
Empire Theatre 31
Even As I.O.U. 149
Extra Girl, The 89-91, 125

Fahrney, Milton H. 67
Fainting Lover 123, 246
Farley, Dot 91, 93
Fat and Sassy 67
Fatty and Mabel Viewing the World's Fair in San Francisco 53-54
Fazenda, Louise 91
FBO 111
Feet of Mud 98
Felton, CA 80, 83
Fiddlers Three 142
Fiddlesticks 104-105
Fields, W.C. 13, 100, 130
Finegan, Richard 10, 108, 114, 130, 187
Finlayson, James 18, 91, 122-123, 168
First National 106
First National Bank 143
Fletcher, Leslie 48
Flood, Frank 187
Foresters 34
Forest Lawn Cemetery 172
For the Love of Ludwig 123
Fort Wayne, IN 109
Forum Café 55
Foxfilm comedies 65
Frank Sinatra Show, The 169
Fraternal Order of the Eagles (See Eagles)
Frawley, William 169
Friedman, Drew 10,
Fremont High School 46, 48
From Nurse To Worse 139
Frum, A. Guy 67
Fuelin' Around 147

Gable, Clark 130
Get the Hook 67
Gibbs, A. W. 83
Gilbert, Billy 136, 164

Gill, Sam 10, 18, 66, 176, 187
Girl Rush The 123
Gilmore, Blanche 120
Gillstrom, Arvid E. 127-128, 131
Girls Will Be Boys 122
Gladstone Entertainers 48
Glaum, Louise 136
Glendale, CA 91, 175
Golden Age of Comedy, The 17
Golden Gate Park 54
Goldfield, Nevada 34
Golf 85
Gone With the Wind 157
Goodall, Grace 136
Good Morning, Eve 130
Grant Elementary School 36
Grant, Ulysses S. 41, 95
Grass Valley, CA 55
Grauman, Sid 32-33
Great Race, The 33
Greenwood, Charlotte 122
Gribbon, Harry 91, 93
Griffith, D.W. 70
Guadalupe River 22
Gum Riot, A 65

Hail the Woman 70-71, 78, 90
Half-Back of Notre Dame 93
Half-Shot Shooters 132, 134, 136, 151, 153
Half-Wits Holiday 141, 164
Hall, Jon 161
Hardy, Oliver 13, 17, -18, 68, 85, 100, 103-104, 111, 116, 118, 163, 249
Harem Hero, A 65
Harte, Bret 61
Hartman, Ferris 46
Haver, Phyllis 89
Hayes, John 67
Healy, Ted 135, 164
Heavenly Daze 144
Heckler, The 164-165
Herbert, Hugh 164
Hiatt, Ruth 91, 109
High and Mighty 67
Higher than a Kite 146-147
Highsmith, Harry 56, 60
Hill, Thelma 109
His First Flame 100-101
His Marriage Mix-up 132

His Marriage Wow, 98, 247
The Hitchhiker 127
Hoboken to Hollywood 109
Hocus Pocus 151
Holley, Francis 26, 51
Hollywood Hotel 71
Hollywood Kid, The 93, 94, 125
Homestead Avenue 56,
Hooks and Jabs 127-128
Horace Mann School 35-36, 70, 78
Horton, Edward Everett 161
Hotel St. James 22
Hotel Vendome 22
Hot Sports 117
Household Blues 116
Howard, Joseph E. 123
Howe's Great London Circus 73, 74
How High Is Up?, 153
Hubby's Quiet Little Game 111
Hudson River 130
Huntington Beach, CA 59
Hurlock, Madeline 91, 109

Iceman's Ball, The 122
Idiots Deluxe 145
Idle Roomers 150
I Don't Remember 132
Idora Park 46, 55
I'll Never Heil Again 146, 161
I Love Lucy 239
In at the Finish 67
Income Tax Sappy 152
In the Morning 112
In the Sweet Pie and Pie 149
Ince, Thomas 69-71, 73, 77-80, 82-85

Jackson, Mary Ann 109, 111
Jamison, Bud 13, 18, 131, 136, 149
Janitor, The 65
Jewell, Frank F. 25
Johnson, Cole 72, 96, 120
Johnson George W. 128
Johnson, H. 83
Jones, F. Richard 89, 111
Joy, Violet (Duane Thompson) 67, 71-73, 78, 159
Jury Goes Round 'N' Round, The 165
Just an Echo in the Valley 129

Keaton, Buster 100, 130-131, 158, 161, 164
Kelsey, Fred 122, 136
Kennedy, Edgar 14, 18, 54, -55, 96, 122, 187, 249
Kennedy, Tom 164
Keystone Comedy Co. 47, 54-55, 91
Keystone Cops 65, 162, 169-170
Kirby, Marge 65
Kolb and Dill 47
Korby, Marshall 168
Kornman, Mary 128
Knight Duty 127
Kurson, Robert 178

Lahue, Kalton C. 18, 177
Lambert, Glen 90
Landis, Cullen 78-80
Lang, Fritz 125
Langdon, Harry 12, 14, 91-94, 97, 100, 103-105, 110, 126, 128, 131-132, 154-156, 159, 162-163, 172, 182, 184-185
Langdon, Harry, Jr. 94
Langdon, Mabel 154, 163-164
Laurel & Hardy 103-104, 111
Lehrman, Henry 33
Lennon, John 128
Lentz, Irene 93
Leslie, Elgin 54
Lesser, Sol 93
Levine, Jackie 112
Lewis, George 143
Liberty Theatre 54
Lick Observatory 22
Light, Ben 61, 179
Lily of Poverty Flat 61, 80
Lincoln Avenue 23, 36
Lion's Roar, The 112-113, 246
Little Robinson Corkscrew 96
Lion and the Souse, The 95-96
Lion's Roar, The 112-113
Lipsky, Dr. William 51
Listen, Judge 145
Little Rascals (Our Gang) 17
Lloyd, Harold 60, 100
Loco Boy Makes Good 149
Long Beach, CA 59
Lord, Del 93, 96, 124, 132, 169
Los Angeles, CA 10, 22, 56, 59-62, 66, 70-71, 77, 79, 84, 86, 95, 109-110, 122, 136, 156, 162-163

INDEX

Los Angeles Letter Carrier's Band 85
Los Gatos, CA 22-23
Los Gatos Creek 24-25
Love's Sweet Piffle 96
Loy, Myrna 130
Lucky Stars 102

Mabel's Willful Way 55
Mace, Fred 91
Mack Sennett Bathing Beauties 17, 89-90, 93
Malice in the Palace 143, 164
Maltin, Leonard 10, 187
Manhattan Melodrama 130
Manly, William Lewis 22
Mann, Gus 58, 60
Mann, Hank (David Willie Lieberman) 136, 168-169-170, 188
Mann, Helen 123
Mann, Horace (School) 35-36, 70, 78
Mann, Sam 47-48
Margaret Herrick Library 10, 64, 69, 141, 187
Market Street 10
Marriage Humor 128
Marx Brothers, The 13
Mason, Helen 48
Massa, Steve 187
Matri-Phony 140-141
McCollum, Rebecca, 23
McIntyre, Christine 13, 141
McKinley, President James 21, 27-28
McLean, Rev. Robert N. 156
Meins, Gus 111
Mendelssohn, Felix 137
Mendelssohn's Wedding March 137
Merkel, Una 164
Mermaid Comedies 127
Messenger, The 65
Metro-Goldwyn-Mayer 111
Michelena, Beatriz 61
Midway Quintet 48
Million Dollar Legs 130
Million Dollar Theatre 109
Milpitas, CA 22
Missed Fortune, A 153
Mission Theatre 70
Mitchell, Margaret 157
Mockoski, James T. 10, 178, 247
Moody, Fred 81-82
Monterey, CA 21, 51, 249

Moran, Polly 164
Morse, Alice 171
Morton, James C. 18, 136
Mossman, Fanny B. (Dent) 21, 25, 34, 45, 51
Mossman, Frances 25
Motorboat Mamas 110
Mr. Noisy 164
Mt. Hamilton 22
Mummy's Dummies 121
Mummy's Nightmare 67
Munzer, John 35, 78
Murder Will Out 112
Murray, Charles 61, 91
Musolff, Rose Frances 91
Mutts to You 152
Mystic Mush 65

Naglee, Henry Morris 34
New Orleans, LA 51
Naughty Nurses 65
No Dough Boys 146, 161
Normand, Mabel 53-55, 60, 89-91, 111
Norton, Jack, 136
Norwalk, California State Hospital 137
No Census, No Feeling 148
Norris, Eleanor 158
Now or Never 67
Numa the Lion 95-96
Nutty but Nice 140

Oak Hills Cemetery 24
Oakland, CA 10, 18, 21-22, 27, 45-48, 52-55, 70, 78, 81
O'Brien, Virginia 155
O'Day, Nell 126-127
O'Dell, Georgia 112
Okuda, Ted 14, 18
Old Chicago Barbershop 9
Ohmart, Ben 10
On Ice 128
On the Jump 67
One-Man Mama, A 109,
Oratorio Society,
Orpheum Theatre,
Oscar the Elephant,
Out West 35
Overseas Club 85
Ovey, George 66-67

Pacific Film Company 66-68
Palace of Fine Arts 53
Pair of Kings, A 85
Panama-Pacific International Exposition (San Francisco) 51
Paper Hanger, The 65
Paramount 128-131, 182
Paris, France 33
Parker, Kit 10, 187
Parlor Pests 114-115
Pasques, Ethel 10
Pathé 111,
Peach Street 156
Pest Man Wins, The 151
Petting Preferred 128
Petty, Angelina 48
Philharmonic Auditorium 85
Philotros Club 46
Pickford, Mary 92
Picking Peaches 93
Pistol Packin' Nitwits 14
Plain Clothes 99, 103
Please 128-129
Plumb Crazy 72-73
Pollard, Daphne 112
Porter, Gene Stratton 95
Portland, Maine 23
Post, Emily 135
Poverty Flat 61, 80, 82
Powell, William 130
Principal Pictures Corporation 93
Prisoner of Zenda, A, 104
Punchy Cowpunchers 147

Quebec, Canada 170
Queen Elizabeth 170
Quillan, Eddie 109, 164

Rambo, Ralph 9
Rappe, Virginia 68
Redwood City, CA 78
Red Oak, IA 71
Remember When?, 99-100
Rhythm Boys, The 124
Riders of the Purple Cows 96
Ripley, Arthur 97, 99-100, 102, 106, 132, 158
RKO 111, 122, 136
Roach, Hal 17, 109, 111, 116, 127
Roaming Romeo 65, 128

Roberts, Steven 116
Romeo and Juliet 96
Roberts, Jay 48
Roberts, Richard M. 10, 187
Rohauer, Raymond 14
Rolph, Jim 53
Rooney, Mickey 130
Rousseau, Grace 109
Rousseau, Benjamin 109
Ryan, Irene 161
Rydzewski, Steve 187

Sacramento, CA 21,
Salinas, CA 19, 28, 249
San Diego, CA 51, 60-61, 131, 158
San Diego, I Love You 161
Sanford, Tiny 136
San Francisco, CA 21-22, 27-28, 31, 33, 45, 51-56, 59-60, 79-80, 146
San Francisco Earthquake 28, 33, 146
San Gabriel, CA 62
San Jose, CA 9, 10, 17, -18, 21-29, 31-36, 39-41, 45-46, 51, 54-56, 60, 70-71, 73-74, 77-79, 81, 122, 172
San Rafael, CA 61, 80, 122
San Lorenzo, CA 81-82
Santa Clara Valley 21-23, 28, 32, 54, 79
Santa Cruz, CA 10, 22, 79-82-83, 85, 90-91
Santa Rosa, CA 28
Sappy Birthday 165
Saratoga, CA 22-23
Saturday Afternoon 102, 104
Sawyer, Sarah L. 59
Scheuer, Philip K. 136
Schilling & Lane 164
Schley, Ida , 39, 41
Seal Beach, CA 56, 59-60
Seattle, WA 27
Semon, Larry 85, 100
Seiter, William A. 89
Sennett, Mack 12, 14, 16-17, 33, 47, 53, 65, 69-70, 89-97, 99-100-102, 104-106, 109-112, 121, 123-124, 127, 132, 136, 138, 168-169-170, 172, 187
Share the Wealth 132
Sherk, Warren M. 187
Shivering Sherlocks 144
Silicon Valley (see also Santa Clara Valley) 21
Sing a Song of Six Pants 144

Sitka, Emil 170
Sleeping Sickness 67
Slippery Silks 148
Slow But Sure 67
Smith & Dale 164
Smith Family 111
Smith, Ron 178
Smith, Sid 91, 95-96
Social Prestige 113
Soldier Man 104
So Long, Mr. Chumps 146
Some One To Love 78-79, 83
Sons of the Desert 104
Soul of the Beast 83-85, 90
Sousa, John Philip 46
Spoor, George K. 81.
Squareheads of the Round Table 142
Steers L. 83
Sterling, Ford 47, 91, 170
Stevens Creek 55
Stockton, CA 55
Studio Stoops 145
Stroheim, Erich Von 125
Stubborn Cinderella, A 123
Studio Theater 17
St. James Park 21-22, 27-28
Strong Man, The 127
Summerville, Slim 165
Sunday Morning 121
Sunkissed Sweeties 123
Swanson, Gloria 91
Sykes, Ethel 182

Taft, William Howard 51, 53
T & D (Turner & Dahnken) 70
Tars and Stripes 131, 158
Tassels in the Air 152
Taylor, William Desmond 89
Terweanor, Celia 52
There He Goes 102
They're Off 67
They Stooge to Conga 146, 161
This is Your Life 169
Thomas, Clarke W. 78
Thompson, Al , 112
Those Two Boys 115
Three Arabian Nuts 151
Three Little Beers 135
Three Little Pirates 142,

Three Little Sew and Sews 153
Three Pests in a Mess 150
Three Smart Saps 149
Three Stooges, The 13-14, 17, 19, 100-101, 116, 130-132, 135, 138, 159, 164, 169, 172, 175
Ticklish Business 116
Tied for Life 127-128
Tillie's Punctured Romance 100
Time, The Place, and the Girl, The 123
Tired Feet 127
Tivoli Theatre 46
Tooth Will Out, The 140
Tower of Jewels 53, 59
Tracy, Bert (Productions) 90-91
Triangle Pictures 70
Turpin, Ben 91, 96

Ullman, Elwood 159
Unique Theatre 32-33, 54
Universal Studios 120-121, 161
Up and at 'Em 67, 71
Up and Down Stairs 121
Urlin, Cleveland 39-41

Vague, Vera 165
Vance, Vivian 169
Vandivere, Elinor 136
Van Dyke, W. S. "Woody" 130
Van Nuys, CA 156, 159, 171
Vernon, Bobby 72
Vernon, Wally 164
Vernon's Aunt 121,
Victory Theatre 32
Vidor, Florence 70
Vose, Howard 48

Yosemite National Park 128-129
Young, George Oscar 48, 50, 52, 55
Youngson, Robert 17
You're Darn Tootin' 115, 130
You're Telling Me! 130

Walker, Brent 10, 187
Wall Street Blues 96
WAMPAS Baby Stars 71
"Waning Honeymoon, The" 123
Ward, Dean 183-185
Warner Bros. 130

Warren, Charles 55-56, 71, 77
Washington Hotel 96
Watch Your Friends 121
Watz, Edward 10, 12, 18, 132, 155, 157, 159,
    163, 166, 178, 187, 205
Weber and Fields 47
Wee Wee Monsieur 143,
We Faw Down 104
Wells, H. G. 53
Westlake Park 163
Weston, William 31
What a Day 116
Wheeler, Bert 164
When Spirits Move 65
White Cap Productions 67
White, Jack (Preston Black) 111-115,
    117-118, 121, 131-132, 159, 178
White, Jules 116-117, 132, 159
White, Leo 136
Whiteman, Paul 124

Willow Glen 22-24, 26
Willow Glen School 23
Willow Street 23-25
Wished on Mabel 54
Wooley, Dr. W. H. 137
Woollcott, Alexander 94-96
Whoopie Boys, The 113-114, 246
Woman Haters Club 101, 131
Worswick, G. D. 28
Wray, John Griffith 70
Wyatt, David 187

Yes, We Have No Bonanza 143
Young, Alan 169

Zandt, Phil Van 141
Zell, Harry Von 164
Zuckerman, Rose 155

Bear Manor Media

Classic Cinema.
Timeless TV.
Retro Radio.

WWW.BEARMANORMEDIA.COM

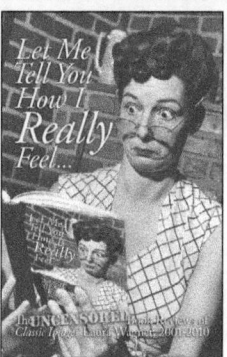
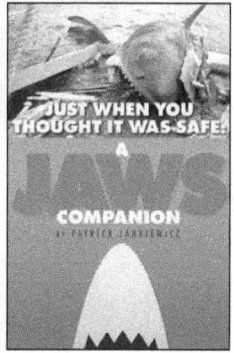

www.ingramcontent.com/pod-product-compliance
Lightning Source LLC
Chambersburg PA
CBHW071228170426
43191CB00032B/1074